AGRICULTURAL POLICY REFORM

AGRICULTURAL POLICY REFORM

Politics and Process in the EC and the USA

H. Wayne Moyer and Timothy E. Josling

Iowa State University Press/Ames

H. Wayne Moyer is Rosenfield Professor and Professor of Political Science, Grinnell College, Grinnell, Iowa.
Timothy E. Josling is Professor at the Food Research Institute, Stanford University, Stanford, California.

Published in the United States, Canada, and the Philippine Islands by the Iowa State University Press, Ames, Iowa 50010.
Published simultaneously in Great Britain by Harvester Wheatsheaf.
Printed in Great Britain.

First edition, 1990

Library of Congress Cataloging-in-Publication Data
Moyer, H. Wayne,
    Agricultural policy reform: Politics and process in the EC and the USA by H. Wayne Moyer and Timothy E. Josling.—1st ed.
        p. cm.
    Includes bibliographical references.
    ISBN 0–8138–1371–9
    1. Agriculture and state—United States.   2. Agricultural price supports—United States.   3. Agriculture and state—European Economic Community countries.   4. Agricultural price supports—European Economic Community countries.   I. Josling, Timothy Edward.   II. Title.
HD1761.M68   1990   66821
338.1′873—dc20   89–48550

CONTENTS

PREFACE

This project had its origins during the 1979–80 academic year, when one of the authors, Wayne Moyer, spent a sabbatical as Visiting Scholar at Stanford University's Food Research Institute (FRI). While there, he and Tim Josling spent many hours discussing agricultural policy in the European Community and the United States. It was clear to both that the political process provides an essential part of the explanation for most agricultural policy decisions. They decided to see whether one could make useful generalizations about the political process, which would both help explain past policy decisions and help predict future ones. They developed some ideas on the subject, but the project had not got to the writing stage by the end of the sabbatical.

In the spring of 1987, with another sabbatical in the offing for Moyer, the project was revived as a comparative study of the politics and process of agricultural reform in the USA and EC. Such a study was clearly timely, with the Uruguay Round of the General Agreement on Tariffs and Trade (GATT) negotiations in progress, and with both the USA and EC grappling with pressures to reform profligate spending on farm subsidies. Each of the authors contributed elements of the analytical framework used in this study. Moyer had used Graham Allison's organizational process and bureaucratic politics paradigms in his teaching of international relations, along with Lindblom's partisan mutual adjustment. Josling brought the perspective of public choice from the economic literature on policy analysis.

The authors worked together at FRI during September and October 1987 to develop the analytical framework and work out the research design for the project. Moyer then spent the period from 22 October until 29 January 1988 as Resident Fellow at the National Center for Food and Agricultural Policy at Resources for the Future in Washington, DC. While there, he did the background research for the chapters on US agricultural policy. He went to England on 30 January 1988, and spent six months as Fellow at the Centre for European Studies at Wye College of the University of London. This provided a base for the European phase of the research. The manuscript was completed after Moyer's return to Iowa in July 1988.

The authors found it stimulating bringing their respective disciplinary perspectives to bear (Moyer as a political scientist and Josling as an economist) in trying to explain the snail's pace of agricultural policy reform in both the USA and EC, by analysing the behaviour of various policy actors and by exploring the interplay between economic trends, politics and the policy process.

The authors are grateful to the many people who have helped one way or another with this project. They wish to thank Denis Britton, Allan Buckwell, Simon Harris, David Harvey, Michel Petit, Ross Talbot and Michael Tracy, each of whom read large parts of the manuscript, providing detailed and very helpful comments. Allan Buckwell and Michael Tracy deserve special thanks in other respects as well. Buckwell served as a marvellous host while Moyer was at Wye College, helping him integrate himself into the academic life there, and providing valuable guidance at every stage. Tracy, who was Visiting Professor at Wye during February and March 1987, took a serious interest in the project, providing encouragement and a wealth of useful advice based on his many years as a European civil servant. He helped immensely with the Brussels phase of the project in identifying the people to interview, even attending some of the interviews, and in providing the overview for interpreting the comments made by EC officials. Tracy is an excellent example of the senior administrator who looks at issues from the perspective of the good of the broader community.

The authors would also like to thank Hans Apel, the former Finance Minister of the Federal Republic of Germany, who had visited Grinnell College as a German Marshall Fund Fellow in the spring of 1987, and who served as host in Bonn, providing the perspective of a senior politician with a vision for Europe, who can relate agriculture to other important priorities.

Thanks are also in order to Ed Rossmiller, director of the National Center for Food and Agricultural Policy for the Future in Washington, DC, who provided office space, publications and all manner of helpful advice during the Washington phase of the research. The NCFAP staff and the Agricultural Economics academic staff at Wye College also deserve recognition for providing stimulating intellectual environments.

Moyer greatly appreciates the assistance provided by Grinnell College, its President, George Drake, and the Rosenfield Program endowment, for providing him with a full year's leave along with generous research support to undertake this project. The project would not have been possible without this support. He also wishes to recognize Ann and Mike Preisig, farmers near Charing, Kent, who provided a wonderful bungalow in an idyllic setting, ideal for writing and research. They also provided the benefit of the grass-roots farmers' point of view, which can too easily become lost in the political process.

At Stanford, thanks are due to Claudia Smith, who cheerfully accepted the task of entering revisions in drafts, keeping track of successive versions of the manuscript and printing out drafts for yet further revision. The age of the word processor makes authorship easier on the author but still requires skilled and dedicated support.

Finally, the authors owe a large debt of gratitude to their wives, Helen and Anthea, for their encouragement, for tolerating the many hours that went into this project, and for helping them maintain a sense of balance.

ACKNOWLEDGEMENTS

A series of 24 in-depth interviews was conducted on a non-attribution basis by Wayne Moyer with participants, former participants and close observers of the United States and European Community agricultural policy processes. These interviews took place: in Washington, DC, during January 1988; in Brussels during April 1988; and in Bonn during May 1988. The interviews focused generally on how agricultural policy is made in the USA and EC, with specific discussion of the 1981 and 1985 farm bills, the 1984 dairy quotas decision and the 1988 agriculture stabilizers agreement. The authors owe a large debt of gratitude to Hans Apel, former Finance Minister of the Federal Republic of Germany; to Michael Tracy, former director in the Secretariat of the EC Council of Ministers; and to Ed Rossmiller, director of the National Center for Food and Agricultural Policy; for their assistance in scheduling the interviews, respectively, in Bonn, Brussels and Washington, DC and for sharing their own considerable expertise in long private conversations. They also wish to thank the various people who were interviewed for giving willingly of their time, for speaking candidly, and for sharing their insights. These individuals were extremely helpful in piecing together the puzzles which are US agricultural policy and the EC Common Agricultural Policy.

Martin Abel: chairman of the Washington consulting firm of Abel, Daft and Early
Graham Avery: director, Directorate F-1, DG-VI, European Commission
John Campbell: legislative assistant to US Senator Rudy Boschwitz (Republican, Minnesota)
Barbara Chow: staff, US Senate Budget Committee
Aldo Ciocioli: Director-General for Agriculture of the Secretariat of the EC Council of Ministers
Kenneth Clayton: Office of the US Trade Representative
Keith Collins: Office of the Assistant Secretary of Agriculture for Economics, US Department of Agriculture
Noel DeVisch: member of Cabinet of EC Agriculture Commissioner Andriessen
Dale Hathaway: former US Under-Secretary of Agriculture for International Affairs and Commodity Programs
Jan Hennekens: President of the Boerenbond Belge (Belgian Farmers

Union) and former President of the Comité des Organisations Professionnelles Agricoles (COPA)

Wilhelm Henrichsmeyer: Professor of Agricultural Economics, University of Bonn, and chairman of the advisory council, Ministry of Agriculture, Federal Republic of Germany

Gerd Jarchow: European Commission staff and former member of Cabinet of Commissioner Pfeffer

Bruno Jullien: former EC agricultural representative in EC Mission to the United States and now member of staff of DG-VI

Walter Kittel: State Secretary, Ministry of Agriculture, Federal Republic of Germany, and former Deputy Chief of Mission of FRG Mission in Brussels

Leo V. Mayer: Deputy US Assistant Secretary of Agriculture for Economics

Eugene Moos: Assistant for agriculture to US House of Representatives majority leader Tom Foley (Democrat, Washington)

Uffe Toudal Pederson: member of Cabinet of EC Budget Commissioner Christophersen

Thomas Schlier: head of the Arbeitsgemeinschaft der Verbraucherverbande (German Consumers' Organization)

Rudolf Schnieders: Secretary General of the German Farmers Union (Deutscher Bauernverband)

John Schnittker: former US Under-Secretary of Agriculture and now a Washington, DC, consultant

Peter Thompson: DG-VI staff member with responsibility for bilateral relations with the USA, Canada, Australia and New Zealand

Craig Thorne: Agricultural Section, US Mission to the EC

Carlo Trojan: Deputy Secretary-General of the European Commission and former chief of Cabinet of Agricultural Commissioner Andriessen

Allan Wilkinson: Adviser to Peter Pooley, Deputy Director-General, DG-VI

INTRODUCTION

The 1980s have been troubled times for agriculture in both the United States and the European Community. Food production has increased steadily in both areas at a time of relatively static international and domestic demand, with adverse consequences for prices and farm incomes. Stocks have increased, at least until trimmed by the 1988 drought in the USA, lending urgency to costly surplus disposal efforts, which, in turn, have greatly intensified the export competition between the USA and the EC. The costs of government price and income policies escalated dramatically over much of the decade, placing strains on the budget, increasing the visibility of agricultural spending and increasing the competition between farm programmes and other priorities. US outlays for farm price and income support increased from $3 billion in 1980 to $25 billion in 1987, while comparable outlays for the EC increased from $16 billion in 1980 to $26 billion in 1987 (see Figure 0.1).[1] As a result, discussion centred, in both Brussels and Washington, on the necessity of drastically transforming those policies which create powerful incentives towards over-production. These reform efforts have so far had only limited success: the basic farm policies which existed at the beginning of the 1980s are still firmly in place today.

While agricultural commodity programmes have become more and more expensive in both the USA and EC, they have not notably succeeded in improving the lot of farmers. Income per worker in agriculture has failed to keep pace with the income per worker in the general economy.[2] Moreover, most commodity programmes, by virtue of the fact that the benefit conferred is in direct proportion to the amount produced, reward large farmers disproportionately.[3] US and EC farm programmes have also failed to stanch the exodus of farmers from the land. Agricultural employment as a percentage of civilian employment decreased between 1980 and 1985 from 8.0 per cent to 7.2 per cent for the EC, and from 3.4 per cent to 3.0 per cent for the USA (Newman, Fulton and Glaser, 1987, p. 4). Indeed, one can argue that government commodity programmes have speeded the exodus by strengthening larger farmers in their competition with smaller ones (see Cochrane, 1986).

The efforts to reform US agricultural policy and the Common Agricultural Policy (CAP) of the EC by cutting costs and increasing market orientation have waxed and waned in the 1980s, strongly influenced by changing economic and political conditions and by the different policy and

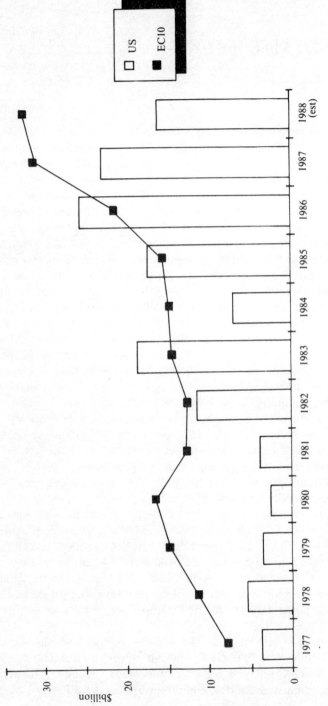

Figure 0.1 Outlays for price and income support, EC and US, 1977–88
Source: Newman *et al.* (1978).

electoral cycles of the USA and EC. In the USA, the two principal opportunities for reform came in the context of the debates over the 1981 and 1985 Omnibus farm bills. In 1981, however, there was little impetus to reform: US agriculture was just ending a period of unparalleled export growth, with government spending on farm programmes running only at levels between $1 billion and $3 billion per year. In addition, a general feeling prevailed that the world food economy might again be entering a period of scarcity.

The situation was far different in 1984 when attention began to focus on the 1985 farm bill. Outlays for price and income support had increased from $4 billion in 1981 to $11.6 billion in 1982 and $18.8 billion in 1983. The actual cost was higher than this: the 1983 Payment-in-Kind (PIK) programme, which exchanged government stocks for idle farmland, had the effect of masking the true costs of the policy.[4] The Executive, Congress and the agricultural community broadly debated changes to commodity programmes. However, the 1985 Food Security Act which emerged largely disappointed those who had advocated reform. Commodity programmes emerged pretty much intact, though loan rates were reduced to make exports more competitive. Target prices were not to be reduced until the last three years of the legislation, and then to drop a maximum of 10 per cent. Weak market prices and lower loan rates raised the prospect of higher deficiency payments and increased budget costs for the main crops. An attempt was made at cost control by freezing the acreage bases and crop yields used to determine farmer eligibility for deficiency payments, but this did not seem enough to constitute a major change in policy.

The pressure for agricultural reform was appeased only temporarily with the passage of the 1985 farm bill. Enormous outlays for price and income support of $17.6 billion, $25.8 billion and $25.3 billion for the years 1985, 1986 and 1987, respectively, rekindled the flame of reform. The cost of support fell in 1988, along with the impetus for reform, largely as a result of the drought in that year. However, with the Bush administration attempting to cut the budget deficit without new taxes, and with harvests returning to more normal levels in 1989, the issue of farm programme spending will still be important in the 1990 farm bill debate. It could return to the top of the agenda rapidly with a fall in world market prices.

Debate on reform has followed a very different progression in the 1980s for the EC. This is partly because the policy cycle is different. Rather than debating agricultural policy every four or five years as in the USA, the EC considers policy modifications at any time, often taking decisions in the context of the annual commodity price package negotiation. Still, the attention given to reform has varied considerably from year to year. Reform was a hot topic in 1980, with agricultural expenditures (constituting about 70 per cent of the total EC budget) threatening to exhaust available Community revenues. However, the heat was off in the years 1981–3 when

CAP spending actually declined. The tide of reform began to rise again in 1984 and increased rapidly until 1988 as outlays for price and income support have escalated upwards. A significant change in the dairy support programme was achieved in 1984 with the imposition of milk production quotas. Other commodity support programmes are finally beginning to yield to increasing budgetary pressures. The February 1988 EC summit in Brussels achieved a measure of budgetary control by explicitly including finance ministers in the agricultural policy process and by instituting limits on agricultural expenditures (stabilizers). The Community instituted automatic penalties for overproduction in a range of commodities, particularly cereals and oilseeds. Spending growth was contained somewhat in 1989, partially because of the operation of stabilizers, but also because of the poor US harvest in 1988, which raised world food prices. Yet, the tide of reform will not recede for long unless production incentives are significantly reduced, a prospect which still seems very much in doubt.

Agricultural policy reform is not just a matter of domestic policy. It has international trade manifestations as well. The declining farm income situation in the 1980s has made it difficult to reduce the level of agricultural protection in importing countries. Growing surpluses have contributed to an escalating warfare of export subsidies on the part of the USA and EC to maintain their respective shares of a declining export market. This competition has had an adverse effect on other exporting nations, including Argentina, Australia, Canada and New Zealand, whose markets have been endangered. It may also have adversely affected the Third World where low world commodity prices appear to impede agricultural development efforts. Increasing efforts have been made, particularly since 1985, to bring agricultural trade more generally into conformity with general GATT procedures and to reduce the level of protection afforded to agricultural commodities. These efforts are currently coming to a head in the GATT Uruguay Round negotiations, scheduled for completion by the end of 1990. Attempts to reform the international trade system are, of course, tied in with the developments in national policy. Reform of the international agricultural trading regime can only take place in the context of changes in domestic policy which reduce protection against imports and avoid the need for export subsidies.

It is not always easy to define agricultural policy reform. The notion of reform is essentially subjective. A policy change seen by one group as reform could be viewed by another as a modest revolution of policy or an improvement in programme administration. The definition used here for reform is *a significant shift in policy direction, usually involving changes in instruments, arising from general dissatisfaction with the current operation of the policy.* Even such a definition leaves ample scope for interpretation, but it is intended to exclude year-to-year policy reactions which neither of themselves nor cumulatively add up to a significant shift in policy. To link reform to changes in instruments may not be necessary – one can presumably use the same set of policy instruments to achieve markedly different effects – but, in general, the policy shift will require new mechanisms. The introduction of new policy devices is in any case the normal focus of debate and the outward and visible sign that the change in 'policy direction' has taken place. Reform may occur through a series of incremental steps (the most likely way to achieve change in pluralistic democratic societies), or it may occur as a sudden non-incremental shift to a completely new policy, as in the creation of a new dairy quota regime for the EC in 1984.[5]

In the following chapters we will identify and analyse in detail the principal agricultural reform initiatives during the 1980s in the EC, the USA and in the international trade arena to gain an understanding of the dynamics of the policy process.[6] We will be particularly concerned with the politics of agricultural reform and with the interplay between economic and political forces in placing reform on the policy agenda; developing options to deal with perceived problems; and deciding how to respond. What makes initiatives succeed or fail? How much can one attribute to the underlying economic and political environments? How much to the structure and function of the policy process? How much to the leadership or obstructive role of individuals? And how much can be attributed to external constraints and pressures, including those generated by the policies of the other partner in the US–EC agricultural relationship?

Before assessing US and EC agricultural policy processes, it is necessary to develop a framework for analysis – the task of the first chapter. Existing decision-making paradigms in the literature include those of the rational national actor, public choice theory, organizational process, bureaucratic politics and partisan mutual adjustment. From these various approaches we develop a schema for analysing US and EC agricultural reform efforts, and hypothesize a general scenario for agricultural policy reform. For those less interested in the analytical framework, this first chapter can be skipped without loss of continuity.

The detailed examination of the agricultural policy process in the EC and the USA is dealt with, respectively, in Chapters 2–4 and 5–7, including a discussion of the 'reforms' of the 1980s. The issue of reform of the trading system is dealt with in Chapter 9, and the final chapter attempts to compare and contrast the EC and US experiences and look for lessons for those charged with reforming farm policies in industrial countries.

NOTES

1. The expenditure figures for the EC do not include agricultural spending by national and local governments. However, most price support programmes operate at the Community level.

2. Income per worker in agriculture is not the same as family income: non-farm earnings have softened the impact on farm families both in the USA and the EC.
3. The US Department of Agriculture, in attempting to persuade Congress to cut commodity programmes in the 1985 Food Security Act, noted that of the $6.6 billion spent in commodity payments in 1984, 39 per cent went to only 5 per cent of farmers, who each received more than $25,000 from the programmes. See Guither (1986).
4. The value of the government stocks given to farmers under the PIK programme did not appear as a budget cost.
5. Incremental change might appear inconsistent with new policy instruments. However, new policy instruments can be created incrementally, as the EC has recently done with set-asides and the USA has done with decoupling. At first, the new instruments have limited applicability, with the scope of the change increasing over time.
6. There has been little previous work comparing US and EC agricultural policy processes. However, insights can be gained from Wilson (1977), which compares the USA and United Kingdom.

PART I

AN ANALYTICAL FRAMEWORK

1 · ALTERNATIVE APPROACHES TO THE STUDY OF THE AGRICULTURAL POLICY PROCESS

The complexity of the public policy in agriculture poses a challenge for those who wish to understand it. A degree of simplification is necessary in order not to get lost in detail, but too simple an account misses much of the flavour of the policy. What is needed is a structure, a framework, on which to hang the detail. Our explanation of the process of agricultural reform will be made easier by the use of such an analytical framework or schema. It will suggest reasons for particular characteristics of policies. It will enable comparisons to be made between EC and US experiences. It will help in distinguishing short-term policy adjustments from long-lasting reforms.

Such an analytical framework requires a decision-making paradigm. Several such models exist in the literature of political science and political economy, ranging from rational choice and public choice to various types of organizational and bureaucratic behaviour model. Each of these models highlights an aspect of public policy, and has some value in understanding agricultural reform. No single model or theory is likely to explain satisfactorily all the twists and turns of a complex policy. And yet, if one does not have in mind some explanation of the motives and actions of decision-makers, then policy becomes a random process subject to description but not understanding. No attempt is made here to 'prove' certain theories, or even to rank them in terms of their usefulness. Our approach is more eclectic. We review the various decision-making paradigms for any insights they may give in understanding the complexity of the real world. After reviewing the various approaches taken by others, we attempt a framework which may help in putting together the many aspects of policy-making and policy-reform in agriculture.

1.1 RATIONAL CHOICE MODELS

Among the most common models used for the explanation of public policy is that of the rational actor. Rational choice models assume a calculating central national actor acting with complete information and with the power to make and implement policy decisions. Such models are the easiest to apply because they do not require information about the workings of the policy process.[1] The rational national actor develops clear goals and priorities on the basis of the interests at stake and then chooses the most efficient from a broad range of alternatives. In the language of the neo-classical economist, the government works to maximize the welfare of the society. Policies are necessary when markets are missing or work imperfectly: in those situations the government has to intervene in well-defined ways to achieve social optimality. For the political scientist, the goals of such a rational actor are more likely to include such things as the preservation of stability and government legitimacy in the domestic arena, and maintenance of the balance of power internationally.

Although rational choice models provide the basis for most economic analysis of policy, such models allow one to consider situations where economic goals are combined with social ones.[2] In agricultural policy, for instance, the government may work to save the family farm, assure a 'fair' income and standard of living for farmers, conserve the natural environment, ensure adequate food at reasonable prices for consumers and maintain vigorous and pleasant rural communities. But to be operational one needs to measure these intangibles in situations where consumers and voters do not readily reveal their preferences. A market demand for environmental quality or price stability may not exist. And if one relies only on the political process to interpret the signals, the argument quickly becomes circular. Anything a government does must be appropriate because it is assumed to have taken fully into account the non-economic goals to weigh against the narrow economic and measurable objectives of policy.

Stripped of this tautological component, rational choice models do not seem adequate in themselves to explain agricultural policy in either the USA or the EC. The rational actor would probably have eliminated commodity price and income support policies to reduce the burgeoning surpluses, allowing the market to clear. The financial resources saved could undoubtedly be more productively employed elsewhere. With regard to the non-economic goals, US and EC policy-makers have expressed general support for distributional and environmental policy objectives, but on both sides of the Atlantic the bulk of support goes to large farmers, the small family farm is declining, environmental problems are multiplying, consumer prices are kept artificially high and rural society is in decay.

One common explanation for the failure of the rational choice model in explaining agricultural policy is that, even though governments try to achieve economic and social rationality, they are incompetent to do so because of defects in the policy process.[3] This explanation has the advantage that it takes politics and process into account. However, it still assumes that the government has clear policy objectives, which may not be the case.

Power is usually divided among organisations and individuals with different interests, goals and perceptions. There may be no consensus about national goals: they may emerge *ex post* from the outcome of the political process. In this case, the 'benevolent dictator' needs to be put in the appropriate institutional environment.

1.2 PUBLIC CHOICE ANALYSIS

An alternative approach to the study of policy is to be found in the theory of public choice. A good deal of scholarly work has been done to explain the behaviour of participants in the policy process.[4] This public choice approach shifts policy rationality from the level of the single actor or government to that of the many participating individuals, trying to maximize egoistic utility subject to constraints. Individuals with common interests combine together to form organizations to protect these interests, which in turn develop their own interests, related to, but not always identical with, those of their constituencies, which their staffs have an incentive to enhance. Government agencies also have their own organizational interests which personnel have a stake in promoting. Policy is the outcome of the way in which the preferences of these institutions and agents are combined in the political process.

According to public choice analysis, participants in the policy process maximize values which are important to them as individuals. They may be concerned with such things as job advancement, security, recognition, or sense of accomplishment.[5] The values maximized would seem to fall along a spectrum ranging from selfish interests on one end to altruistic interests on the other. Table 1.1 (p. 16) gives a general categorization of motivating concerns along this spectrum. What seems clear is that priorities vary from moment to moment, sometimes in predictable ways. One might hypothesize, for example, that a policy crisis helps individuals to transcend narrow selfish concerns. Personal insecurity probably has the opposite effect. Policy context would appear to play a very important role in determining value priorities.

Role is very important in that it influences the incentives for individual behaviour. Thus, one would expect politicians to show greatest concern about re-election, particularly as an election approaches. Lower and middle-level bureaucrats seem likely to further the goals of the organizations where they work. Top officials with broad policy responsibilities will probably focus on national or community interests. Leaders at any level of the policy process can influence the priorities of those working below them by the way they structure performance rewards and penalties.

It also makes a difference where in the policy debate action is occurring. When participating in a debate inside an organization, the individual will

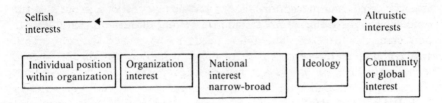

Figure 1.1 The range of individual motivations

probably work to improve his or her position within the organization. As the arena shifts to bargaining between organizations, the bargainers will attempt to maximize the benefits for their organizations. In international negotiations between nations, the negotiators will pursue the national interest as it appears from their organizational perspective. When an international organization participates in negotiations, its representatives can be expected to further the broader community interests as perceived by the international secretariat (see Figure 1.1).

Policy-makers often have serious problems with maximizing in that they have multiple values to consider in a given policy situation. Often these values are in conflict with each other. There is a good deal of literature to suggest that individuals have great difficult in making value trade-offs (see, for example, Jervis, 1976; George, 1980). They may go for one value at one minute and another value the next, or even pretend no conflict exists.

The responsiveness of the policy process to various inputs depends on the openness of the system, how closely the interests of policy-makers coincide with those of other actors, how much the policy-makers are committed to a particular strategy, the opportunities the political system offers for gratifying the interests of a particular group, and the ability of a group to reward or punish the decision-makers (Senior Nello, 1984, pp. 270–1).

The policy process in democratic societies creates incentives for decision-makers to respond to special interests. Elected officials try to maximize their chances for re-election by seeking votes. If all voters knew and communicated their interests there would be no problem because politicians would respond to the majority view of the community. However, not all voters know or express their preferences. Anthony Downs's (1957) classic *Economic Theory of Democracy* provides a persuasive explanation. Information and signalling costs are involved in forming and expressing preferences. It costs a voter time, energy and money to find out how a proposed policy affects him or her and to attempt to influence the political process. Assuming rational behaviour, the individual has no incentive to incur these costs unless he or she can be persuaded that the benefit is larger than the cost. Only those individuals with more than a general stake in the outcomes of particular policy decisions have an impetus to try to influence politicians.

A typical public choice analysis of policy would contain three elements: identifying those economic agents who expect the policy to affect their interests, and estimating how strong they expect the effects to be; exploring how and whether the economic agents do indeed respond to the supposed effects of the policy, along with how they translate these effects into efforts; and understanding the way in which the political system responds to these efforts on the part of the economic agents.[6]

In agricultural policy the main economic agents can be readily identified. Farmers, food manufacturers, exporters, fertilizer and chemical producers, seed producers, middlemen, merchants, the general public in the roles of taxpayer and final consumer, and members of government with responsibility for agricultural policy would all be on such a list. The quantification of the economic and financial impacts of agricultural policies confirm a priori reasoning. In general, farmers and agri-business feel the effects of agricultural policy most directly.[7] Current government programmes confer large special benefits (rents) on farmers and agri-business which are not shared by other groups. These benefits can only be preserved if the programmes are retained. Farm subsidies also create a dependency on government policy decisions. Some of the 'benefit' of continued support is avoidance of the cost of adjustment to unsubsidized conditions. This may prove an even stronger incentive for political activity.

Farmers respond vigorously to agricultural policy issues. Individual farmers cannot easily shift their fixed capital resources out of farming to more productive endeavours. Moreover, most farmers do not want to leave the land. Their efforts to make a living are frustrated and this frustration leads to expression through interest group activity or direct attempts to influence the government. This activity can be explained in terms of Hirschman's (1975) concepts of 'exit' and 'voice' (see Senior Nello, 1984, p. 269). Farmers denied easy opportunities for 'exit' and those unwilling to 'exit' rely heavily on exercising political 'voice'. The notion of 'rent-seeking' has also been applied to interest groups which benefit from farm programmes.[8] Farmers turn to political action or political rent-seeking particularly when their efforts at economic profit-seeking are frustated. The political economic-seeking transfers (PEST) activities of large farmers and agri-business deriving large special benefits from current agricultural policy have also been called 'rent-protection'.[9] These benefits are worth a good deal of time, effort and money to protect.

How vigorously groups respond depends not only on how much they are affected, but also on how easy it is to organize. Individuals join organizations if the benefits exceed the costs. To understand this relationship in any policy context one must understand the structure of the interest groups. Important features are homogeneity of preferences, size, strength, economic structure of the membership sectors and political party affiliation (Senior Nello, 1984, p. 265). Farm groups generally find it easier to organize than consumer groups because they are more homogenous. They also seem less vulnerable to the 'free-rider' effect described by Mancur Olson (1965). Farm organizations tend to be dominated by large prosperous farmers with a large stake in the 'public goods' provided by agricultural policy. As a result they appear to be induced into accepting responsibility for safeguarding and enhancing farm benefits (Senior Nello, 1984, p. 267). Farm organizations co-opt support from smaller farmers by making available benefits such as low-cost life insurance and detailed information about current farm programmes.

Thus, one would expect agricultural policy in both the USA and EC to show responsiveness to farm and agri-business interests, even when such interests represent a small minority of the voting population. Agricultural policy has become extremely complicated. Only large farmers and agri-business derive sufficiently large benefits to justify the enormous costs involved in understanding and attempting to influence farm programmes. Smaller farmers join the effort because their information costs are often reduced by farm interest groups which provide detailed information about current and proposed policies. Consumers and the general public with much smaller individual stakes have little incentive to attempt to influence policy formation.

Bureaucrats also tend to respond to special interests. Rather than trying to win votes, it is rational for non-elected officials to seek power, prestige, income and security (see Downs, 1967; Tullock, 1965). Bureaucrats responsible for making agricultural policy need good information and a base of outside support to be effective as well as to enhance their positions. Farm organizations and agri-business can provide this information and support much better than consumer and other public interest groups. Civil servants also tend to respond to the vocal outside forces to increase their legitimacy. It is easy for them as it is for politicians, to confuse vocal inputs with more general public opinion.

1.3 ORGANIZATIONAL PROCESS AND BUREAUCRATIC POLITICS

Graham Allison (1971), the political scientist, has formulated two alternative analytical paradigms to the rational actor which he labels 'organizational process' and 'government (bureaucratic) politics'. These paradigms have elements consistent with public choice theory, but focus more on process than on individual behaviour.

The organizational process paradigm (Allison, 1971, Ch. 3) assumes that government action reflects organizational output. It is based on the extensive literature of organizational theory which shows many common characteristics required for the functioning of large complex organizations (see especially March and Simon, 1958; March, 1965; Cyert and March, 1963). This paradigm sees the actor not as a monolithic 'nation' or 'government' but as a constellation of loosely allied organizations on top of which government leaders sit. Government acts only when the component organizations, like the US Department of Agriculture or the Office of Management and Budget, perform routines. Power is fragmented and problems are factored. Factoring permits more specialized attention to particular facets of problems than would be possible if government leaders looked at problems in their totality. Primary responsibility for a narrow set of problems encourages organizational parochialism. Organizations see problems in accordance with their own interests, which leads to different perceptions and priorities. Action is understood as organizational output characterized by programmed response, with goals considered sequentially, policy repertoires, uncertainty avoidance and 'crisis coping'. Organizational goals, of which the most central is organizational health (defined usually in terms of bodies assigned and dollars appropriated) define the parameters of acceptable performance.

In the organizational process paradigm, the best predictor of what an organization does today is what it did yesterday. Organizational budgets, structures and personnel change only incrementally, so the possiblities of policy change are limited. Moreover, organizational priorities, perceptions and issues appear relatively stable. Organizations tend to act on the basis of rules and standard operating procedures which are themselves slow to change. Only a limited number of options can be considered, with a tendency to satisfice (i.e. to be satisfied with an acceptable option, not the best possible option) (Allison, 1971, p. 72).[10]

Allison notes several other factors which hinder an organization's ability to respond adequately to problems. Long-range planning tends to become institutionalized and then disregarded. Trade-offs (i.e. hard choices among goals) are neglected. Organizations tend to ignore conflicts between goals. They can handle this by imagining that the conflicts do not exist, or by ignoring some goals while giving attention to others. Projects which demand that existing organizational units depart from their established programmes to perform unprogrammed tasks are rarely accomplished in their designed form. Projects that require co-ordination of the programmes of several organizations are rarely accomplished as intended. When an assigned piece of a problem is contrary to existing organizational goals, resistance will be encountered. Government leaders can expect that each organization will 'do its part' in terms of what the organization knows how to do. They can also expect incomplete and distorted information from each organization about its part of the problem.

The government politics paradigm (Allison, 1971, Ch. 5) focuses on bargaining among players in positions. Allison applied it strictly to the bureaucracy, but it seems with some adaptations, to fit bargaining in any context. The bargaining stance each player assumes depends on his or her role and interests ('where you stand depends on where you sit') (Allison, 1971, p. 176). Different actors are likely to have different perceptions of the problem, what is at stake, and the feasible options. Political action is seen as the result of bargaining. The assumption is that each actor will act in accordance with self-interest; but the nature of self-interest varies. When an individual participates in a bargaining game his motivations change from what they would be if he had the power to make the decision in question himself. He must think not only about his policy goals, but also about what it will take to 'win' in the bargaining game. Acceptability becomes the most important criterion.

This paradigm pays very close attention to the bargaining process. Understanding the rules and procedures for bargaining is very important because they determine how open or closed the process is, what gets on the agenda, who is involved in the decision, the action channels and how the process proceeds. Bargaining rules heavily influence policy outcomes. For instance, a voting rule of unanimity lengthens the decision-making process, but ensures that no decision will be taken which violates the fundamental interests of any actor.[11]

Government politics analysis also requires assessment of the distribution of power among bargaining actors to explain policy outcomes, where power is a function not only of capabilities, but also of the relative stakes the actors have in the policy decision. Power appears also as a function of the norms and rules governing the process. Individuals seldom bring their full resources to bear. The process may deny them access to the bargaining table at the critical moments, or they may not think the situation is critical enough to commit scarce political resources.

It is also important to understand how winning coalitions are formed and how they operate. To achieve a winning coalition, an actor must reward those who join, which may mean compromise or side payments. Coalitions do not just happen when there are shared interests; the environment must be conducive, and someone must form them. Strategy is very important. The person forming a coalition must recognize that others will generally delay making concessions until they are sure they have achieved the best possible deal. When a coalition has been forged, it usually does not have much flexibility, because any change in position implies bargaining costs to achieve a new consensus. Significant change may endanger the very existence of the coalition. The literature on bargaining gives some insights about how to build winning coalitions (see especially Schelling, 1960). The proposed outcome must be better for all participants than no agreement at all. The person forging the coalition must make credible commitments in terms of threats and promises, where credibility is a function of power, incentive and reputation for carrying out commitments. Ability to control information and to control the bargaining agenda appear very important, along with the ability to spot the 'prominent' solution to which all actors are inexorably drawn (see Schelling, 1960, Parts I and II).

When one analyses the policy process using the conceptual lenses of both these approaches, the structure of the process becomes critically important. How many actors are there? Who are they? What do they represent? How many steps does the process have? Who is involved at each stage? How decentralized is the decision-making? We could suggest certain general hypotheses. For instance, one could argue that the more decentralized the process, the greater the number of steps, and the greater the number of actors, the stronger the bias towards maintaining the status quo, because the bargaining costs of achieving change increase with the complexity of the process. Decision-making under these conditions seems inherently reactive and incrementalist. The analysis on the part of any participant probably is limited, self-interested and directed towards winning the bargaining game. Each step in the policy process is severely constrained not only by past policy decisions, but also by previous steps in the process. An interesting paradox seems implied by this approach: as the process proceeds vertically towards decision-makers whose overview seems more likely to be comprehensive, the options available to them become more and more severely constrained.[12]

1.4 PARTISAN MUTUAL ADJUSTMENT

Charles E. Lindblom (1959; 1965; Lindblom and Braybrooke, 1963) has developed a model of partisan mutual adjustment similar to Allison's bureaucratic politics paradigm, except that it takes a normative position. He argues that policy reached through bargaining and consensus-building – partisan mutual adjustment – is likely to be of better quality than policy based on comprehensive cost-benefit analysis – central synoptic decision-making. This argument includes a number of elements. First, central synoptic decision-making (considering all the variables) tends to fail for complex problems in that there is often no agreement on the values to be pursued. Even assuming agreement over values, variables with measurement uncertainties too often appear, thus preventing effective analysis. Second, partisan mutual adjustment has the advantage that agreement can often be reached over means even without consensus on the ends. Indeed, heated bargaining over means often facilitates consensus over ends. Third, in partisan mutual adjustment, the analysis is more limited and hence more manageable. It is also more tentative, which makes policy more receptive to negative feedback and amenable to change. Fourth, though the incrementalism of partisan mutual adjustment may not allow rapid responsiveness to changing conditions, it will prevent drastic mistakes. Fifth, central synoptic decision-making tends to underplay the importance of consent to the continued viability of a democratic society, while partisan mutual adjustment emphasizes this value by taking into account the intensity of feelings. Sixth, one cannot say that partisan mutual adjustment simply reflects a consensus among special interests, because, inevitably, some of the participants in the process reflect the larger public interests. Lindblom postulates that the requirement of building a winning coalition encourages moderation on the part of special interests.

Lindblom's analysis suggests that, though the progress of change achieved through a political bargaining process may appear painfully slow and inefficient, progress is much surer than if reform is adopted without partisan mutual adjustment. Decisions reached through partisan mutual adjustment are likely to have a high degree of legitimacy in that they are based on consensus – efficiency is sacrificed for legitimacy. But, one could raise the issue whether important interests are excluded from the process and whether the public interest is adequately represented by such procedures. Democratic political processes seem inherently slow to act and slow to change because decisions are usually made through partisan mutual adjustment or bargaining between pluralistic political interests, rather than through cost-benefit analysis by central decision-makers. It is much easier to preserve the status quo than to implement reform because of the high bargaining costs implied in forging a new policy consensus. Those who would prevent change have merely to prevent a new policy consensus from emerging. Reform can be achieved, but usually only incrementally, except when the economic or political environment becomes so adverse that it undermines the position of those who would prevent change. It usually takes a serious crisis to achieve rapid change.

Where the arena for partisan mutual adjustment is a legislative body, as it often is, change seems especially difficult, because the legislators often have more political interest in taking a position and in being noticed than they have in seeing effective policy developed. Their electorates will notice and hold them responsible for the positions they take, but will not normally hold them accountable for either success or failure of policy, which is after all the responsibility of the Executive.[13] In addition, power in legislative bodies is likely to be compartmentalized into committees whose members tend to represent constituencies which have a vested interest in the current policy. Such committees are almost never the source of reform ideas which do not benefit their parochial constituencies and tend to resist reform directed to more general interests.[14]

1.5 A PROCESS SCHEMATIC APPROACH

These various approaches to policy-making emphasize the way in which decisions are made. Each highlights a particular aspect of the decision-making. But the various actors in the policy system interact in a policy process, often specific to a particular country or type of policy. The identification of this process, including both political and bureaucratic actors, the relationships among them and the forces that impinge upon them, provides a framework for the examination of policy reform. Michel Petit (1986), in comparing agricultural policies of the USA and the EC, has developed a process schematic which allows one to take into account some of the insights of public choice theory and the organizational process and bureaucratic politics paradigms.

This schematic is reproduced in Figure 1.2. According to Petit's model, policies are viewed as 'political resultants' of a bargaining process in which policy debate plays a central role. As Petit (1985, pp. 29–30) describes the process:

> Policy decisions during period (*t*) come out of the black box called 'political bargaining', a process that takes place among organizations, shaped in period (*t*) both by the state of economic interests and that of institutions. Long-term economic forces at period (*t*) influence the state of economic interests. Long-term economic forces are assumed to be exogenous, although they are partially influenced by policy decisions.

Long-term economic forces are defined as trends in key economic variables changing because of the general evolution of the national economy or of world trade. Similarly institutions are mainly autonomous. Long-term economic forces and institutions directly influence the bargaining process in the short run, but are only influenced by the policy process in the long run (Petit, 1985, p. 19).

Petit's schematic is helpful but incomplete in a number of respects. First, it plays down the influence of past policy in shaping current policy decisions. Second, it ignores the influence of political developments, such as the changes in legislative strength of the farm lobby caused by population movements and the evolution of public attitudes on farming.[15] Third, it neglects political interests such as preserving political stability, increasing government legitimacy and enhancing the relationships with other countries.

Petit's approach also does not consider the impact of economic shocks and the political environment in which policy is made. Both these factors influence the way individuals see and make operational their multiple interests. Group and national interests tend to be very broad-ranging and nebulous – such things as security, stability and prosperity. As one attempts to get more precise, different dimensions of these general interests appear.

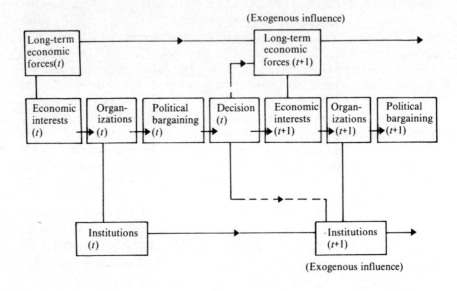

Figure 1.2 Recursive representation of the dynamic policy-making process
Source: Petit (1985)

For instance, when an actor in the system has an interest in prosperity, this could be a concern about GNP growth, the trade balance, job creation or farm income. No individual can pay attention to all his interests and all the dimensions of each interest at any one moment. The political environment helps establish what should get attention and what should be the priorities. Similarly, economic shocks will bring certain interests to the front of the political stage at any particular moment.

Finally, the Petit schematic does not show explicitly how important outside political inputs, such as the press, public opinion, lobbies, and the writings of scholars, fit into the bargaining process. The roles played by these political inputs and the influence each has on the decision-makers would appear strongly influenced by the political environment. If farmers are blocking a highway, policy-makers will tend to listen. If an academic produces an idea which will help solve a political problem, it may get attention.

For the purpose of exploring agricultural policy reform, we have developed a new schematic, which builds on Petit's work but tries to incorporate the missing elements noted above. This schematic is shown in Figure 1.3. The policy from the previous period represented by the Decisions (*t*–1) box has a direct effect on bargaining at time (*t*) which takes

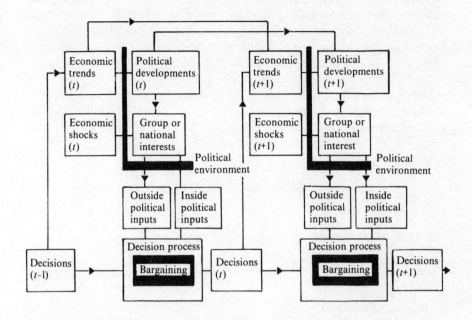

Figure 1.3 Modified representation of the dynamic policy-making process

place inside the decisions process. It also impacts on economic trends (which include changes in key economic indicators such as gross national product, rate of inflation, exchange rate, trade balance, food production, and farm income). Past policy may also have an effect on economic shocks, which include such things as a sudden drought or a policy decision by another nation to dump food commodities on the international market. Economic trends have a strong impact on political developments, such as the movement of the EC to a single European market in 1992. But, political developments, such as changes in the legislative strength of the farm lobby and evolution of public attitudes toward farming, may be independent of direct economic inferences. The nature of the impact of economic trends is conditioned by the political environment, defined as the problems policy-makers face at a given moment (such as a budget crisis or an imminent election). Political developments and economic shocks have a strong influence on how policy actors perceive their individual, group and national interests and on how they prioritize these interests.

Policy actors fit into two groups: *outside* political inputs and *inside* political inputs. Examples of the former type are farm, agri-business and consumer organizations, academics, the press and public opinion. They are considered 'outside inputs' in that they influence the policy process, but are not participants in the actual decision-making. The latter group consists of actors in the decision-making process, including politicians and officials. The positions which actors take and the intensity of their commitment are strongly influenced by their conceptions of political and economic interests. They seem also conditioned by the current political environment. Bargaining outcomes reflect both the positions and intensity of commitment of outside and inside political inputs and the structure of the decision process. Economic trends and political developments at time (t) are, of course, directly related to the economic trends and political developments in time $(t+1)$.

Table 1.1 Scheme for analysis of US and EC agricultural reform

1. The policy background
    (a)   Economic trends
    (b)   Economic shocks
    (c)   Political developments
    (d)   The political environment
    (e)   Conceptions of individual, group and national political and economic interests
    (f)   Past policy decisions

2. Outside political inputs
    (a)   International — pressures from allies and other trading partners
    (b)   Academic — proposals in books and articles
    (c)   Farm groups: which ones? How broadly based? How democratic?
    (d)   Agri-business and trade interests
    (e)   Consumers
    (f)   Government
    (g)   How groups construe their interests and form their positions

3. Inside political inputs
    (a)   How officials construe their interests
    (b)   The positions of the various policy actors and how they are formed
    (c)   Sensitivity of policy-makers to various inputs
    (d)   Quality of information exchanged
    (e)   Quality of analysis
    (f)   Differences between civil servants and elected officials
    (g)   Responsiveness of actors to external and internal influences
    (h)   Political accountability
    (i)   Position as a reflection of interest (political and economic) (global, community, national constituency, bureaucratic and personal)

4. Structure of the decision process
    (a)   The role and authority of the various policy actors
    (b)   Steps a proposal goes through before reform can be achieved
    (c)   What actors are involved and when
    (d)   Inherent constraints and biases of process
    (e)   The parameters for action at each stage of the process
    (f)   Constraints introduced at each stage for subsequent stages
    (g)   Biases of the policy process

5. Bargaining structure
   (a) Statutory policy goals
   (b) Rules for forming the bargaining agenda
   (c) Rules for access
   (d) Rules for introducing options
   (e) Rules for bargaining
   (f) Rules for voting (unanimity, majority, consensus, etc.)
   (g) Policy leeway
   (h) Power of the various actors, where power is conceptualized in terms of resources (inherent bargaining advantages, etc.) and in terms of influence (stake, skill, will)
   (i) Pluralism in the process
   (j) Differences between bargaining among approximate equals and bargaining to get the ear of a superior

6. Bargaining
   (a) What is put on the agenda
   (b) The critical issues
   (c) Bargaining outcomes and their explanation
   (d) Interplay between actors
   (e) How coalitions are formed
   (f) Strategies for winning and avoiding defeat
   (g) Impact of contextual economic and political variables
   (h) Role of external influences
   (i) Differences between international and domestic bargaining
   (j) Complexities introduced by perceptual differences and bureaucratic interests
   (k) Importance of precedents
   (l) Incrementalist tendencies

7. Outcomes
   (a) What they are
   (b) Who wins and who loses
   (c) Repetitive patterns
   (d) Reasons for success or failure of initiatives
   (e) The near-misses
   (f) Instances of reform

8. Outcomes and value priorities
   (a) Which interests prevail (global, community, national, constituency or individual)
   (b) Situational variability of interests
   (c) Relative importance of political and economic interests
   (d) Importance of agricultural interests. Which ones?

9. Implications of outcomes
   (a) For structure of farming
   (b) For farm income
   (c) For consumers
   (d) For general welfare
   (e) For legitimacy of the political process
   (f) For future reform

The analysis of agricultural reform in the following chapters will follow this approach. In particular, it will be concerned, first, with what is put on the policy agenda as well as when and why. It will also examine why certain obvious reform measures never make it onto the policy agenda. We will discuss how the policy process handles reform issues when they get attention: how the issues are perceived; what options are developed; how decisions are made; what factors are influential; how outcomes can be explained; and when and why some reform initiatives succeed and others fail. An analytical scheme has been developed with nine basic elements to correspond to the modified recursive representation of the dynamic policy-making process: the policy background; outside political inputs; inside political inputs; structure of the policy process; the bargaining process; bargaining; outcomes; value priorities; and implications of outcomes. The detailed development of this scheme is shown in Table 1.1.

The analytical framework developed in this chapter takes into account the insights of public choice, organizational process, government politics and partisan mutual adjustment. Consideration of economic trends, economic shocks, political developments and the political environment allows assessment of interests and positions using public choice. Elaboration of the decision structure permits assessment of the impact of organizational process on the policy process. Detailed discussion of the elements of bargaining facilitates evaulation of the importance of government politics and partisan mutual adjustment on policy outcomes.

1.6 HYPOTHESES ABOUT REFORM PROCESSES IN THE EC AND THE USA

The analytical scheme suggests a number of hypotheses about the policy processes and agricultural reform in the USA and EC. We would anticipate initiatives for reform to come primarily from high-level central decision-makers somewhat removed from the partisan mutual adjustment of legislative bodies and from the inertia of bureaucracies. We would expect legislative actors almost never to take the initiative in reform given their incentives to posture rather than produce. Bureaucratic actors are not much more likely to be in the vanguard of reform given the uncertainty avoidance and incrementalism of complex organizations, except, of course, when their jobs or programmes are somehow at stake.

What factors could make legislative and bureaucratic actors overcome their basic inertia and resistance to change? It would seem that a budget crisis where expenditures exhaust available revenues would provide the most potent stimulus. For bureaucratic actors, a budget crisis not only threatens their jobs and programmes, but also portends the loss of organizational autonomy. When agricultural ministries increase their spending too rapidly, their programmes are likely to come under much tighter scrutiny than usual from both prime ministers and finance ministers. An incentive is created to make the most of a bad situation and preserve as much organizational autonomy as possible. The motives are similar for legislative actors. A budget crisis inherently has the potential to disturb the compartmentalization previously created to protect constituency interests. The preservation of power requires responsiveness. For example, a budget crisis in agriculture tends to get legislators who normally have little interest in agriculture involved in policymaking. This is intimidating to the agricultural representatives, because they represent minority interests and could never hope to prevail except when there is disinterest among the majority. What makes a budget crisis so threatening to both agricultural bureaucracy and agricultural legislative actors is that it turns the policy process into a zero-sum game where agriculture's demand for new resources is seen as coming at the expense of other programmes. No other crisis is likely to create the same kind of outside interest.

Prior to discussion of the EC and US policy processes, it may be useful to postulate a general scenario for response to a crisis in agriculture generated by over-production. The initial indicator of a problem will probably be increasing stocks with increased spending for commodity programmes. The first responses will deal only with symptoms, not the basic problem. A logical first step would attempt to increase food exports. This does not offend any domestic constituencies as it tends to 'export' the problem. Import restrictions on competitive products are cheaper, but they tend to bring about retaliation and may get the foreign ministry interested in agricultural policy.

A second response would cut commodity prices, but the constraints are likely to be severe, because this offends the agricultural interests central to the partisan mutual adjustment process. Increases in commodity support may be forestalled, but cuts seem almost impossible at this stage, because they imply sacrifices by farm interests which their representatives have every incentive to oppose. Expedients may be tried which do not fully address the causes of surplus.

Only when continued over-production brings about a serious expenditures crisis, when the whole system of farm supports is threatened, will the underlying problem of overproduction be addressed – then only in piecemeal fashion. The normal agricultural policy process will probably not make the necessary reforms because farm interests will block them. Rather, the process will be temporarily changed either by broadening the range of participants to include budgetary and other actors more representative of the general community interest or by shifting the locus of decisions upward to top political levels.

Changing the process may change the rules for bargaining. It may also vary the mix between the forces which must be accommodated and their relative strength. Thus, the final consensus outcome may shift significantly. The decision-makers, ever mindful of the importance of maximizing consensus, will probably not change agricultural policy any more than they must, first attempting new expedients. Significant change will occur only when no other way out of the crisis seems evident. Legislative actors, inherently unable to handle decisions to redistribute resources, may be unable to act themselves, which may allow executive agencies to exercise discretionary authority.[16]

NOTES

1. For a thorough discussion of the assumptions made by rational actor models see Allison (1971, especially Chs. 1 and 2).
2. For a discussion of the problems associated with social rationality models, see Winters (1987, pp. 290–1).
3. For a discussion of limited social rationality, see Winters (1987, pp. 291–9).
4. Susan Senior Nello (1984, pp. 261–83) gives a useful summary of this approach applied to agriculture, and a full bibliography.
5. Much of the public choice literature tends to emphasize narrow self-interest as motivation for individual behaviour. But John Quiggin (1987, pp. 10–21) shows the need to emphasize a broad spectrum of motivators including a degree of altruism.
6. This categorization follows that in Susan Senior Nello (1984, p. 264). See also Josling and Moyer.
7. Merchants, middlemen, machinery dealers and input suppliers may not recognize their dependence on policy as clearly as they might. On the other hand, they may recognize their dependence but prefer to keep their policy influence covert.
8. For more general discussion of rent-seeking, see Buchanan *et al.*, (1981).
9. For a detailed discussion of PESTs, see Rausser (1982, pp. 821–33).
10. The concept of satisficing was developed by Harold Simon (1957). Satisficing can be seen as constrained optimization given the institutional costs of considering all options.
11. For an interesting discussion of voting rules in the EC context, see Runge and von Witzke (1985).
12. Two factors probably operate here. On the one hand, subordinates tend to constrain the options as they pass a decision upward. On the other hand, top-level decision-makers are more likely to see that all decisions are interrelated and that these relationships themselves constrain the options.
13. This argument is eloquently made for the US Congress by Mayhew (1974, p. 138).
14. On this point, see Mayhew's (1974, pp. 81–105) discussion on congressional committees.
15. Long-term trends in the strength of the farm lobby may be very long-term. The rapid decline in the farm population in the last 40 years leaves many people no longer in farming with fond memories of what farming was like and with romantic and family connections with the industry.
16. Lindblom (1965, pp. 217–20) mentions this as a very likely outcome in partisan mutual adjustment processes when legislative actors cannot afford the political consequences of voting directly for the necessary reforms.

PART II

AGRICULTURAL REFORM IN THE EUROPEAN COMMUNITY

2 · DECISION-MAKING IN THE EUROPEAN COMMUNITY

2.1 INTRODUCTION

In March 1957, six countries in Western Europe took the unprecedented step of setting up a common market designed to lead to eventual economic (and political) union. This experiment was intended to stimulate economic progress based on a large home market and to establish an influence on the world scene to rival that of the USA. They decided that agricultural markets could not be excluded from the process of integration. Existing national support systems were not compatible with a common market in agricultural products, but continued support to farmers was a political necessity. As a result, a common agricultural policy was thought necessary to manage the integrated European market for farm goods. The Treaty of Rome, which set up the European Community, explicitly mandated such a policy, and set up the machinery to put it in place. By 1962, the new CAP began to replace the plethora of support schemes used in the six member states. By 1968, the introduction of the policy was essentially complete, with harmonized prices and the removal of most national price support measures. Arrangements were made to finance the policy from a central EC fund, the European Agricultural Guidance and Guarantee Fund (FEOGA). This was financed initially through national contributions, but later supported by revenue from duties and levies on imports into the EC and by a national tax based on the 'value added' in member states.

This seemingly reasonable set of decisions paved the way for the present-day Common Agricultural Policy (CAP). But, along the way the CAP acquired notoriety at home and abroad and attracted more critical attention than any other policy of the European Community. The CAP has usually accounted for 60 to 70 per cent of the EC's common budget, and a similarly disproportionate share of administrative costs. Together with rapid technological progress in agriculture, it has stimulated EC food production well beyond self-sufficiency in many commodities, creating expensive surpluses and distorting international commodity markets. Once viewed as a notable achievement, cementing the EC together, it now drives a wedge between countries. The reform of the CAP has ranked high on the political agenda in Europe in recent years.

The CAP has also performed two roles. On the one hand, it is an agricultural policy for an integrated European Community. As such, it has the task of stablizing markets and supporting farmers' incomes, much like the policies of other industrial countries. On the other hand, it represents a delicate compromise between member governments, each attempting to use EC regulations to achieve national ends. Success in the first role is hampered by preoccupation with the second. Policy reform hovers between the impossible and the inevitable. The policy clearly does not achieve its aims and it imposes unsustainable burdens on EC finances and institutions. Yet agreement on reform has proved difficult as governments continue to block even modest progress where it conflicts with domestic self-interest. This element of inter-country bargaining makes the politics of the CAP particularly complex and interesting.

This chapter deals with the question of what constitutes reform of the CAP, why the CAP is under pressure to reform, and how the policy process deals with reform. Chapter 3 explicates the positions of the decision-makers, (inside political inputs) and external groups (outside political inputs), and discusses attempts over the years to reform the CAP. The discussion focuses on the political and the economic conditions which stimulate reform, and the particular interaction of political, bureaucratic and economic factors which shape this particular policy issue. Chapter 4 turns to case studies of the EC in crisis: the 1984 decision to institute dairy quotas; and the 1988 Brussels accord to institute agricultural stabilizers. It concludes with some generalizations about CAP reform.

2.2 PRESSURES FOR REFORM

The economic pressures for agricultural policy reform in the EC at present come largely from the high financial cost of the policy. The recent escalation of CAP costs, relative to the resources available to the EC to spend on all common policies, provides the most urgent signal that change is necessary. Spending on the CAP for market price support (FEOGA guarantee expenditures) is shown in Figure 2.1 for the period since 1970. In the early years, expenditure increased in part as a result of the transfer of spending obligations to the EC from national budgets. It increased later in the decade as a consequence of enlargement in 1973 to include the UK, Denmark and Ireland. Agricultural spending over the 1970s stayed well within the limits set by the available resources, and by 1980 had reached about 10 billion ECU (European Currency Units).

The problem of CAP expenditure became more severe in the 1980s. Spending doubled between 1980 and 1986, largely because of increasing costs for market intervention, storage and surplus disposal. In addition, the EC picked up more members. Greece joined in 1981 and Spain and Portugal were admitted in 1986. In 1984, the EC ran out of money for the first time

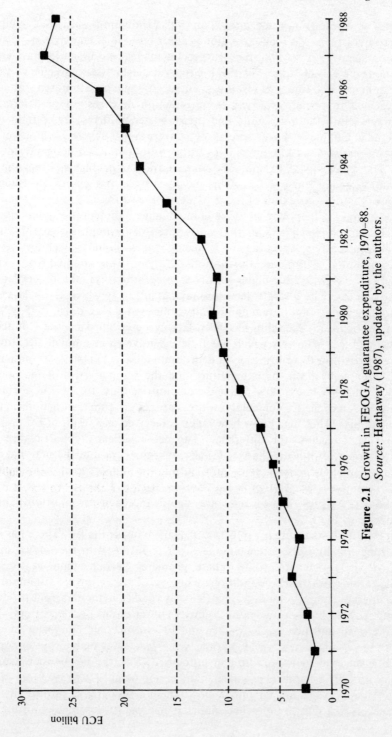

Figure 2.1 Growth in FEOGA guarantee expenditure, 1970–88.
Source: Hathaway (1987), updated by the authors.

and, as a result, imposed quotas on milk production and raised available resources from VAT-based national contributions. The extra money was soon spent, and by 1987 the prospect of inadequate funds loomed again. The response this time was the February 1988 Brussels agreement, which again increased financial resources, but at the same time imposed stabilizers designed to penalize farmers for production in excess of predetermined targets. Both the milk quota and the stabilizer 'reforms' are considered in detail in Chapter 4. Future pressures for reform will depend on how well the stabilizers succeed in controlling surplus production and budgetary costs.

The financing of EC policies poses particular problems. First, the EC cannot legally run a deficit. This means a stark and immediate trade-off between competing uses of funds. Second, the sources of revenue available for financing the policy are defined in advance – though the actual amount may vary somewhat from that anticipated. This implies that the choice between cutting spending and raising taxes is not available to the Community. Third, EC institutions are not well adapted to keeping agricultural spending under control. Integration has not proceeded far enough to create a single decision-making authority which can balance the funding claims of different community policies (see Hagedorn, 1985, pp. 42–3). Agricultural spending has been largely determined by the Council of Agricultural Ministers which has little incentive to give much attention to non-agricultural priorities.[1] Fourth, individual countries are impacted differently by both the expenditure and the revenue sides of the budget. Governments know how much their countries 'pay' to the EC, including how much of the EC financial resources are raised from transactions in their economies. They also know how much is received as a result of EC policies, and can calculate the difference. The net beneficiary countries are well positioned to prevent change. Finally, marginal costs at the national level decline with increasing agricultural output and support levels, thus creating an incentive to increase price support (see Ritson, 1979). For these reasons, budgetary issues take on an extra significance and are more difficult to resolve in the EC.

Not all the pressure for reform comes from inside the EC. There has been a long-standing discontent among other countries with the impact of the CAP on agricultural trade. These problems become acute at times of depressed world market conditions. The level of protection against imports of temperate-zone commodities, particularly cereals, dairy and meat products, and sugar, has always been a target of criticism for exporters, both developed and developing. When the EC was a major importer of these products, and when world markets were readily available, the exporters' criticism appeared sporadic and unfocused. But, the EC became a major exporter of agricultural products in the period from 1976 to 1981 (see Figure 2.2). As the EC moved into a position of considerable surplus in these markets, the reaction of other exporters became strident and co-ordinated.

In 1986, the EC agreed to enter into trade negotiations in the GATT (the Uruguay Round), aimed, among other things, at reducing the influence of export subsidies on world trade in agricultural produce. The extent to which these talks will help to translate outside concerns about the CAP into domestic policy changes is discussed in Chapter 8.

One long-time observer of agricultural policy has remarked that the CAP was based on two assumptions, both of which have proved false: that the EC would continue as a major importer of agricultural products; and that the price of such products on world markets would be steady or rise over time (Hathaway, 1987, pp. 73–4). A flexible political and administrative system might have coped with the changing domestic and foreign realities. However, the build-up of surpluses and the cost of their disposal indicate that the policy has not responded fast enough to these events. Reform, in the CAP, consists of the delayed response to accumulated pressures. The inertia of the policy process as much as market events has made reform a pressing issue. In terms of European unity, the CAP has become not the solution but a part of the problem.

The pressures on the budget and the tensions in the trade system essentially arise from the same set of underlying forces. Structural change and the adoption of new farming methods lead to a steady increase in farm output from year to year. Demand for farm products in the EC, as in other affluent countries, does not grow fast enough to prevent markets from becoming saturated. At certain times the growth in demand in other countries is enough to provide export markets to absorb the excess capacity. When that export demand becomes slack, governments face a political dilemma: buy stocks and dump them on world markets; or control production by lower prices or by quantitative controls. The first reaction is the easiest, at least at first. The problems arise when the period of reduced demand lasts for some years. The second reaction takes time to accomplish, and requires considerable political capital and bureaucratic energy.

Weak demand in the face of steady productivity increase leads eventually to lower farm prices. In periods of rapid inflation the underlying price trends can be obscured: in the 1980s, the downward trend became apparent to all. The trend in real prices is indicated in Figure 2.3 for the largest EC member states. On average, prices fell nearly 20 per cent over the period 1980–7. The policy of limiting price rises to less than the rate of inflation and of weakening the intervention system clearly has had an effect at the farm level. Incomes stagnated over this period, the price declines offset by changes in output and productivity and some reductions in input prices (particularly those based on petroleum) in the post-1982 period (see Figure 2.4). But, at a time when non-farm incomes increase with general economic growth, stagnation in incomes is not good news. As a consequence, it is probably true to say that both price and income trends contributed to the pressure on the policy over this period.

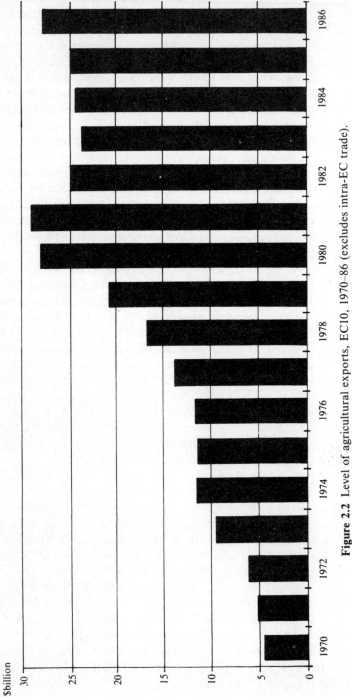

Figure 2.2 Level of agricultural exports, EC10, 1970–86 (excludes intra-EC trade).
Source: Newman *et al.*

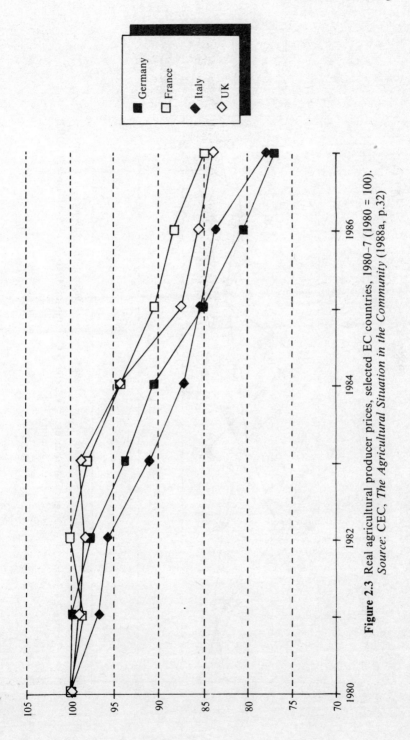

Figure 2.3 Real agricultural producer prices, selected EC countries, 1980–7 (1980 = 100).
Source: CEC, *The Agricultural Situation in the Community* (1988a, p.32)

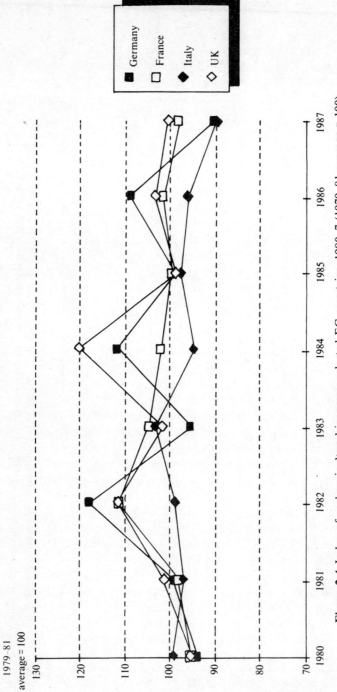

Figure 2.4 Index of real agricultural incomes, selected EC countries, 1980–7 (1979–81 average = 100).
Source: Agra Europé, 8 January 1988

2.3 THE AGRICULTURAL POLICY PROCESS AND REFORM

Decisions on policy changes have not come easily for the EC. A major reason for this is the highly compartmentalized decision-making structure of the EC, which essentially prevents rapid policy responses to events. To examine the link between structure and reform, this section explicates the EC agricultural policy process, including the relationships among EC institutions and between these institutions and the national governments. A discussion of the 'inputs' into the policy process follows in Chapter 3, along with an analysis of the positions of the main actors in the drama.

2.3.1 Decision-making bodies

The formal chain of consultations, proposals, and decisions is indicated in a simplified form in Figure 2.5. The four main EC bodies are the Commission, the Council of Ministers, the Parliament, and the Court of Justice. In recent years a fifth body, the European Council (the heads of government meeting at periodic 'summits'), has become important in taking decisions on contentious issues, though it has no formal role in governance of the Community.

The European Commission

The Commission of the European Communities holds a strategic place in the constitution of the EC. It acts as both the initiator of proposals (a task which the Council of Ministers cannot perform), and the administrator of decisions. It controls the major part of the bureaucracy, the Directorates-General, which run the day-to-day business of the EC. Much of the internal action on reform consists of proposals by the Commission to the Council of Ministers. At the head of the Commission are the Commissioners, who supposedly take a 'community' view of issues, separated from mere national advantage. They are appointed for four-year terms by the member states. The Commissioner holding the agricultural portfolio is responsible for submitting proposals for changing the CAP to the other Commissioners, meeting weekly as the 'College' of the Commission. He develops these proposals with the assistance of his Cabinet[2] and the Directorate-General for agriculture (DG-VI). How they are developed depends to a large extent on the preferences and personality of the Commissioner. There are no established procedures. When the Commissioner is assertive (as was Frans Andriessen, from 1985-8), he can dominate the process along with his Cabinet. When the Commissioner is less assertive, (as was his predecessor, Poul Dalsager), the locus of policy formation is centred much more on DG-VI.

Reform proposals are usually developed in response to a 'crisis' and

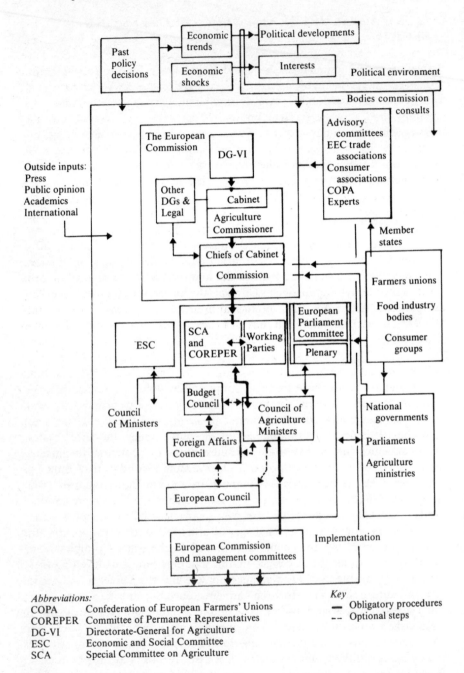

Abbreviations:

COPA   Confederation of European Farmers' Unions
COREPER Committee of Permanent Representatives
DG-VI   Directorate-General for Agriculture
ESC   Economic and Social Committee
SCA   Special Committee on Agriculture

Key
— Obligatory procedures
-- Optional steps

Figure 2.5 Decision-making process for EC agricultural policy formation under Article 43 of the Treaty of Rome

contain elements from a general pool of ideas circulating within the EC policy establishment. Specific ideas for change are promoted by individuals, usually on the basis of feasibility. In the past, proposals for reform have generally been considered in conjunction with the annual price review. But consideration of policy changes has recently come at other times of the year. The 1986 dairy and beef policy changes were agreed in December, for example, and the February 1988 Brussels agreement instituting stabilizers was concluded before the Commission made its price proposals for 1988-9.

Before submitting his proposals to the College of the Commissioners, the Agriculture Commissioner must clear them with affected Directorates-General and with the Commission's legal staff. They then face screening in the weekly meeting of the chiefs of the various cabinets to set the agenda for the weekly session of the full Commission. The chiefs try to streamline the Commission debate by identifying key issues as well as areas of probable agreement.

The full Commission then debates the proposals and may approve, modify or reject them. Even though decisions are made by simple majority vote, agreement does not always come easily. There are a number of reasons why this is the case. First, the College appears a rather unwieldy body. Since the enlargement of the Community in 1986 to include Spain and Portugal, it now consists of 17 members, which makes it a rather large forum for debating detailed proposals. Second, agricultural reform proposals have become so complex that the Agriculture Commissioner and his Cabinet must spend a good deal of time simply familiarizing other Commissioners with the details. Third, it is not easy to build support for a new idea among the Commissioners who reflect the full diversity of the member nations and who have different backgrounds, ideologies and constituencies.[3] Fourth, it takes time for the Commission to examine the implications of the proposal not only for the CAP but for other Community priorities as well, and to consider whether the proposal is politically feasible in the Council of Ministers.

The Commission submits its final proposal to the Council of Ministers. The Council Secretariat refers it for an opinion to two bodies which give advice, generally of a non-binding nature, to the Commission and Council. One is the Economic and Social Committee, comprised of 189 individuals from various walks of life divided into three groups, broadly representing employers, trade unions and 'independents'. This branch of the institutional tree has withered over time, and now plays no crucial role in policy-making. Another branch, the European Parliament, has flourished into a directly elected forum with limited but growing powers, both constitutional and political. Its main influence has been in its role in budget-making: it has to agree to spending on 'non-obligatory' items. Most expenditure on agriculture, however, is 'obligatory', meaning that it is directly mandated by the Treaty obligations and the consequent legislation, and cannot be blocked by the Parliament. More recently, the European Parliament has been integrated further into the decision process under the 'co-operation procedures' agreed in 1987 (see below). However, the most important roles for Parliament will probably remain those of well-informed watchdog, inquisitor of the Commission and the Council, and sounding board for ideas outside the normal government channels.

In preparation for discussion in the Council of Ministers, Commission proposals are scrutinized in one or more committees made up of national and Commission officials and chaired by an official from the member state holding the presidency. The Commission representative can speak but cannot vote, though formal votes are taken only rarely (see Harris, *et al.*, 1983, pp. 17–18). These committees operate at three levels. At the first level working parties deal with the details and technical aspects of the proposals. At the second level, sectoral aspects of proposals are examined. At the third level, the Committee of Permanent Representatives (COREPER) assigns Commission proposals to other committees for study and analysis and prepares the agenda for Council meetings.[4] It makes recommendations on non-controversial matters, thus facilitating formal council decision ('A-points').

COREPER does not consider agricultural issues unless they affect other Community policies. Instead, they are considered by the Special Committee on Agriculture (SCA), consisting of permanent officials from the member states plus a senior representative from the Commission who is there to explain and defend Commission proposals (Harris *et. al.*, 1983, pp. 18–19). The SCA can forward Commission proposals to the Council after discussion or send them first to a technical working party. The SCA never votes formally. Where agreement develops on specific items ('A-points'), the SCA can make preliminary decisions subject to later confirmation by the Council. A Commission proposal may be substantially modified as it is considered by SCA: such changes are often made to increase the chances of a proposal's acceptance by the Council. Normally, the Commission accedes to these modifications and on occasion takes the initiative (Harris *et. al.*, 1983, p. 19). In fact, a close informal working relationship usually exists between SCA and the Commission. Where the Commission does not agree, the modification must receive unanimous approval by the Council.

The Council of Ministers
The Council of Ministers, as the decision-making body, controls the direction and the pace of the Community. Each member state has a seat on the Council, which it fills with a minister from the national government. Discussions in the Council are structured by subject matter and attended by the ministers responsible for those subjects. Hence, the EC has, for example, an Agriculture Council, a Finance Council, and a Foreign Affairs (or General) Council. This decision-making structure has led to a serious lack of

co-ordination, which undoubtedly makes more difficult both the budget and the external trade problems. Such fragmentation by subject limits the scope of negotiation among countries, and creates an unrealistic separation between policy actions and their domestic (or overseas) costs.

Council decision-making, until recently, came largely through consensus or unanimity. This has no basis in the EC Treaty, which provided only for voting by 'qualified majority',[5] (the votes of member states being weighted roughly according to size of population), but developed as a result of the Luxembourg Compromise (see Tracy, 1989, pp. 263–5) reached in January 1966, after President de Gaulle had withdrawn France from the Council for six months. In the 1980s, decision by qualified majority voting has become increasingly prevalent. This trend has been caused in part by the increased unwieldiness of the Council, with the expansion of the EC to 12 members, and, in part, by the need for prompter action. Greater use of qualified majority voting is mandated in the Single European Act (SEA), though the SEA's applicability to agricultural policy is limited.[6]

All Commission CAP proposals under Article 43 receive their primary consideration in the Agriculture Council. However, they may also receive consideration in the Budget Council, which can examine their cost implications, especially since the February 1988 agreement on financial limits, and the Foreign Affairs Council, which may analyse the ramifications for external policy. When the agriculture ministers cannot agree, the Foreign Affairs Council (as the 'senior' ministerial body) sometimes has the last chance to forge consensus before the proposals are submitted to the European Council (of heads of government) for final decision. Neither the Budget Council nor the Foreign Affairs Council has much agricultural expertise, so both bodies hesitate to tinker with the details worked out by the Commission and Agriculture Council.

The European Council
The emergence of the European Council comes largely as a response to the fragmentation of authority among the various Councils of Ministers, although it also serves the need to discuss future directions for the EC. Made up of heads of government (or, in the case of France, the head of state), together with the Commission President, and, recently, with the President of the European Parliament, the European Council holds 'summit' meetings at least twice a year. Questions that cannot be resolved at the regular Council of Ministers meetings are referred to the summit. In turn, the prime ministers and President of France generally make decisions in principle, which are passed back to the Council of Ministers for action. Agricultural reform issues have figured prominently on the agenda of the European Council in recent years.

Management Committees
When the Council of Ministers has approved a proposal for a change in agricultural policy it becomes legislation and is sent on to the Commission (where the locus of action is DG-VI) and management committees for implementation (see Harris *et. al.,* 1983, pp. 25–7). The management committees administer the various commodity regimes. There are separate committees for each commodity, many of which meet weekly. They usually bring together two or three officials per delegation from the Ministry of Agriculture of each member state under the chairmanship of a senior Commission official. The management committees consider an agenda and proposals drawn up by the Commission. Voting is by 'qualified majority'. The Commission can go ahead and implement its proposals whatever the management committee decides, but in the case of a negative finding, it must inform the Council of Ministers which has the power to override the Commission within a period of a month (Harris *et. al.,* 1983, p. 26).

The Court of Justice
As an arbiter of the legality under EC law of actions brought to its attention, the Court of Justice has a significant role to play in agricultural policy. Some of its rulings have constrained the Commission where policies have been introduced which violate aspects of the Treaty of Rome. Others have been against individual member countries, when they have acted contrary to EC law – which is binding in all member states. The Court's actions have been particularly important in the area of food standards, and have accelerated the movement toward freer internal trade in food products. However, the Court is not strictly part of the policy-making process, and hence is not discussed further in this chapter.

2.3.2 Recent changes in decision-making

The SEA which came into force in July 1987, has modified the EC's decision-making process in that it establishes a 'co-operation procedure' between the three main EC institutions. This procedure is detailed in Figure 2.6. Under its provisions, the Council of Ministers can no longer act on a proposal of the Commission until the European Parliament (EP) has given an opinion. After the EP has rendered its opinion, the proposal goes to the Council which then seeks a 'common position' on the proposal. Having reached a 'common position' by weighted majority voting, the Council informs the EP of its position. The Council's new rules of procedure allow for the Commission as well as the member states to call for a vote. If the EP concurs after a second reading, the draft legislation becomes the EC law in the form of a Regulation or Directive. If the EP rejects the proposal, it can only become law if the Council approves it by unanimous vote within three months. The EP can amend the Council's position by an absolute majority of members (260 votes), in which case the amended proposal goes back to the Commission. If the Commission incorporates the EP's amendments, the amended proposal becomes law if approved by a weighted majority in the Council. If the Commission does not accept the EP's amendments, the proposal can only become law if accepted by unanimous vote in the Council in three months.

The impact of the 'co-operation procedure' is not yet clear. The Council still remains the ultimate decision-maker. It is under no time limit to produce its common position after the EP's first reading. It is under a time limit after the EP's second reading, but if it fails to act the proposal simply lapses. However, the increased use of qualified majority voting and new rules for procedure should produce some general time constraint on the Council to produce its common position. The Commission also seems to maintain most of its powers. It remains in the driver's seat throughout the process. It is the Commission's proposal which is subject to majority voting in the Council. If the Council amends the Commission's proposal, either in arriving at its common position, or, in final adoption, then unanimity is automatically required. The role of the EP appears somewhat enhanced in that it can put pressure on the Commission to modify its proposal in accordance with the EP's wishes by delaying giving its opinion after a first reading (there is no specified time limit for giving an opinion). The EP may also gain some influence over the Council with its powers to delay action after a second reading by rejecting or amending the Council's common position. The fact that the Council needs unanimity to overturn EP amendments may prove significant. Although the requirement of an absolute majority of votes in the EP makes amendment extremely difficult, there is some evidence of the increased role of the EP in shaping policy. The Commission has gone out of its way to accommodate Parliament in shaping policy, and has incorporated several EP amendments into its proposals since the SEA came into effect.

The effect of the new 'co-operation procedure' on agricultural policy seems limited in that it does not apply to questions falling under Article 43 of the Rome Treaty which covers all CAP matters. Thus, any changes in agricultural commodity programmes (FEOGA guarantee expenditures) are excluded, as are changes in agricultural structural programmes. However, the Council and the EP have reached an agreement which says that the EP will be 'fully associated' with future revisions of the 'stabilizer' regulations, using 'concertation procedures' when appropriate (EC press release 5418 f/ 88 (Presse 44)). This 'concertation procedure' should not be confused with the 'co-operation procedure'. The former is a relatively formal affair which gives the EP the chance to make its views known, perhaps more effectively than through the formal 'opinion' required under Article 43, but still does not give it any real power over the outcome.[7] Though agricultural policies are excluded from the new 'co-operation procedures', regional and social policies are covered.

First Reading:
No Time Limit

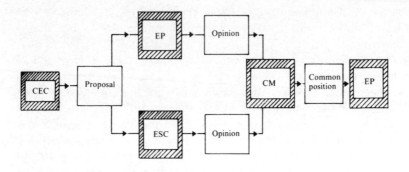

Second Reading:
Time Limits

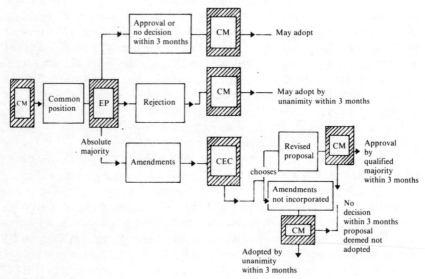

Abbreviations:
CM: Council of Ministers
CEC: Commission of EC
EP: European Parliament
ESC: Economic and Social Committee
Source: Paul Adamson, 'Lobbying and the
   Single European Act', *Commerce in
   Belgium*, April 1988.

Figure 2.6 Co-operation procedure under the Single European Act

NOTES

1. This may be changing, as evidenced by the 1988 Brussels stabilizers agreements: but, it is too soon to say definitely that the process has changed.
2. The EC uses the term 'cabinet' in the French rather than Anglo-Saxon sense. A high official's Cabinet is his personal and professional office staff.
3. This will be explained in more detail in the subsequent section on the positions of the various actors.
4. The COREPER has two parts: Part I, consisting of the deputies to the ambassadors, which may deal with certain agricultural issues, especially budgeting implications, and Part II, consisting of the ambassadors, which rarely handles CAP matters, concentrating on more general issues.
5. A qualified majority is the number of votes which will prevent the four largest member states (France, West Germany, Italy and the UK) from acting without support from the smaller members (see Harris *et. al.*, 1983, p. 26). The votes are distributed in the following manner: France, Italy, the UK and West Germany have ten votes each; Spain has eight votes; Belgium, Greece, the Netherlands and Portugal have five apiece; Denmark and Ireland have three, and Luxembourg has two votes. Out of a total of seventy-six votes, a qualified majority requires fifty-four and a blocking minority twenty-three votes.
6. See the subsequent discussion on the impact of the Single European Act on the EC policy process.
7. We are indebted to Michael Tracy for pointing out the distinction between 'co-operation procedures' and 'concertation procedures' in a personal communication of 29 July 1988. The 'concertation procedure' will also probably apply to agricultural structural programmes. However, its net overall effect on CAP decision-making is not clear.

3 · INPUTS INTO THE POLICY PROCESS IN THE EUROPEAN COMMUNITY

3.1 INTRODUCTION

The explanation of bargaining outcomes in the CAP requires an understanding of the interests, incentives and postures of both the decision-makers (inside political inputs) and the groups attempting to influence policy from the outside (outside political inputs). This chapter examines both sets of inputs to identify bargaining parameters and constraints. We then turn to a general discussion of the attempts over the years to reform the CAP.

3.2 ACTORS IN THE POLICY PROCESS

3.2.1 The decision-makers

Each of the institutions involved in decision-making in the EC is subject to pressures and influences from outside. These pressures include requests or demands from producer groups, from processing and trading sectors, from consumers, from member governments and from foreign countries. They are brought to bear on the actors through lobbying and through the threats and sanctions of the political process. However, the mix and impact of pressures varies among institutions because different institutions have different responsibilities, constituencies and conditions for appointment or election and tenure in office. To put it in terms of public choice theory, individuals working in different institutions have diverse individual and organizational interests which influence their behaviour. It is important to distinguish between those institutions where loyalty is primarily directed towards the EC and those where it is primarily directed towards national governments. It is also important to distinguish between technical, political and administrative functions. Figure 3.1 places the main institutions involved in agricultural decisions in the categories suggested by these distinctions.

National politicians have uncertain tenure in their occupation: every move must be weighed on the balance of political forces that they represent. Journalists in the relatively open environment of Brussels will see that

National governments	Community institutions	
Management committees	Commission services	Technicians (career positions)
Special Committee for Agriculture	Commissioners	Senior administrators (political appointees)
Council of Ministers	European Parliament	Politicians (elected representatives)

Figure 3.1 Classification of EC and national institutions by primary loyalty

domestic constituencies have the information on which to judge performance. By contrast, Community politicians – the members of the European Parliament (EP) – are subject to much less public scrutiny and party discipline. Their contribution to the debates can be less circumspect, a direct function of their lack of influence.

At the technical (rather than political) level, the national civil servants have considerable influence over policy detail, though less over broad policy directions. This influence is exercised both in their role as advisers to administrators and politicians (in particular as guardians of the information base) and as participants in day-to-day decision-making in the management committees. Community civil servants also influence the administrators (the Commission) through their advice and directly make policy through their management functions. With good tenure and promotion prospects if they provide careful and sensible advice, both national and Community technicians provide a source of stability rather than change in the system. Their job security protects them from the direct pressures of special-interest groups, but bureaucracies develop their own agendas and interests which clearly influence policy.

Caught somewhere between the technical and the political policy-makers are the administrators. At the national level these would include senior ministry personnel sitting on the Special Commission for Agriculture (and, for non-agricultural issues, the Committee of Permanent Representatives (COREPER)); at the Community level the Commissioners (with their hand-picked Cabinets) and the most senior officials in the various Directorates-General of the Commission. They do not have to stand for re-election to their present position, but they are generally appointed by politicians who do have to run for office. They are therefore subject to indirect pressures arising from electoral politics and interest-group activities. But, in general, the position of senior administrators is the least circumscribed and the most open to the possibility of policy change. Since they are associated – often personally – with the direction of policy, they may have a more direct stake in its success. Though often politicians themselves, they commonly feel frustrated at the national political constraints on policy imposed through the Council of Ministers.

Though it is very hard to measure, a 'European spirit' may modify the motives assumed by the public choice paradigm. There are officials at all levels of the EC civil service who are motivated by a vision of a strong united Europe, even though it is not clear how this benefits them, except in the sense of working for a good cause. This 'European spirit' appears to motivate some of the Commissioners. It may even be present to some degree in the Council of Ministers among national policy-makers. To be sure, it is the job of members of the Council to defend national interests in Community negotiations, but, subject to this constraint, some ministers will exercise what leeway they have to promote agreement. As an example, Joseph Ertl, the former West German Agriculture Minister, after forcefully fighting for German agricultural interests, would often exert himself to avoid a breakdown of negotiations.[1]

3.2.2 Lobbies

In addition to the decision-makers are the institutions which bring outside political input into the agricultural policy process. These can conveniently be thought of as 'lobbies' including farm groups, agri-business, and consumer groups.

These lobbies generally have their base in the political structure of member states. However, the creation of the EC changed the role of such domestic lobbies. Common policy-making in Europe weakens the direct influence of national lobbies by removing certain aspects of policy decisions, such as agenda-setting, from national control. It allows ministers to use the position of other members as reasons why a particular lobby cannot always be satisfied. As a result, at the EC level, lobbies tend to form in Brussels, both to influence the agenda and to put collective pressure on EC institutions – particularly the Commission, but increasingly also the EP. These lobbies also provide a service in improving the flow of information from Brussels to industry and national groups. In the agricultural area, COPA, the federation of Community farm organizations, fulfils this function.[2] National lobbies have not withered away in the process, though they have altered their modes of operation. They now work at three levels: to influence national governments to represent their positions in Brussels; to influence EC officials directly; and to influence the EC lobbying organizations with which they are affiliated. The overall balance of these forces has probably acted to obstruct CAP reform.

The Commission, not directly responsive to any electorate, maintains a good deal of freedom of action with respect to lobbies. In fact, the strongest lobbying influences come from national governments themselves. After all, national governments appoint (and may reappoint) the Commissioners and the top levels of the Directorate-General. Officials in national governments maintain very close ties with their compatriots working in the Commission, who often share common backgrounds and values, and who understand the problems their home countries face.

The farm lobby
By far the most important source of outside inputs into the EC agricultural policy process is the farm lobby. This lobby consists of national farmers' organizations and of the EC confederation of national farmers' organizations, COPA. These organizations generally have proved highly successful in mobilizing support among European farmers, thus generating strong financial and other organizational resources. They have also been successful in forcefully conveying their positions to both national and EC policy-makers.

This success can be explained by public choice theory. EC farmers are joined together by a strong collective interest in the existence and enhancement of the CAP. The CAP conveys enormous special benefits to farmers (economic rents), which provide the incentive to support farm organizations dedicated to preserving these benefits. The existence of protection provides an impetus for the development of institutions to preserve it.[3] European farmers did not have to develop new organizations to support their interests when the EC was established, because ready-made vehicles already existed in the form of their national farm organizations. These organizations had strong ties to farmers both in terms of benefits delivered from national farm policies and in terms of other benefits, such as insurance and dissemination of farming information, delivered directly to farmers. Creating COPA was not a difficult step because the national farm organizations had an interest in co-ordinating their positions to maximize their bargaining position with EC officials. At the same time they could easily provide the requisite financial and organizational resources. As the benefits to farmers under the CAP increased, as they did until the 1980s, the farming lobby thrived. Paradoxically, the general technological and economic pressures to shift human resources out of farming, present throughout the industrialized world, strengthened involvement in farm organizations. Farmers, a group not easily mobile given their large fixed investments, and hence denied an easy economic 'exit', had a strong incentive to mobilize a political 'voice' to protect their positions (see Hagedorn, 1985, pp. 31–3). Their strong attachment to the land strengthened this incentive.

The agricultural policy environment of the 1960s and 1970s seemed highly conducive to unity among farm organizations. Europe thrived, with sustained economic growth that created increasing resources for the EC. When the EC was formed, it depended heavily on food imports. This, along with the remembrance of serious food shortages after the Second World War, stimulated a broad social consensus for greater spending on agricultural commodity programmes. Increasing expenditures on agriculture created a positive-sum game which encouraged the farm organizations to work together. The size of the budgetary pie was growing so new benefits for one farm group did not have to come at the expense of another. Co-operation seemed logical in that it created the maximum pressure on policy-makers to enhance the share of agriculture, which could then be divided among the various farm interests. All groups could gain without any group having to sacrifice what it already had.

The climate of increasing expenditures on the CAP perhaps helped to inhibit the growth of commodity groups which could have challenged the dominance of the national farm organizations inherited from the pre-EC era. As long as the size of the budgetary pie increased, it was relatively easy for each national farm organization to serve as a forum for accommodating different commodity interests. Trade-offs did not appear particularly difficult and all groups could be broadly satisfied. The problem, after all, was one of distributing new resources, rather than redistributing existing resources. Thus, little incentive existed for specific commodity interests, at least at the farm level, to organize on their own. By contrast, EC-wide associations among processing firms have generally been along commodity lines.

The EC farm lobby has been extremely successful in influencing the development of the CAP and instrumental in preventing reform of commodity programmes. Until recently it even succeeded in preventing price cuts in the annual price negotiations. At first glance, this may seem surprising given that European farmers constitute only a small percentage of the EC population. A number of factors contribute to the political strength of agricultural interests. First, a strong corporatist tradition appears in

European agriculture marked by very strong links between agricultural ministries and farm organizations (see Cox, *et. al.,* 1986). This tradition can easily be understood in terms of public choice theory. Governments and farm organizations have strong mutual interests in working closely together. Farm organizations can deliver the political legitimacy and policy support which governments need from farmers in return for participation in policy-making which strengthens the tie between farm organizations and their members. The general weakness of the EC's public legitimacy as an authoritative political institution made it absolutely imperative for Commission officials to establish a new corporatist relationship with farm organizations at the Community level. The farm lobby has had every reason to oblige, given that Brussels is the primary source of benefits.

The development of the CAP did not undercut and may even have strengthened the corporatist relationship between national agricultural ministries and farmers. National interests are broadly represented in the deliberations of the Council of Ministers. Prior to the CAP, agricultural ministers had to fight the demands of their national farm organizations in order to avoid overspending the national budget. Now that EC financing has obscured the domestic political costs of budget overruns, agriculture ministers and national farm organizations have a mutual interest in securing as much benefit as possible for farmers. This convergence of interest is strengthened for most member nations in that they are net recipients of EC funds. Only West Germany and the UK have consistently been net contributors.[4]

Farm organizations have the incentive to use their full resources in opposing commodity price cuts. The rents delivered by the CAP provide the most important basis for the legitimacy these organizations have with their members. Price cuts reduce the rent and hence threaten this legitimacy (Hagedorn, 1985, p. 33). Farm organizations also cannot easily accept direct income support in compensation for price reductions. Direct income support appears as welfare payments, which implies that farm payments ought to be made on the same basis as other welfare payments – to each according to need. This principle is in direct contradiction with the principle normally used to defend farm payments – equal treatment of all farmers. Such direct payments would also be more visible as budget items. It would be natural for interest groups receiving benefits to wish to keep hidden the full cost of those transfers. Moreover, acceptance of direct income payments could also endanger the legitimation of farm organizations with their members (Hagedorn, 1985, pp. 37–40).

The influence of the EC farm lobby has been strengthened by the political importance of the 'farm vote'. How the farm community votes can determine the outcome of elections in a number of member countries where other political forces are relatively evenly balanced. Farmer support is currently crucial to the continuing political rule of the Christian Democratic

Union/Christian Social Union (CDU/CSU) coalition with the Free Democrats (FDP) in West Germany. The 'farm vote' not only consists of farmers and their families, but also includes many others who work in the farm support sectors and those whose roots are in farming and who still are sympathetic to the apparent plight of farmers. Farm organizations have demonstrated the ability to 'deliver' the farm vote, which strengthens their position with policy-makers. The support for farming in public opinion, which legitimizes the power of farming organizations, derives in part from the rapid decline in the agricultural population in the recent past and the resulting 'rump' of non-agriculturalists who still have romantic and favourable, though often not accurate, views on the merits of farming.[5]

The influence of national farm organizations on their governments' positions varies considerably among the EC member nations. Petit *et. al.,* (1987, p. 111) argue that the degree of influence is determined by four factors: cohesion within professional farm organizations; the functional relationship between the professional organizations and the ministry of agriculture; the importance attributed by national governments to agriculture; and the political power of the minister of agriculture within his or her own country. The influence of the farm lobby appears strong in West Germany, where the first three conditions are all met. It is less strong in France, where the cohesion among farm organizations seems weaker, and the relationship between the ministry and farmers' organizations more problematical, even though the importance attributed by the government to agriculture is strong. In the UK, the farm lobby is cohesive and the relationship with the ministry close, but the government attributes little importance to agriculture and the agriculture minister does not usually appear to be an important figure in the Cabinet. The farm lobby seems especially weak in Italy, where none of the four conditions is met.

The incomplete integration of EC political institutions strengthens the political power of the farm lobby. Agricultural interest groups achieve a significant advantage in that the lack of a regular central policy co-ordination mechanism in the Council of Ministers allows the agriculture ministers to be the final authority on agricultural policy in all situations short of crisis. The Agriculture Council constitutes a forum where farm interests are necessarily privileged. Agriculture ministers have no incentive to work closely with non-farm groups which can offer them nothing comparable to the political support of the farm lobby. The general complexity of the EC farm legislation further weakens the impact of non-farm interests. Mastering this complexity requires the commitment of significant human and financial resources. Only farm organizations, which receive special benefits, have the incentive to make the requisite investment.

The success of the EC in instituting milk quotas and budget stabilizers provides some evidence that the influence of the farm lobby has peaked and is now beginning to wane. An important reason for declining farm group influence is the tendency of EC policy to gravitate toward a zero-sum game caused by escalating CAP expenditures and revenue exhaustion. When revenues are exhausted, new spending on agriculture can only come at the expense of other programmes since the EC cannot legally run a budget deficit. There are at least three consequences which together work to shift the balance of political forces against the farm lobby in the bargaining process.

First, greater incentives exist for prime ministers and finance ministers to increase their involvement in agricultural policy-making, both to find new revenues, and to balance agricultural spending with other priorities. These actors are generally much less likely to do the bidding of farm interests than agriculture ministers. Second, Commissioners in charge of non-agricultural policies have increased incentives to limit agricultural spending to protect their own programmes. They are thus likely to challenge proposals from DG-VI and the Agriculture Commissioner which do not work to contain CAP costs. Third, the increasingly zero-sum game character of policy tends to divide the farm lobby and weaken its ability to present coherent positions in policy debates. At the national level, segments of the farm community develop conflicting interests not easily resolvable within national farm organizations. As a result, national farm organizations are slow in developing bargaining positions within the COPA framework. When national positions are developed they tend to be inflexible. Bargaining at both the national and COPA levels is hindered further in that the perception of a zero-sum game breeds mutual suspicion among farm groups whose interests diverge.

Ample signs of all three of these trends appear in the CAP reform debate of the 1980s. Prime ministers and finance ministers have at times become heavily involved in policy-making. The 1983 decision to impose milk quotas, the 1986 decision to tighten them, and the 1988 decision to impose stabilizers for cereals and oilseeds all went to the European Council. Indeed, on occasions even the annual price package had to be decided without the help of European Council action. Perhaps the most significant change in 1988, the direct involvement of finance ministers in the price negotiations whenever the guidelines on agricultural spending are approached, is especially important in that it gives a new 'bite' to the commitment to restrain agricultural spending. The substantially increased budget resources provided by the February 1988 summit in Brussels makes spending discipline critically important. Farm policy probably would have consumed the bulk of the increase without the severe restraint of the February 1988 agreement. Second, proposals to the Council and administrative action by the Commission have progressively become tougher on farm interests. Third, evidence exists of fragmentation of the farm lobby in individual nations and in COPA. COPA's incoherence has been aggravated by the expansion of the Community from nine to twelve members which has added a whole new range of divergent national farm interests into the bargaining process.

Agri-business

European Community agri-business is a rather divided constituency, which limits its ability to influence the CAP price policy process. It contains elements representing trading, food processing, fertilizer and chemical production and farm machinery production. The interests of these various elements are by no means convergent. Many food traders, for instance, have an interest in an increased market orientation of the CAP which would lead to increased food trade, though others benefit from surpluses and subsidized exports. Input and implement producers probably have less interest in policy reform, because increased liberalization of the CAP is likely to lead to less food production in the EC and hence will reduce demand for their products. Input producers will also have an interest in preventing the spread of quotas as a means of curbing production.[6] The food-processing community has divided interests within itself. Oilseed processors have a clear stake in liberalizing CAP reform, but sugar, olive oil, and milk processors could see their businesses hurt.

Other factors restrict agri-business influence. First, the Commission has little incentive to cultivate close ties. Commissioners and Commission bureaucracy are relatively isolated from elective politics and hence do not depend on political contributions from agri-business. Second, the Commission does not need agri-business support in the same way as it needs farm group support to legitimize its policies. Third, even though specific agri-business interests may influence individual national agricultural ministries, the characteristics of agriculture differ so widely in member nations that no one agri-business interest can easily influence the entire Council of Agriculture Ministers. Indeed, agri-business interests may to some extent cancel each other out at the Council level. Finally, the impact of commodity policies on agri-business appears generally indirect. Thus, no incentive exists to commit large resources in an attempt to influence the policy outcome.

Consumers

EC consumer groups have never constituted an important force in influencing the development of the CAP. At first this may seem puzzling since the CAP holds farm prices considerably above where they would be in the absence of price supports. Public choice theory gives insights as to why the consumer voice is weak. Individual consumers do not easily perceive the impact of the CAP. Most of the food they buy in the shops comes only indirectly from farmers, through processors and the marketing chain. Raw material costs are generally less than one-half of retail prices. Losses to each individual consumer are therefore small relative to total income. The effect of the CAP in maintaining stable consumer prices (even if at a higher level) has been publicized as a benefit to consumers, along with the presumed advantages of a high degree of self-sufficiency. As a result, consumers have had little incentive to organize and contribute the resources necessary to influence the policy debate. Only recently has the issue of excessive food costs been linked to issues of family poverty and industrial wage costs, and then only in certain countries. Moreover, consumer interests appear so diverse, that consumer organizations have difficulty in forming positions generally acceptable to their membership.[7] All this means that consumer organizations cannot make credible threats or promises to policy-makers. Consumer organizations cannot deliver effective political support or opposition. As a result, neither the Council nor the Commission has much incentive to pay much attention to their views, except on specific issues such as food quality and safety.

3.2.3 Other outside political inputs

The press
The press in EC nations does not seem to have played a critical role in either stimulating or obstructing CAP reform. EC agricultural policy debates are not very well covered except in such elite publications as *The Economist, Financial Times* and *Agra Europe*; hence, they do not generate political groundswells which policy-makers must heed. This is partly a question of incentives. It takes both journalistic commitment and agricultural expertise to cover and clearly explain the complexities of the CAP. Elite publications, with a readership that sees the importance of the CAP, can justify committing the requisite resources. The mass media, with a readership not much interested in following complex policy debates, have no such incentive. To the extent that the mass media cover the CAP at all, they tend to focus on more sensational aspects, such as sales of butter at bargain basement prices to the Soviet Union or cheating by Italian farmers in gaining olive oil subsidies. Such coverage does little to generate informed public debate. The press has managed, to some extent, to convey the moral outrage of EC food surpluses, while other parts of the world suffer from famine, to a public which is beginning to take these issues seriously. The elite press does contribute to the intellectual debate inside and outside the policy process, but one cannot easily attribute specific policy outcomes to this influence.

Public opinion
Public opinion does not play a direct role in EC policy-making as unorganized individuals cannot enter directly into decision-making. However, the 'climate of opinion' does seem to have an influence in setting agendas and constraining national policy-makers. Public opinion in the EC

does not appear well informed about the CAP, though there is consensus that agricultural issues are important. A recent large-scale cross-sectional study of European views on agriculture found a high 'don't know/no answer' rate of up to 36 per cent when the respondents were asked a series of 20 questions on the CAP (Commission of the European Communities (CEC), 1988c, p. 23).[8] When asked whether they had heard or read about the Common Agricultural Policy, only 35 per cent said that they had heard or read about it recently. Yet, two-thirds of the sample indicated interest in agricultural matters and virtually the entire sample considered agricultural issues important.

Europeans have a genuine affinity for the countryside and a strong basic sympathy for farmers. Given a list of seven activities implying contacts with the countryside, 90 per cent of the respondents in the survey indicated that they pursued activities implying contacts with the countryside and agriculture (CEC, 1988c, p. 21). Eighty per cent indicated that they consider farmers disadvantaged nowadays compared with other citizens (CEC, 1988c, p. 25). Europeans do not agree that it is more sensible to buy some of their foodstuffs from abroad than to subsidize farmers to produce them in EC countries (CEC, 1988c, p. 28). They do not agree that farmers' organizations have far too much influence.

The general public shows an awareness that EC agriculture faces serious difficulties. For the European population as a whole, surpluses constitute the biggest problem (CEC, 1988c, p. 25). This view is not shared by farmers, who think the principal issue is decline in farm incomes. Two other problems strike both non-farmers and farmers alike as serious: the abandonment of certain regions; and the widening gap between big and small farmers. Europeans seem aware that agricultural problems are long-term and international. Three-quarters of the survey respondents thought that the problems affecting European agriculture were the same as those affecting agriculture in the USA and the Soviet Union and that the solution would take time (CEC, 1988c, p. 35). Eighty-three per cent thought agricultural problems merited the most serious attention (CEC, 1988c, p. 25).

Contradictions appear in public attitudes to CAP spending. According to the survey, Europeans do not think that the level of CAP spending is excessive. One in two respondents favoured keeping expenditures on agriculture at least at present levels, or even increasing it (CEC, 1988c, p. 29). Yet the majority thought that the CAP proportion of the EC budget was too high. The public also feels it is not acceptable for individuals as consumers to pay high prices for foodstuffs and at the same time, as taxpayers, to pay subsidies for farming (CEC, 1988c, p. 33). A general awareness exists of the need for a better balance between food production and consumer requirements, even if some people in farming are obliged to change their employment (CEC, 1988c, p. 32).

Attitudes to trade policy also seem contradictory on the general notion of CAP reform. On the one hand, 71 per cent of the general public in the recent survey thought that the EC should defend its position as the world's second largest exporter of agricultural products, though opinion appeared very divided about the merit of export subsidies. Seventy-five per cent of the sample favoured protection against foreign imports even if the consumer has to pay more for certain products (CEC, 1988c, p. 35).

These survey results confirm that the EC public has a generally positive overall view of the CAP. There exists a general sentiment that the price of food is too high, even though one of the goals of the CAP is to pitch prices at a reasonable level. But most people think that consumers have benefited from the CAP. There is a sense that the CAP preserves the economic conditions necessary for the preservation of the environment. Yet, at the same time a strong sentiment exists that the EC should do more to improve food quality, cut the use of fertilizers and pesticides and help those farmers who need it (CEC, 1988c, pp. 33–40).

European public opinion does not appear as a strong force for agricultural reform. The general public is not demanding radical change for the CAP. It expresses some general preferences, though a few of these are mutually contradictory. Policy-makers appear to have a good deal of leeway with regard to the specific policies they adopt. Some pressure seems evident to keep costs from exploding, to do more to reduce surpluses and to protect the environment. The deep-seated sympathy for farmers explains in part why farm organizations have succeeded in mobilizing public support while consumer organizations have not.

Academics
It is difficult to assess the impact of academics on the EC agricultural policy process because much of this impact is indirect. Academics have access to policy-makers when they provide useful technical and analytical expertise. The various studies conducted by scholars and the books and articles they write clearly do much to set the tenor of the policy debate. Most of the writing by agricultural economists is based on the premise that market efficiency is good. This belief has general acceptance in EC member states, in particular in the northern members. Policy-makers, who recommend action that increases market efficiency, can easily find an intellectual argument that justifies their actions. The EC's surplus and budget crisis strengthens the general weight of market efficiency arguments, though policy-makers do not necessarily feel constrained to follow them. The Commission, removed from the constraints of electoral politics, and having an interest in maintaining the financial viability of the EC, has appeared more receptive to market efficiency arguments than the Council.

Academics influence the process both by contributing proposals to the general pool from which policy-makers will make their choice and by their assessment of the consequences of different courses of action. Academics generally have no political base, so cannot compel Commission or Council to consider the proposals. To the extent that their ideas are adopted, it is because these ideas fit the interests of the decision-makers. Policy-makers, according to the theories of public choice and organizational process, have little incentive to pay much attention to new ideas unless these ideas help them cope with their current problems. When a policy-maker faces a crisis, through a process of selective perception, he searches for a potentially feasible option which will allow him to 'cope' with the situation. If an academic provides such an option, he or she will have had some influence over policy.

3.3 THE POSITIONS OF THE ACTORS

3.3.1 The Commission

The balance between national and EC interests is at the heart of the tensions apparent in the CAP. This is true in particular in the debate on reform. Of the EC institutions, the Commission has been pressing for reform for many years. Table 3.1 shows the sequence of documents published by the Commission, all of which deal with significant changes to the CAP. In some cases the papers were written in response to a request from the Council of Ministers (the 1975 'Stocktaking' and 1985 'Perspectives' papers are of this type) but in other cases the Commission has initiated the discussion expressly to try to create the climate for change. The Commission uses these discussion documents to try out ideas for policy changes, to establish the need for action, and to pave the way for its own submissions to the Council. On the other hand, the Commission clearly cannot be too harsh on the workings of a policy for which it is in part responsible. It has to paint a picture of a reasonable and necessary policy liable to be blown off course by the winds of world price changes, technical progress, and monetary instability.

Decision-making within the Commission usually proceeds slowly because power is divided and action emerges only after considerable bargaining. Different actors have diverging interests and, hence, differing perceptions and incentives for action. For example, DG-VI and the Agriculture Commissioner's Cabinet do not have the same incentives to promote CAP reform. DG-VI staff have strong reasons to want to maintain the status quo for the CAP. Normally so overwhelmed with the complex tasks of managing the various market regimes, they really do not have much time to consider new ideas which would change the CAP. Besides the possibility always exists that a proposal for change would further complicate the already difficult administrative burden, or shift the balance of power in an unsatisfactory way between different departments of the Directorate-

Table 3.1   Major EC reform discussion documents (1968-87)

1.	1968	'Memorandum on the Reform of Agriculture in the EEC' (known as the 'Mansholt Memoranda (COM (68) 1000)
2.	1973	'Improvement of the Common Agricultural Policy' (COM (73) 1850)
3.	1975	'Stocktaking of the Common Agricultural Policy' (COM (75) 100)
4.	1978	'Future Development of the Common Agricultural Policy' (COM (78) 700)
5.	1980	'Reflections on the Common Agricultural Policy' (COM (80) 800)
6.	1982	'Guidelines for European Agriculture' (COM (81) 608)
7.	1983	'Common Agricultural Policy – Proposals of the Commission' (known as 'COM 500') (COM (183) 500)
8.	1985	'Perspectives for the Common Agricultural Policy' (COM (85) 333)
9.	1985	'A Future for Community Agriculture' (COM (85) 750)
10.	1987	'Making a Success of the Single European Act (COM (87) 1000)
11.	1987	'Review of Action taken to Control the Agricultural Markets and the Outlook for the Common Agricultural Policy' (COM (87) 410)

General. Even if an idea seems good, the prospect of pushing it through a complex bureaucratic structure must always seem forbidding. These tendencies are probably much stronger at the lower technical levels of DG-VI where the perspective is likely to be extremely parochial and where the tasks of selling a new idea seem insurmountable.

Members of the Agriculture Commissioner's Cabinet find themselves in a rather different position. Cabinets tend to be small, informal and free from cumbersome bureaucratic procedure.[9] The members, chosen directly by the Commissioner rather than through seniority, are likely to be young and action-orientated, with little inherent commitment to current policies. Not burdened with heavy tasks in managing market regimes, and with responsibility directly to the Commissioner, they can maintain a broad perspective. They have more incentive to pay attention to political feasibility than to the problems of policy implementation. Cabinet members, by virtue of their positions, would seem more receptive to new ideas for agricultural reform than their colleagues in DG-VI. However, they are limited in what they can do by what the Agriculture Commissioner is willing to consider. They have no independent power base.

The Agriculture Commissioner, the key actor in the Commission process, must maintain the confidence of a number of often conflicting constituencies, which include the other Commissioners, the Agriculture Council, the farm lobby and DG-VI. This implies that he must first establish his credibility by showing he is in control of agricultural policy and can get things done.[10] Since power is divided in the EC, this requires skill at political persuasion. To succeed, he must provide each of his constituencies with at least part of what it wants. He must work to contain agricultural spending to satisfy the other Commissioners. This promotes their collective interest in safeguarding the EC's future financial viability, at the same time guarding the funds needed for other EC programmes. To satisfy the interests of DG-VI, he must not recommend changes which, on the one hand, will create unmanageable new administrative burdens, or, on the other, will reduce DG-VI's overall authority. He must also take care not to recommend changes which will require major restructuring of the bureaucracy. In short, strong organizational incentives exist to proceed incrementally.

Satisfying the Agriculture Council means that the Agriculture Commissioner must not recommend any change offensive to a majority of Council members. Policy measures must broadly be acceptable to the larger states (the UK, France, West Germany and Italy) although with the increase in the use of majority voting, proposals need not appeal to all member countries. In practice, the Commissioner formulates proposals mutually acceptable in that they contain elements for which each agriculture minister can claim credit. This argues for comprehensive proposals. Finally, to satisfy the farm lobby, the Agriculture Commissioner must make the case that his proposals for reform damage farm interests in the minimum way consistent with maintaining a viable CAP. Sacrifices must be equitably distributed among agricultural interests.

When an agricultural reform proposal comes before the full Commission, the individual Commissioners share a collective interest in containing agricultural spending to maintain the viability of the EC. However, they also have individual interests which can complicate the bargaining process. Each Commissioner has an interest in protecting and enhancing the programmes for which he has reponsibility and, as a result, is likely to examine agricultural proposals in light of this interest. Each will also probably consider the effect of the proposal on his country's national interests, even though as an international civil servant he is sworn to uphold the common interests of the EC. Commissioners who desire reappointment cannot afford continuously to antagonize their home governments. Those who plan to resume domestic political careers must consider the consequences of their actions. Only those Commissioners who have decided to retire from their posts are likely to be free from the domestic political constraint. Even then they can never completely avoid a national bias, because their evaluative frame of reference, experience and contacts are all likely to centre on their home state. Conceptions of national interests are also influenced by ideological factors, so individuals from the same country may see the 'national interest' rather differently.

3.3.2 The European Parliament

The EP has an ambivalent attitude towards reform, in part as a result of its own structure. Its members (MEPs) group themselves into 'parties' which represent broad coalitions of parliamentarians from like-minded national parties. These parties, however, tend not to form consistent views on issues such as the CAP: national interests within the parties are often too diverse to make such consistency possible. Instead, the main ideas on agriculture come from the Agriculture Committee. The EP does much of its work in committees, which then report back to the full assembly.

The Agriculture Committee contains a wide range of different viewpoints, but in general supports policies which raise prices and incomes in agriculture. This is easily explained by public choice theory. MEPs from agricultural constituencies have an incentive to choose service on the Agricultural Committee over other assignments so they may influence the benefits accruing to their constituencies. This incentive is weakened by virtue of the fact that the EP's real powers with regard to agriculture are very limited. Still, MEPs from non-agricultural constituencies have little to gain from agricultural committee service.

The Agricultural Committee does, however, actively explore ways for improving policies: in this sense it can constitute a constructive element in the reform process. The EP, when meeting in plenary session, has an increasing tendency to emphasize wider issues such as the budget cost of policies and their overseas implications, including their impact on developing countries. As a result, the EP often modifies Agricultural Committee proposals to reflect general Community interests.

3.3.3 The Council of Ministers

As the body responsible for making decisions, the Council of Ministers plays the dominant role in policy change. Although only the Commission can propose legislation, the Commission obviously takes into account the probability of passage through the Council. This process of co-ordination works in particular through the Special Committee on Agriculture, which acts as a permanent subministerial organ of the Council. Draft legislation, as opposed to discussion documents, is crafted with an eye to political acceptability. Each successive version moves closer to the position of the Council. In the long run, the importance of the exclusive power of initiation held by the Commission may not be as great as it appears: the EC essentially moves at the pace of the Council of Ministers.

Voting
This pace in turn is set by the inclinations of the most reluctant country. The long-established practice of time-constrained unanimity implied that the Council would never act in such a way as to violate the vital national interests of any member nation.[11] In practice, this meant that no action could be taken which visibly reduced the farm income of any country. Thus, the Council was unable, until 1987, to take action to reduce the nominal prices of any commodity. The practice of unanimity has had other implications as well. First, it created significant pressures to increase budgetary expenditures. By increasing the size of the pie, conflicts over distribution of resources were mitigated. Second, it ensured that no decision

was taken until the last possible moment. Nations, by holding out the prospect of a veto, could hope to induce concessions from other nations. Finally, the practice of unanimity ensured a reasonably *even* distribution of benefits. Thus, it was not possible to approve a package which differentiated greatly between nations in new benefits or new sacrifices. However, *even* distribution of benefits should not be confused with *equal* distribution, since certain members benefit far more than others from existing policy. In short, unanimity prevented much redistribution of benefits between member states.

It should be clear that the practice of unanimity in the Council creates powerful disincentives to agricultural reform. However, this practice has served an important legitimizing function in that no nation has been forced to accept policies which might have led to its withdrawal from the EC. It has also helped ensure that nations carried out EC policies of their own volition, which is important given the lack of any community police powers. The practice of unanimity may now have a delegitimizing function as well, given that the EC's rich northern nations receive far more agricultural support benefits than the poor southern nations.

It should thus not be surprising that the rule of 'qualified majority' voting is now becoming more the norm.[12] This development has undoubtedly speeded decision-making and may contain the pressure to increase expenditures. However, it has some limitations of its own. The possibility always exists that only limited shifting will occur between coalitions; that for many issues there will be a permanent majority and a permanent minority. If this happens, a serious risk develops that the CAP, and even the EC, may lose legitimacy for the minority. Qualified majority voting does not, in itself, imply a more equitable distribution of benefits. While the EC's Mediterranean members (Spain, Portugal, Italy and Greece) constitute a blocking minority, they need help from the northern members to form a weighted majority to increase their share of CAP benefits. This seems highly problematical given that the current agricultural policy situation is close to a zero-sum game. Qualified majority voting has another problem in that it removes the ability of individual nations to challenge seriously the existing 'system'. This could lead to even more rapid agreement on the lowest common denominator solution than the practice of unanimity and reduce the prospect of significant policy change. For instance, in the present policy context, qualified majority voting would appear to reduce the ability of the UK government to demand a more responsible agricultural policy.

The national interest
Among the present member states, enthusiasm for significant agricultural policy reforms varies widely. In large part this has reflected perceived national interest. For any particular commodity, the national interest often corresponds broadly to the net-trade status. Exporters of a commodity will tend to favour protection against imports, subsidies on exports, and no

restriction on domestic production. Though such countries may reject price cuts, they often realize that generally high prices (including higher prices in other EC countries as a result of the agricultural exchange rate conversion rules – the 'green money' system) will cut down their export potential within the EC and make the cost of exporting more visible. Exporting countries have thus tended to be strict on adherence to the rules of the CAP, but have not always advocated higher prices. It is importers, as often as not, who have pressed for price increases for CAP commodities, under pressure from their domestic lobbies. The original price level for cereals and other products was set with the interests of West German farmers in mind, and this sectoral pressure has exercised, through the West German minister of agriculture, a profound influence on the CAP ever since.

The structure of agriculture seems to have an influence on a member state's attitude towards the CAP and hence on its support of policy reform. Countries with a small average size of farm often push for higher prices. This is one reason for West German pressure in this direction. By constrast, the United Kingdom, with its larger farms, would probably advocate price level moderation even if it were not a major importer and contributor to the budget. Associated with farm size is the average level of farm income, relative to that in the rest of the economy. Again one sees a clear distinction between West Germany, with low incomes per farm (a combination of small farms and considerable off-farm work) and high non-agricultural incomes, and the UK, with larger full-time farms earning for their owners a roughly comparable income to that of the rest of the economy. This strengthens the pressure for high prices on 'parity' grounds in West Germany.

A third factor influencing national positions with respect to CAP reform is the extent to which the country contributes to the budget cost of the policy. At a general level, net contributors (West Germany, the UK, and now France) will tend to show more concern about budget cost increases than net recipients. However, in any particular situation, a policy change will have a budget cost or benefit to each member country which depends upon the distribution of receipts as well as on the incidence of costs. The complicated system of budget rebates set up for the UK (and, to a lesser extent, for West Germany) obscures the source of finance for increasing budget expenditures. It is possible that exporting nations, always thought to benefit from additional spending by the European Agricultural Guidance and Guarantee Fund (FEOGA), may now feel the pinch of additional contributions.

This combination of factors, from trade balance and farm size to budgetary contributions, helps to shape the attitude of member states toward CAP reform. In addition, each country has its own set of political circumstances and historical experiences which colour the position taken by its agriculture minister. This can include traditions for enhancing farm incomes through price supports, deep-seated cultural values associated with the countryside, environmental concerns, trade relations with overseas countries, expectations about inflation, and the power of particular farm groups to influence politicians.[13] Each member state faces its own political constraints. For instance, governments which depend heavily on the 'farm vote' have great difficulties supporting major CAP reform proposals. Governments facing an imminent election feel strongly constrained to delay action or oppose action on agricultural reform which cuts benefits to farmers in their country. Support for such reform is guaranteed to lose votes in the agricultural community without compensating votes being gained elsewhere.

The Council presidency

Our discussion on the Council of Ministers did not address the question of leadership. In fact, the Council has a presidency, rotated among the various members and held for a six-month period. An individual serving as Council president has somewhat different incentives than when serving as a mere minister. Most important, he is expected to move the Council through the business it has to conduct. This implies muting his national position and assuming a posture of impartiality. Stalemate, even in in the interest of his constituency back home, reflects adversely on the Council president's leadership and leaves him vulnerable to both international and domestic criticism. Forging an agreement, on the other hand, tends to increase the political stature of the Council president and of his country. As a general proposition, a minister can make concessions while acting as president of the Council that he cannot make at any other time. Depending upon the subject under consideration, he may be able to be more flexible. A consequence of this proposition would be that favourable action on a reform proposal is most likely when the minister from the nation most opposed to the proposal sits in the Council president's chair.

The Council president has important prerogatives which increase his ability to catalyse an agreement. First, he can schedule and set the agenda and control the Council meetings. The strategy employed may have a significant effect on the outcome. Second, he can often act as broker. He can take the initiative in informal conversations to see what is acceptable to the various member states and then develop a compromise proposal of his own. Indeed, a norm seems to have developed for the Council president to shuttle back and forth between national capitals prior to a crucial meeting to stimulate consensus. Strictly speaking, only the Commission can make proposals, but the Commission is strongly constrained to accept any compromise developed by the president of the Council. Third, the Council president has available the services of the Council Secretariat, a small bureaucracy independent from the Commission, whose responsibilities generally are to see that the Council gets the information it needs, to co-ordinate with the Commission, and to help the ministers develop consensus on various proposals. The Council Secretariat combines the perspectives of national interest and Community interest. Often, the Director-General of the Council Secretariat and his subordinates can make suggestions to the Council president which facilitate the Council process or ease relationships with other EC bodies including the EP and the Commission.

The success, or otherwise, of a country's six-month presidency depends not only upon the agenda during that period but also on the effectiveness of that country's national civil service. Countries with weak domestic administrative systems, or those with little experience in Community matters, face formidable difficulties in steering major reform proposals through the Council. Small countries have an additional problem, with severe difficulties in finding experienced individuals to take on the task of chairing the various Council working groups. Hence, the best chance for reform will tend to be when the presidency resides with one of the larger member states, such as West Germany, France, or the UK, or a small state, such as Denmark or the Netherlands, with strong administrative capabilities and long European experience.[14]

3.4 ATTEMPTS TO REFORM THE COMMON AGRICULTURAL POLICY

3.4.1 1968–80

If reform is a significant shift in policy direction stimulated by general dissatisfaction, the question arises whether any such reform has taken place in the CAP so far. For convenience it is useful to separate the 25 years of the CAP into three time periods.[15] The first period extended until 1968, when unified markets and policies were established. Although this was an era of significant change in EC agriculture, it would be confusing to talk of 'reform' of a policy still being developed and introduced.

The second period covers the years 1968–80, a time of turbulence in both agriculture and the rest of the economy. A number of 'reform' efforts were initiated over this period, but little progress occurred.

The year 1968 saw the first 'reform' proposal, the Mansholt Memorandum, emanating from the Commission (CEC, 1968). Having set up the CAP, and seen it introduced over the transition period, the Commission recognized that it could only be kept viable if adapted to new circumstances. These circumstances appear somewhat similar to those existing in the 1980s – with surplus production, high stocks and weak world prices. As Neville-Rolfe (1984, p. 298) points out, the focus of the Mansholt Memorandum was not so much on changes in policy as on changes in agriculture. Policy changes were suggested to assist the development of a healthy and competitive agricultural sector. In this the document is unique:

all subsequent Commission reform plans concentrate on saving the policy from its own implications – surpluses, budget costs – and largely ignore development of the agricultural sector *per se*.

The Mansholt 'reforms' comprised a 'prudent' price policy coupled with a strong programme of structural adjustment. After three years of wrangling, the Council agreed to a weak version of the structural policy – embodied in the three so-called 'socio-structural directives' of 1972. These directions dealt with assistance for farm modernisation (Directive 72/159); early retirement for farmers (72/160); and retraining for agricultural workers (72/161).[16] They had little impact on the major structural change that occurred over the following decade, and never achieved the central place in the CAP that Mansholt had in mind. His price policy fared better, in that prices remained unchanged for the first three years of the 'harmonized' policy. Subsequent price increases were modest until 1972, when inflation became a factor. Moderation in price-setting may create sound policy, though in itself it hardly constitutes reform. Had subsequent Commissioners for Agriculture persevered with Mansholt's notion of de-emphasizing price support, the subsequent need for major reform might have been much less.

The mid-1970s were a confusing period for policy-makers. Both world prices and inflation rose to historically high levels. At the same time, the EC had to cope with the absorption of three new members, including a divided and hesitant UK. Following the prevailing view that agricultural markets were entering a period of scarcity (though no serious shortage actually materialized) EC support prices were allowed to rise by an average of 9 per cent per year over the four years 1973–7. The Commission adopted an 'objective method' of calculating the annual price increase which would be necessary to propose to the Council in order to preserve farmers' incomes. This built in inflation trends and made sure that the real value of Community prices did not fall too fast.

In contrast to the sweeping view of the Mansholt Plan, the two reform documents produced by the next Agricultural Commissioner, Lardinois, were focused on the management of the policy. The 'Improvement' paper of 1973 dealt with such seemingly mundane issues as price ratios among support prices (as it turned out, a key problem), and more flexibility in the commodity market organizations (CEC, 1973). It did, however, introduce the political notion that farmers should bear some of the cost of surpluses, by proposing the application of a co-responsibility levy to dairy producers. This somewhat toothless attempt at reform was introduced five years later.

The second document from Commissioner Lardinois was the 'Stocktaking' paper of 1975 (CEC, 1975). This attempted to explore the appropriateness of the CAP, and its success in achieving the aims of the Treaty of Rome. The Commission concluded that the CAP had indeed been successful, but that certain changes were needed. In the turmoil surrounding the renegotiation of the UK's terms of entry and the temporary rise above

CAP levels of world cereal prices, any reforming intentions of the 'Stocktaking' exercise were soon abandoned.

Serious discussion of reform occurred in the late 1970s. The Commission in which Gundelach held the agricultural portfolio produced a document on 'The Future Development' of the CAP (CEC, 1978), which kept alive some of the Commission's ideas for policy change. But Gundelach put his faith in a strict price policy rather than a reform of instruments. In effect, he had to remove from the agricultural sector the additional incentives thrust upon it by four years of generous compensation under his predecessor. The issue of the UK's budget contribution and the collapse of the common price system as a result of currency changes kept reform on the back burner. The steady rise in budget costs, particularly in the dairy sector, did prompt some action. Producer co-responsibility levies, introduced in 1977, represented an attempt to reduce production incentives and budget exposure. However, their impact was muted by the tendency of the Council of Ministers to raise support prices to offset the impact of the levies.

In 1980, the Commission published a further document called 'Reflections on the Common Agricultural Policy', significant in part for its rejection of both direct income aids and renationalization of financial obligations (CEC, 1980). Earlier that year the Commission was asked by the Council to consider the range of agricultural and budget problems and to lay out its suggestions for their resolution – the so-called Mandate of 30 May 1980. The reply to that request started a chain of events leading to a more radical set of adjustments to the CAP that continue to the present.

3.4.2 Since 1980

The third period, from 1981 to the present, has been one of growing realization of the inevitability of change in the policy, and of halting steps in the reform process. It started quietly, with a brief respite from budget pressures. Events in the world markets for dairy products and the strengthening dollar led to a reduction in budget cost in 1981. The next year support costs for cereals dipped slightly and CAP spending again appeared under control. The biggest institutional push for reform was temporarily frustrated by a sudden relaxation of economic pressure. Sentiment shifted towards the view that world prices would rise again; and that the policy would be rescued by external events.

This optimistic view was short-lived. In 1982 the budget cost of the CAP had jumped by 11 per cent, and the policy was back in crisis. Intervention stocks started a heady climb to the levels of today. Generous price awards in 1981 and 1982 ensured an upward trend in production, just as world markets became saturated. The debt problem and slower world growth halted the growth in world trade that had characterized the previous decade.

Surpluses in other countries exacerbated the situation, particularly in the USA, where expansion had been based on a growing export market.

The response to the Council's Mandate came from the Commission in 1981 (the 'Mandate Report', CEC, 1981): the particular proposals relating to agricultural policy were elaborated in the paper 'Guidelines for European Agriculture' (CEC, 1981). These two documents introduced some important new notions into the reform debate. One of these was that the level of support prices in the Community should be brought into line with those of major competitors (particularly the USA) over a period of time. This radical notion of basing price upon something other than internal farm cost changes or parity incomes with non-farm groups was not embraced with enthusiasm by the Council. It came not so much from a sudden conversion to the doctrine of neo-classical economics as from the realization that the Community was now a major exporter of agricultural products. The Commission also emphasized the need to limit the scope of guaranteed prices to 'basic quantities' of production, thus changing the open-ended nature of the unconditional price policy. This theme became a dominant one in the reform struggle over the rest of the period.

The 'budget issue' addressed in the Mandate was wider than just increased spending on agriculture. Importantly, it also included the distribution of budget burden by member state and the limits imposed by the formula used to apportion 'own resources' to the EC. The UK budget share provided the main focus of the political debate, which absorbed considerable attention from Community institutions. But the need to take action came in 1983, when the increase in spending came up against the budget limit. The Commission proposed an increase in the funds available, and was forced to incorporate a limit on CAP spending – that it should not increase by more than the rate of increase of the budgetary resources. The document that laid out the policy changes for agriculture, simply known as 'COM 500' (CEC, 1983), also specified a super-levy on levels of milk production above 1981 levels and the introduction of an oils and fats tax. Both ideas recurred in later Commission proposals: the super-levy was finally adopted in 1984, but the oils and fats tax is still 'on the backburner'.

Reform in the CAP proceeds from general notions to specific commodity applications. The system finds it difficult to deal with more than one major sector at a time. That time had come for the dairy industry. The notion of 'guarantee thresholds', as advocated in the 'Guideline's' document (CEC, 1981), had been introduced in a somewhat ineffective way in the 1982 review. These applied to milk and to cereals, as well as to some oilseeds. They served the function of suggesting price cuts for the following year based on production relative to the guarantee threshold amount. They were, however, not automatic, and the 'reductions' were merely to be taken into account in fixing the prices. As a reform instrument, this policy hardly threatened the status quo, but it did serve to rally the supporters of price decreases – and reinforce the notion of 'producer co-responsibility', largely an empty phrase until that time.

The main problem with applying the notion of guarantee thresholds to the dairy industry was that it would have implied a price drop too large for contemplation. In a major policy shift, the Commission reconsidered its opposition to the use of quotas (the sugar quotas have always been considered 'temporary') and recommended their application to the dairy sector. The Council agreed to the proposal, in March 1984, as a temporary device. The Commission considered the quota as a particular way of administering the guarantee threshold through the use of its 'super-levy' on above-threshold production – and more generally as a way of strengthening producer co-responsibility. Shorn of the rhetoric, it actually constituted an admission that prices had got so far out of hand that a switch to quantity-fixing rather than price-fixing was needed in this sector.

The link between price decisions and policy changes appears at the heart of the CAP. The level of prices serves as the main determinant of the tensions and pressures that build up within the policy. High prices promote production, restrict consumption, and promote surpluses: they also maintain farm incomes and attract rural votes. Policies, such as intervention buying, deficiency payments, export restrictions, and import levies, work perfectly well to stabilize domestic producer prices when these are set close to 'market' levels. With the appropriate domestic support prices almost any policy can be made to work. Conversely, all policies become difficult when the prices are set at too high a level. Intervention becomes expensive as producers unload their output on the intervention agencies in preference to finding a market. Producer subsidies become significant budget items, even for commodities that account for a small share of agricultural output. High import levies and export subsidies arouse the displeasure of exporting countries and promote the search for alternative sources of inputs into food and feed processing industries. Disharmonies arise between supported sectors and unsupported ones, and between agricultural and non-agricultural industries. In this sense, an appropriate price policy obviates the need for reform.

The 1984 dairy quotas agreement temporarily took the milk sector off the agenda, to be replaced by cereals – along with beef, wine and oilseed – as the main problem area. Spending continued to rise despite a strong dollar and hence high world prices. The new Commissioner, Andriessen, revived the notion of a prudent price strategy, with a new twist. Prices were actually decreased in ECU terms, though this was less dramatic than it appeared, since the ECU had been retied to the Deutschmark. Yet another set of policy documents came from the new Commissioner – the 'Perspectives for the CAP' (CEC, 1985a) – and its follow-up paper called 'A Future for Community Agriculture' (CEC, 1985b). These documents backed the notion of price discipline, through the mechanism of co-responsibility levies for cereal and other products. One of the most wide-ranging reviews of the options for policy came up with a narrow view of the options.

By 1986 it was clear that even the dairy quotas had not really led to a satisfactory solution to the budget cost problem: a cut in the quotas of 9.5 per cent, along with a weakening of the beef intervention price, was needed in December 1986 to contain spending in those areas. The focus then turned to quotas in cereals, and to alternative types of policy – in particular to set-asides.

In July 1987, the Commission submitted a package of agricultural stabilizers designed to penalize farmers for overproduction, by imposing automatic price cuts if production thresholds were exceeded. This package also proposed increased co-responsibility levies, which could be refunded if production stayed under the thresholds. After heated discussions, a stabilizers' package along with set-asides was approved by the European Council in February 1988, as part of a larger package which also included increasing EC revenues and extending the UK budgetary rebate. The recent changes in the CAP have probably been facilitated by the 'blame shift' provided by the idea of European solidarity which seems increasingly important since the ratification of the Single European Act in 1986.[17] Ministers, at least in principle, have the opportunity to sell unpalatable packages at home on the grounds that they are good for Europe. This is clearly a much more realistic option among those countries with questioned loyalty to the concept and continuation of the EC. The 'blame shift' appears most useful when the Community is in a state of crisis with current policy unsustainable. The GATT negotiations may alter the perspective of European solidarity somewhat in that they insert international reciprocity and benefits for third countries as justifications for policies not very acceptable to European farmers.

NOTES

1. We are indebted to Michael Tracy for this example.
2. The initials stand for the Comité des Organisations Professionnelles Agricoles. They work closely with the federation of agricultural co-operatives, the Comité General de la Coopération Agricole des Pays de la Communauté (COGECA), and the two organizations generally co-ordinate their views on agricultural policy.
3. Harvey (n.d.) has noted that since political institutions are the natural outcome of the workings of the economy, and are an integral part of the economy, any realistic theory of economic theory must include an explanation of political behaviour and vice versa.
4. This situation may be changing in that France recently became a net contributor to EC finances.
5. This is discussed in the treatment of public opinion in Section 3.3.
6. When, in 1987, pressures developed for a tax or quotas on nitrogen usage, the British chemical giant, ICI, launched a major advertising campaign in the UK

press to counteract it, which, among other things, showed cricket pitches being ploughed up to feed the country. We are indebted to David R. Harvey for bringing this to our notice.

7. The label 'consumer' itself is misleading. Since food commodities pass through so many hands on the way to end use, the 'consumer' is as much agri-business and other farmers as the housewife in the supermarket.

8. This study is based on interviews between 17 March and 8 May 1987 of a sample of the general public consisting of 1,000 persons per country, except in Luxembourg, where 300 persons were questioned. Three hundred persons were questioned in Northern Ireland. Respondents were all given the same questionnaire, consisting of 60 questions, in their homes by professional staff. Another part of this survey was based on interviews of 3,140 farm heads in all 12 EC member countries.

9. The EC uses the term 'Cabinet' in the French rather than Anglo-Saxon tradition. A high official's Cabinet is his personal and professional office staff.

10. For a discussion of political credibility see Neustadt (1980).

11. This discussion of the implications of the rule of time-constrained unanimity draws on the analysis of Runge and von Witzke (1985).

12. As we have indicated the practice of unanimity is still in force for questions under Article 43 of the EEC Treaty of Rome, which includes all market regulation policies. But individual nations are showing increasing reluctance to insist on this rule, at least in part to avoid blame for preventing EC action to deal with the current crisis. What should be emphasized is that the Treaty Rule for Article 43 provides only for 'qualified majority' voting, although the practice since the 'Luxembourg Compromise' has been unanimity. The Single European Act does not change Article 43 procedure, but with regard to Council voting did not need to do so since here – in contrast to others where the SEA did make a change – qualified majority applied anyway.

13. For a very detailed discussion of the various factors which influence the national interest, see Harvey (1982).

14. We are indebted to Simon Harris for communicating this point.

15. For a very comprehensive discussion of the development of the CAP, see Michael Tracy (1989), Ch. 14.

16. For a discussion of the socio-structural directives see Harris, Swinbank and Wilkinson (1983) Ch. 9.

17. We are indebted to David R. Harvey for emphasizing the concept of 'blame shift' in this connection.

4 · EUROPEAN COMMUNITY AGRICULTURAL POLICY REFORM, 1980-8

To get a better sense of the capacity for the EC to reform its agricultural policy it is useful to look in some detail at the policy process as it functioned in the two most recent crises. The cases presented are the imposition of milk quotas in 1984 and the imposition of stabilizers and set-asides in 1988. The discussion uses the analytical framework developed in Chapter 1 to examine the events surrounding the reform efforts and the roles of the actors in the process.

4.1 THE IMPOSITION OF MILK QUOTAS

On 31 March 1984, the Council of Agriculture Ministers approved the establishment of dairy quotas to check burgeoning milk production. This action was taken along with a package of other agricultural measures including the extension of the system of guaranteed thresholds; the dismantling of positive Monetary Compensation Amounts (MCAs) and a shift to a new agricultural unit of account (or green ECU) based on the Deutschmark; a price decrease for EC-supported products averaging 1.8 per cent; and a mandate to the Commission to negotiate a limit on grain substitute imports with trading partners. This package, in turn, was part of a broader deal which increased EC revenues by raising the ceiling on national VAT-based contributions to the budget from 1.0 per cent to a maximum of 1.4 per cent. At the same time, the UK contribution burden was reduced. The imposition of dairy quotas constituted reform in that it involved both a significant shift in policy direction and the creation of new instruments in the face of an untenable situation.

4.1.1 Economic trends and economic shocks

The most significant long-term economic trend operating at the time of the milk quotas debate was overproduction of agricultural products, induced partly by technological advances and partly by the CAP's high price incentives. This had led to rapidly increasing expenditures on EC farm programmes. The underlying trend was obscured during 1981 and 1982 by an economic shock caused by the strengthening of the dollar. The strong dollar resulted in higher world prices (in ECU terms) which temporarily reduced export subsidies and European Agricultural Guidance and Guarantee Fund (FEOGA)[1] expenditures. However, in 1983, agricultural commodity programme expenditures rose rapidly again, creating a budgetary crisis. Dairy farmers had particularly strong incentives to produce a surplus in that they could use low-cost cereal substitutes and soybeans for feed while the EC guaranteed them a high price for whatever amount of milk they marketed. Dairy stocks, by 1983, exceeded all other EC stocks in value and were increasing rapidly (see Figure 4.1). The CAP dairy programme, by far the most expensive of all the EC agricultural commodity programmes, consumed 32 per cent of FEOGA expenditures in 1984.

4.1.2 The political environment

The formal decision-making process leading to the establishment of milk quotas began at the Stuttgart summit in June 1983, when the European Council initiated a major review of EC policies under a special emergency procedure (Petit *et al.*, 1987)[2]. The Commission was instructed to submit, by August 1983, 'concrete steps compatible with market conditions . . . to ensure effective control of agricultural expenditures' (Petit *et al.*, 1987, pp. 27–8). A general sense of crisis prevailed. FEOGA costs skyrocketed, after a level period between 1980 and 1982, caused by the appreciation of the US dollar. Unless something was done, the increased revenue agreed in 1981 would have become exhausted at some time before the end of 1984. The dairy sector constituted a natural target for action, with intervention costs predicted to increase from 3.3 billion ECU in 1982 to 4.4 billion ECU in 1983 and 5.8 billion ECU in 1984 (see Figure 4.2; see also Petit *et al.*, 1987, p. 28). Reform proposals could expect considerable opposition from the farm lobby in that farm incomes were declining in a number of member countries. Adding to the pressures facing it, the EC had to give a definite answer to the membership applications of Spain and Portugal. This was difficult as long as the budget crisis went unresolved.

4.1.3 Interests and inputs

The interests to which the EC decision-makers had to pay attention were directly linked to the long-term economic forces and the political environment. Economically, something had to be done to control the growth of agricultural spending, particularly on dairy products. New revenues also had to be sought. At the same time the need to protect agricultural incomes militated against drastic change. Politically, the enlargement of the EC could not proceed without agreed limits to spending growth.

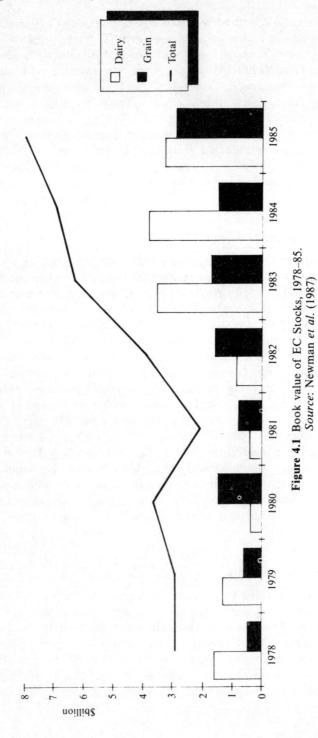

Figure 4.1 Book value of EC Stocks, 1978–85.
Source: Newman et al. (1987)

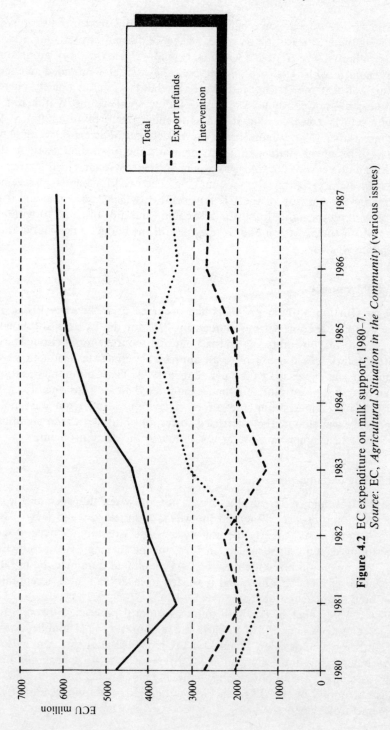

Figure 4.2 EC expenditure on milk support, 1980–7.
Source: EC, Agricultural Situation in the Community (various issues)

The need to take action created an important impetus for policy-makers, allowing them to resist the influence of the EC farm lobby, particularly the dairy interests. The trade-off was a stark one – either the dairy programme was changed or the CAP would collapse. The crisis also provided an excuse for agricultural interests not to fight to the end. It was clear that the current regime could not continue. The farm lobby was able to justify directing its policy efforts towards shaping the impending reform to minimize the damage rather than attempting to prevent change. The crisis strengthened the position of the Budget Commissioner and the finance ministers in that the escalating cost of the CAP gave them both incentive and justification for intervening in agricultural policy-making. The need for increased revenues enhanced the position of the UK government, which had demanded fiscal responsibility for agriculture; the UK could (and did) threaten to withhold support for the provision of new revenues for the budget unless agricultural spending was cut.

4.1.4 Past policy

Overproduction of dairy products had occurred since the early 1970s. The situation had become serious enough by 1977 for the EC to institute a 0.5 per cent co-responsibility levy in that year to discourage production. The co-responsibility levy did not have an appreciable effect on production even though it was increased to 2.5 per cent in 1983. The Community had also attempted price restraint, but had encountered fierce resistance from the dairy lobby, undermining the effort. The implication from past policy experience was that neither increased co-responsibility levies nor significant price cuts held much promise as a solution to the dairy problem.

4.1.5 The decision process

The budget and milk surplus crises not only set the agenda for the Commission, but also influenced the way Commissioners and DG-VI staff saw their interests. Clearly, the survival of the Community depended on containing expenditures, which, in turn, meant curbing dairy production. Any action should not endanger the CAP; it should minimize the negative impact on farmers' incomes; and it needed to meet the test of acceptability to all ten member nations.

The development of the milk quotas proposal proceeded through four stages (Petit *et al.*, 1987, p. 30): the elaboration and publication of Commission proposals on 29 July 1983 (CEC, 1983); discussion in national governments and in the Council of Ministers prior to the Athens summit of 4–6 December 1983; bargaining between the Athens summit and the Brussels summit of 19–20 March 1984; and final negotiations leading to the agreement of 31 March 1984.

The task of formulating the Commission's agricultural proposals devolved primarily to top-level officials in DG-VI, particularly the strong and experienced Director-General, Claude Villain (Petit *et al.*, 1987, p. 30). Villain, as a senior administrator removed from electoral politics, was in a position to entertain new ideas. As the top civil servant responsible for the CAP, he had very strong incentives to propose action which would allow the CAP to surmount its current crisis. Not surprisingly, the subordinate bureaucrats in DG-VI played a minor role in the policy debate. Some of the individuals managing the milk programme were in fact quite surprised when quotas were approved, and were unprepared for the task of administering them. The Agriculture Commissioner, Poul Dalsager, could have taken charge, but apparently did not. He had become Agriculture Commissioner 'by accident' only after the untimely death of Commissioner Gundelach in 1981. Often he appeared to work in Villain's shadow.

The DG-VI policy formulators appear to have behaved as predicted by organizational theory, in that they satisficed by arriving at the decision for milk through a process of elimination. DG-VI, as the managing bureaucracy of the CAP, had every incentive to adapt the existing co-responsibility policy to achieve the agreed objectives, had not this policy already proven itself a failure. In fact, there is evidence that DG-VI did consider increasing the co-responsibility levy to curb production, but rejected this option on the grounds that the necessary increase would be so large that its impact would have to be differentiated among producers of different sizes (Petit *et al.*, 1987, p. 125). The necessary differentiated increase would have shifted the national distribution of benefits and hence, would probably have proved unacceptable to the Council. It would also have compromised the unity of the market mechanism. Decreasing the intervention price was also considered, but rejected on the grounds that the necessary price cut would have an unacceptably large immediate effect on farmers' incomes and only a longer-term effect on production.

The third option considered and then adopted was the imposition of milk quotas. Quotas had advantages in that they could cut production immediately, and could easily be administered through dairies. They would also safeguard farmers' incomes and, hence, would have a greater chance of acceptability to farm groups and the Council of Ministers.

According to Petit, *et al.* (1987, p. 29) the Commission discussion seemed very pragmatic and not dominated by any theoretical economic frame of reference. The imminent crisis created an atmosphere highly conducive to a problem-solving approach. The budget and milk problems demanded resolution and dairy quotas looked both feasible and promising. For largely tactical reasons, the formulators put the dairy quota proposal into a larger package which included a proposed tax on the consumption of fats and oils other than butter, reduction of the differences between EC and world market grain prices and authorization to negotiate reductions in the imports of cereal substitutes. A comprehensive package increased political feasibility because it allowed maximum trade-offs to satisfy the various interests. The Commission's package was set forth in 'COM 500' (CEC, 1983). This document presented the options in such a way as to cast the best possible light on the proposal for quotas. Moreover, the price cut option was presented so that rejection appeared inevitable.

When the dairy quotas proposal went to the full Commission, it was approved by only one vote (Petit *et al.*, 1987, p. 19). This seems surprising given the gravity of the crisis. In fact, as often is the case, consensus on the necessity for action did not lead to agreement about what to do. Several Commissioners would have preferred price cuts. They feared that continued emphasis on such products as milk and cereals would leave very little resources for Mediterranean products and the Integrated Mediterranean Programmes (Petit *et al.*, 1987, p. 19). It seems clear from this outcome that the Commission collectively did not constitute a driving force for quotas. Had DG-VI suggested another viable alternative, it might well have been approved for submission to the Council of Ministers.

4.1.6 Discussions before the Athens summit

Once COM 500 was released, the locus of action shifted to individual countries where farm groups and others reacted to the Commission proposals and national governments formulated their responses. Initial responses corresponded very closely to national agricultural interests, not surprising from the perspective of our analytical framework, since the arena of negotiations had shifted to the Council of Agriculture Ministers. However, in some instances, the national agricultural interests did not appear clear, with some elements of agriculture gaining from the quota proposal and other elements losing. Governments with divided interests found it difficult to make a coherent reaction to the Commission's proposal, which limited their bargaining effectiveness.

Though a broad consensus emerged that the current situation was untenable and that the dairy regime required significant modification, only West Germany greeted the milk quota idea enthusiastically. Both the agriculture minister, Ignaz Kiechle, and the German Farmers' Union – the Deutscher Bauernverband (DBV) – had previously come to the conclusion that only quotas could save the incomes of West German dairy farmers.[3] The French appeared rather negative, with the farm community rather divided.[4] Quotas were unacceptable in western France, particularly Brittany, where dairy production had increased rapidly. They were more acceptable in eastern France, particularly the mountain regions, where production had remained stable or declined. The agriculture ministry looked very hard for, but did not find, an alternative which would hurt French milk producers less than quotas.

The Italian farmers' organizations also had a very divided response.[5] While the dairy sector is strong only in northern Italy, much of the rest of the country would have been quite happy to cut dairy expenditures and increase funds for Mediterranean products. In fact, the Italian Agriculture Minister, Pandolfi, came out for a dairy price cut. Neither the British nor the Dutch farm organizations and governments showed much enthusiasm for quotas. They did not show unalterable opposition either.[6] On the other hand, the British and Dutch raised serious objections to an extension of the co-responsibility levy on the grounds that it would inevitably discriminate against larger producers, important in the UK and the Netherlands. The British government, with the support of the Milk Marketing Board, pressed for significant price cuts, though UK dairy farmers opposed them.

In a special procedure to prepare for the discussions in the Council of Agriculture Ministers, a top-level committee of experts from national ministries of agriculture (and, in some instances, from other ministries as well) was formed to conduct the preliminary negotiations (Petit *et al.*, 1987, p. 29). It was hoped that this committee could speed the process so that a final proposal could be ready for the forthcoming December summit in Athens. The accomplishments of this committee are difficult to assess. As key civil servants with an expertise in agriculture, the members were in a position to explore all the ramifications of the Commission's proposal for their own national agricultural interests. They could also understand the similarities and differences between their national interests and those of other EC members. This could help in preparing for the general Council debate and formulating a final consensus. This committee probably did not resolve any of those major differences between the EC members, or between the Commission and the Council. However, it probably played a significant role in facilitating conflict resolution. It may also have helped ensure that the agriculture ministers stuck closely to national agricultural interests, rather than simply responding to farm group pressures. The creation of the *ad hoc* committee of high-level experts would appear as a rational organizational response to the exigencies of 'crisis-coping'.

In another departure from normal procedure, a Special Council consisting of agriculture, finance and foreign ministers held meetings on 30 August and 9 November 1983 to discuss both agricultural and financial aspects of the reform package. Hence, the predicted broadening of the policy process occurred in time of crisis. Pressure increased for spending moderation and consideration of international concerns by agriculture ministers. However, since neither finance ministers nor foreign ministers generally have much agricultural expertise, they were more in a position to prevent certain things from happening than in one to make a positive contribution to developing the quota proposal.

By the 14 November meeting of the Council of Agriculture Ministers, there was clear movement towards acceptance of a system of milk quotas (see Petit *et al.*, 1987, p. 31). Quotas were still favoured only by West Germany, but none of the other member nations adamantly opposed them. The other two options had both proponents and opponents. The UK and Italy favoured dairy price cuts, but West Germany found them unacceptable. France and Belgium supported progressive co-responsibility, but the UK and the Netherlands registered strong opposition to this option. Consensus eluded the ministers with many details still to be worked out about how the system of quotas would operate. To complicate the process, other related issues needed resolution, including those concerning MCAs, cereal policy and budgetary contributions. The ministers, sensing that the summit could not deal with the full range of agricultural issues, selected only the dossiers for milk, cereals, MCAs and the proposed oils and fats tax for consideration by the European Council. Consideration of measures to enhance the EC structures programme was postponed until afterwards.

In the negotiations prior to the summit, the West German delegation seemed to exercise considerable influence, because its national position was clear (the government and the farm union agreed), and close to that of the Commission. With less clear national positions, the French, Italian and Dutch delegations appeared less influential. The continued resistance to the emerging consensus for quotas by the UK and France isolated these governments. The British did force a decision by refusing to approve new resources until agricultural spending was brought under control and the British rebate extended. As anticipated, EC member nations moved slowly in making concessions, perhaps motivated by the not unreasonable expectation that holding out might engender more generous offers from other parties anxious to see the necessary consensus achieved.

4.1.7 The Athens summit

The December 1982 summit in Athens failed to resolve the EC's agriculture and budget problems and plunged the Community into a deep crisis. The debate on the dairy dossier consumed almost two full half days in the 48-hour meeting, a disproportionate amount of time by any account. All delegations but the French apparently accepted the principle of dairy quotas, the Irish assuming throughout that they would be exempt. The budget issue created the greatest dissension, particularly the British rebate and the length of time it would be valid (Petit *et al.*, 1987, pp. 33–4).

There were at least two instances at this meeting where the behaviour of the actors suggested that the individuals concerned may have superimposed their own interests and concerns on national interests. The first instance was President Mitterrand's resistance to milk quotas. It has been suggested that he acted to delay agreement until the French Council presidency which followed, though Petit *et al.* (1987) believes it is more likely that Mitterrand did not think French public opinion was yet willing to accept dairy quotas.

In the second instance, the Italian Prime Minister Craxi contradicted his agriculture minister and accepted quotas without receiving visible concessions because he wanted to 'get rid of agricultural problems' (Petit *et al.*, 1987, pp. 75-6).

4.1.8 Bargaining between the Athens and Brussels summits

The failure of the Athens summit gave new impetus for the agricultural and budget negotiations in that it shifted the political environment. The member governments were all deeply embarrassed. Confronted by a serious crisis, they had been found wanting in their ability to resolve it. Continued failure would have reflected adversely on their overall competence (Petit *et al.*, 1987, pp. 34-5).

The Commission, in demonstrating that bargaining strategy can make a difference, increased the pressure by delaying intervention payments, by proposing a six-month suspension of dairy aids and by submitting a very strict price package. This served notice on all of the binding nature of the budget constraint. The Commission also insisted that the Council stick closely to its proposals in the absence of unanimity to amend them.

After the Athens failure, the Council of Agriculture Ministers moved steadily towards agreement on a dairy quota package, though the discussions appeared chaotic on occasion. Many meetings were held to resolve the differences, some formal while others were informal, some multilateral between agricultural ministers and their associates while others were bilateral. By 17 March 1984 elements of a package to impose milk quotas, dismantle MCAs and establish prices for 1984-5 were ready for European Council approval, contingent on a balance between agricultural problems, control of budget spending, 'own resources' for the budget and new policies.

4.1.9 The Brussels summit and final agreement

The European Council met in Brussels on 19-20 March 1984. It endorsed the agricultural package, but there was still no overall settlement, because of the inability to reach agreement on the British budget rebate and Ireland's demand for special treatment with regard to milk quotas. On 26-27 March the agricultural ministers resumed their deliberations. On 31 March after 26 hours' uninterrupted discussion, the ministers reached final agreement on a package, which Petit *et al.* (1987) observe was strikingly similar to the Commission's original proposals. A major difference appeared in the allocation of quotas to dairies rather than to individual farmers. The shift of the MCA base to the Deutschmark, and the special treatment for Ireland, Italy and Greece on milk quotas, constituted less significant changes. The final package was approved with quasi-unanimity, even though Greece dissented on fruits and vegetables, and the Netherlands protested against special treatment for Ireland on dairy quotas (Petit *et al.*, 1987, pp. 35–6).

Much of the credit for the successful conclusion of the negotiations goes to the French Minister of Agriculture, M. Rocard, who served as President of the Agriculture Council after 1 January 1984. He effectively used his prerogatives to call meetings and set the agenda. As Petit *et al.*, (1987, pp. 132–3) observed:

> By fixing a very busy schedule of meetings, he infused among his colleagues a sense of urgency as well as a conscience that this was an opportunity to seize after the failure of the heads of state and government in Athens. In the final stages of negotiations, nobody dared to leave the Council meeting room during the informal breaks used for bilateral discussions between the President and each national delegation, because the Council was still formally in session and critical multilateral discussions could resume at any time.

Rocard's leadership in the final stages of the process depended not only on his Council presidency, but also, paradoxically, on the failure of the Athens summit. Prior to that time, he could not assert himself for fear that he might be undercut to his political disadvantage by President Mitterrand, with whom he had a long-standing rivalry. Once the summit had failed, and with this threat removed, Rocard could devote all his energies to forging an agreement (Petit *et al.*, 1987, pp. 45–7).

The final agreement contained something for everybody. West Germany seemed to get most with both the achievement of milk quotas and the shift of the MCA base to the Deutschmark, which came along with compensation to West German farmers in the form of a VAT tax reduction for the resulting decline in their prices. France and Italy achieved the promise of price increases through the phasing-out of MCAs and Commission action to reduce cereal substitute imports. France, in addition, succeeded in creating the option for quotas on dairies rather than on individual farmers. Finally, the UK and the Netherlands got budgetary discipline and a restrictive price policy. No government had to accept provisions which it implacably opposed. Thus, the outcome seems to fit very well into Lindblom's paradigm in which all represented interests reach mutual accommodation. The EC interest was satisfied to the extent that action was taken which allowed the Community to 'cope' with its budgetary and agricultural crises. Of course, some important interests, such as economic efficiency and consumer welfare, were not fully represented by either the Commission or any of the national actors and hence did not fare particularly well.

Only the four large nations of the EC (France, West Germany, Italy and the UK) have the authority to affect significantly the course which a major set of negotiations will take. In the case of the milk quotas decision, West Germany appeared particularly influential for a number of reasons. First, the West German government made its position strong and clear from the beginning, with a high degree of convergence between a cohesive farm lobby (the DBV) and the government. Second, this position seemed close to the recommendations of the Commission and not diametrically at odds with the interests of other nations. France lost an opportunity to influence the course of the discussions at the beginning, when it failed to come up with a mutually acceptable alternative to milk quotas. France's position was hindered by disunity among French farmer organizations. France exercised more influence in the final stages of the negotiations when it was able to use the Council presidency to forge a final agreement and to determine the type of quota package which would be implemented. Italy was unable to exercise much influence at any stage in the process because both farm organizations and government were divided about what course of action to take. The UK exercised primarily a negative influence – to prevent the continuing escalation of budgetary expenditures. The British claim for a budget rebate weakened its bargaining position.

Could the 1983-4 dairy policy debate have resulted in another outcome? Certainly the imposition of quotas had a certain element of inevitability in that no other viable option was suggested. However, the implementation of quotas might have ended up differently had the British government accepted the quota concept from the outset. Then, the UK might have made a stronger case for making quotas tradable and not tied to the land, though the British bargaining position would still have been weakened by the need to achieve a budget rebate. The Ministry of Agriculture, Fisheries and Food appears to have had leeway in determining its policies. The Milk Marketing Board adamantly opposed quotas, but British farmers strongly opposed the price cuts advocated by the UK. Perhaps the ideology of the government was the determining factor.

4.1.10 Milk quotas and the analytical framework

The analytical framework developed in Chapter 1 is helpful in explaining the milk quotas decision. The long-term economic trend of overproduction, in part created by high price supports, forced reform on the political agenda by creating the political environment of budget crisis. The existing policy could not be sustained. The political development of enlarging the EC from ten members to twelve with the prospective admission of Spain and Portugal, contributed to the need for change. The atmosphere of crisis facilitated action in that it stimulated consensus about the high priority of the budget interest. It also weakened the bargaining position of the farm lobby and strengthened the influence of the Commission.

The structure of the decision process also exercised a strong influence. The compartmentalization of decision-making in the Commission and Council slowed the bargaining down. However, the Commission's exclusive prerogative to submit proposals gave it leadership capacity to stimulate consensus among member governments. The institution of the Council presidency also served a useful function in brokering the final agreement, when the situation had deteriorated to the point where action was inescapable. The practice of voting unanimity in the Council strung the process out and created a complicated but balanced package of benefits. It probably also contributed to reform since it enabled the UK government to demand more responsible agricultural policy in return for allowing an increase in budget revenues. Unanimity also ensured a policy which did not undercut the legitimacy of the EC with any member country. Milk quotas, in the last analysis, proved acceptable to everyone.

Public choice theory helps explain the positions and inputs of the various actors. Farm groups took positions quite consistent with their interests and committed resources consistent with their high policy stake. As predicted, consumer groups exercised little influence. Senior administrators in the Commission, as anticipated, took the initiative in developing the quota proposal. Members of the Agriculture Council took positions which balanced national interest (corresponding to net-trade status, structure of agriculture and budget contributions) with pressures from domestic farm groups. However, the threat to EC survival presented by the budget crisis, in the last analysis, forced an accommodation between national interests and the Community interest in containing the growth of agricultural spending.

The organizational process paradigm also provides insights for the milk quota decision. Most important, it helps explain the policy inertia in the lower levels of DG-VI and the reluctance to impose quotas which implied new organizational standard operating procedures. It also accounts for development of the Commission proposal through a process of elimination – satisficing. The establishment of an *ad hoc* body of national experts to prepare for the Council debate shows some organizational flexibility and innovativeness.

Government politics and partisan mutual adjustment paradigms are also useful. Illustrating the former paradigm, French Agriculture Minister Rocard's shift in behaviour when he became Council president clearly shows that 'where you stand depends on where you sit'. The latter paradigm explains the pragmatic focus on agreement over means without attempting to reach consensus on the ends.

4.2 THE ESTABLISHMENT OF BUDGET STABILIZERS

The establishment of milk quotas marked a significant change in the CAP, and can be seen as a step on the road to reform. There is somewhat less certainty about the changes introduced in 1988, under the name of 'budget stabilizers'. If political and diplomatic effort were an indicator of the magnitude of policy change, budget stabilizers would qualify as a major departure. In practice, the policy changes may prove less than dramatic, depending upon how the new policy is administered. Taken with the budgetary decisions, however, the 'February package' was a significant event for the CAP and the EC. This section looks at the anatomy of that decision, as an indication of the reform process at work.

On 13 February 1988, the European Council, after two days of deadlock, approved a framework for a package of measures. These included increasing the revenues available to the EC; creating a new fourth budgetary resource based on GNP shares; imposing a strict limit on the growth of agricultural spending at 74 per cent of GNP increase; and doubling the funds available for regional, social and structural programmes. This package established a system of budget stabilizers for agricultural commodity programmes designed to keep them within budgetary targets and to prevent overproduction (see *Agra Europe*, 15 February 1988; 19 February 1988). At the same time, the British budget rebate was continued, keeping the UK contribution from vastly exceeding the benefits received by British farmers.[7]

The Brussels agreement was the culmination of a year of intense negotiations within both the EC and member governments. The debate formally began with approval by the Commission of its paper, 'Making a Success of the Single European Act: A New Frontier for Europe' (Commission of the European Communities (CEC), 1987a) in February 1987. This document (often referred to as COM 100) pointed out the EC's dire financial situation, along with the need to increase both budgetary resources and budgetary discipline. The proposed key to budgetary discipline was controlling the escalation of agricultural expenditures through the imposition of production stabilizers.

The context of the stabilizers debate was one of serious crisis. The 'budgetary discipline' laid down under the 1984 Fountainebleau agreement clearly had not worked. Agricultural spending in the subsequent period had increased by more than 18 per cent per year, despite the 2 per cent limit allowed under the Fontainebleau formula (see Figure 4.3; see also *Agra Europe*, 26 June 1987, P/1). The growth of agricultural spending had prevented other Community programmes from developing and had exhausted all available revenues. Indeed, the budget shortfall for 1987 was estimated at 4–5 billion ECU, though the deficit had been concealed by clever accounting. The Commission estimated that, by 1987, the Community had accumulated net liabilities of 17 billion ECU, with a rapid upward trend (see Figure 4.4). Things could not continue much longer without significant change. Unless something was done to lower CAP costs and/or increase revenues, funds would run out at some time in 1988 and the EC would not be able to meet its obligations. Cereals programmes appeared as the central target for action because of their escalating high costs. The oilseeds programmes, also suffering from rapidly increasing costs, were also to receive attention.

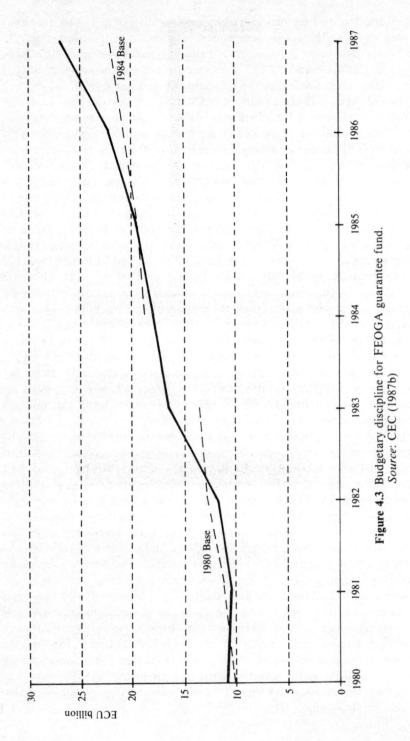

Figure 4.3 Budgetary discipline for FEOGA guarantee fund.
Source: CEC (1987b)

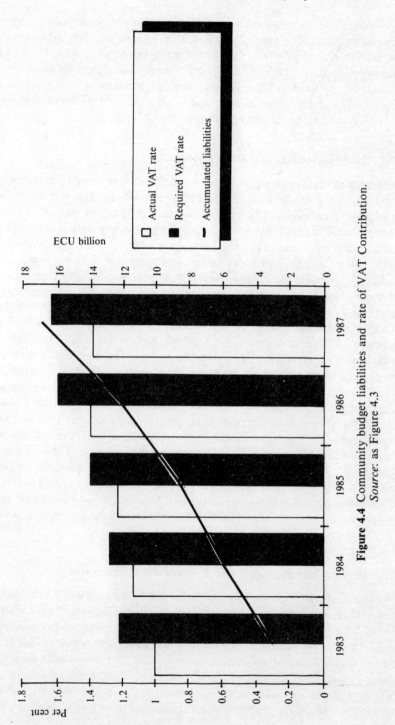

Figure 4.4 Community budget liabilities and rate of VAT Contribution.
Source: as Figure 4.3

The farm income situation did not make it easy to contemplate reform, as farm income for 1987 was declining. The real net value added at factor cost per labour unit dropped by 3.6 per cent between 1986 and 1987 (*Agra Europe*, 8 January 1988, E/2). There was a wide deviation around this figure, ranging from -17.2 per cent for West Germany to -3.2 per cent for France and +11.1 per cent for Ireland. This suggested different degrees of receptivity to change in different countries.

4.2.1 Economic trends and economic shocks

Overproduction appeared still the most important long-term economic trend operating at the time of the stabilizers debate. The imposition and tightening of milk quotas had contained milk production, but other sectors were not yet under control. Commodity support prices were still well above market clearing levels. The most serious problems came from the cereal sector where stocks and costs were increasing rapidly (see Figure 4.5). Cereal programme costs were severely aggravated by increased export restitutions caused by increased competition from the USA for international markets. Two economic shocks, both of which worked to lower US food export prices, aided the USA in this competition. The first came from the decline in US commodity loan rates legislated in the 1985 farm bill (see discussion in Chapter 3). The second came from the precipitous decline in the dollar's value with respect to the ECU. Cereal programme expenditures for 1987 were forecast to reach 4.6 billion ECU, rapidly closing the gap with milk expenditures which had previously dominated CAP spending. Oilseeds expenditures were also increasing rapidly, but were still well below cereal expenditures. EC farmers generally were no better able to take advantage of the increased CAP expenditures than they were at the time of the milk quota debate in 1983-4. At the same time as commodity programme costs increased, real farm prices dropped sharply, particularly in West Germany which could not take advantage of the MCA system to limit price cuts in the annual price fixing negotiations. The agricultural income trend appeared in a slow steady decline.

4.2.2 Political developments and the political environment

Politically, the EC needed to consolidate the Community of 12 to compete more effectively with the USA and Japan and to deal as an equal with the Soviet Union. The EC had made a commitment to reduce national barriers and form a single European market by 1992, but progress was threatened by CAP expenditures, which still consumed more than two-thirds of the EC budget, thus denying resources badly needed to speed the transition. The extensive public opinion survey to which we have referred in Chapter 3 indicated that public support for farmers remained remarkably strong

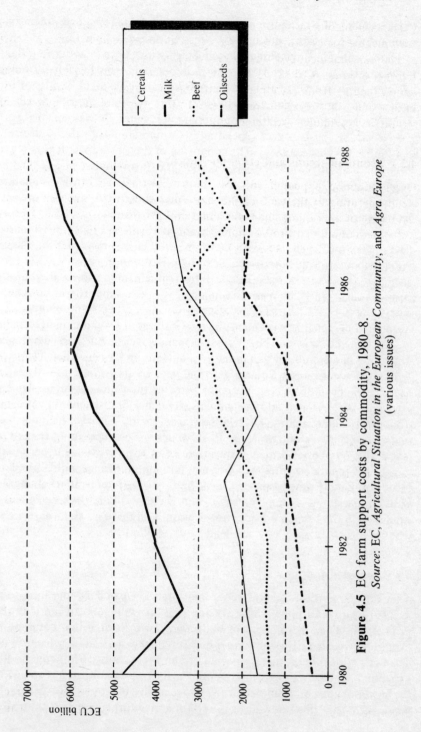

Figure 4.5 EC farm support costs by commodity, 1980–8.
Source: EC, Agricultural Situation in the European Community, and Agra Europe (various issues)

(CEC, 1988c, 59–61). The centrality of the farm vote remained potent in a number of EC nations, particularly West Germany.

The political environment had elements both favourable and unfavourable to reform. At an international level, the EC felt increased pressure from the USA and the Cairns group[8] to negotiate reductions in agricultural support policies. However, this was not accompanied by demands from domestic public opinion, which generally was satisfied with the level of agricultural spending (Commission of the European Communities (CEC), 1988c). The expansion of the EC to include Spain and Portugal had increased the diversity of the farm lobby, weakening its capacity for unified action to resist reform. The balance in the Council of Ministers shifted against the northern products which receive greatest protection from EC agricultural commodity programmes.

Electoral considerations seemed important with a French presidential election in April 1988 and West German *Land* elections in 1988 in Baden-Württemberg during March and Schleswig-Holstein in early May. On the one hand, these elections suggested caution on reform to avoid antagonizing farmers, particularly in West Germany where their support was critical to the ruling CDU/CSU–FDP coalition. On the other hand, both West German and French governments had an interest in reaching an agreement to resolve the crisis. The West German government had developed something of a credibility gap in the eyes of German farmers when it resisted cereals price cuts – particularly with the veto by its Agriculture Minister, Kiechle, of the 1985 price package only to see the Commission implement price cuts of 2 per cent administratively. Evidence of disenchantment came from abstentions among CDU/CSU farm voters. Clearly the policy of obstructionism was not working. Positive action to shape an agreement as favourable to West German farm interests as the environment permitted might prove more acceptable to German farmers. In France, both President Mitterrand and Prime Minister Chirac had a strong interest in resolving the crisis to forestall a strong challenge from Raymond Barre, who also was a candidate in the French presidential election. Failure to reach an agreement would reflect adversely on their leadership abilities.

4.2.3 Interests and inputs

The most important general economic interest created by the long-term trend towards surplus was reducing the growth rate of agricultural production. The environment of budgetary crisis dictated that commodity programme costs be brought under control quickly, particularly for cereals. The net political interests also pointed to an agreement to limit commodity expenditures. Such an agreement could work to the political advantage of the governments of France and West Germany. It would also provide a response to the USA and Cairns group (of agricultural exporting countries) pressures to remove agricultural subsidies in the Uruguay Round of trade negotiations in the GATT (see Chapter 8). Equally important, an agreement could remove a significant obstacle to a single European market in 1992. However, the declining indicators of farmer welfare militated against any changes which would significantly reduce farm income.

4.2.4 Past policy

Guarantee thresholds had been introduced by the EC in the early 1980s to reduce the price incentives to overproduction. These were intended to penalize farmers when certain production limits were reached, but had never been very effective because the penalties were not automatic. Agriculture ministers under pressures from farm communities had been positively ingenious in circumventing the penalties by raising prices and adjusting MCA rates. Co-responsibility levies had also been introduced, but at levels too small to have much bite. Still, guarantee thresholds and co-responsibility levies were two standard operating procedures which could be enlarged with minimum organizational difficulty.

The budgetary crisis strengthened the positions of those in the EC who wanted commodity prices set closer to market levels with strict limits on agricultural spending. It put the farm lobby very much on the defensive. The current system was untenable and change was inevitable. The problem for farmer groups was one of damage control. Divisions in the farm community were hence exacerbated at the same time as the Commission resolve hardened to resist farm interests.

4.2.5 The decision process

The bargaining process can be divided into three stages. The first stage comprised the development of the stabilizers proposal in the Commission. This was completed when the Commission's proposals were submitted to the Agriculture Council on 22 September 1987. The second stage consisted of the negotiations in the Council of Ministers culminating with the collapse of the Copenhagen summit in December. In the third stage, which concluded with the Brussels agreement on 12 February 1988, the efforts of the Commission and the German presidency were successfully directed to developing a generally acceptable compromise acceptable to all. In what follows we will examine, in sequence, each of these phases with an eye to understanding how the policy process operated.

4.2.6 Commission formulation

The Commission began work on developing a reform package soon after the approval of COM 100. Changes in agricultural support policy were seen as part of a much larger strategy induced by non-agricultural considerations. For the Brussels officials, the questions were how to secure peace in the budget field and assure a funding base for priorities besides agriculture. To do these things there was an awareness that the agricultural house had to be put in order. The initiative clearly came from the Commissioners and their Cabinets rather than from the Directorates-General. A central group developed in the Commission consisting of Jacques Delors, the Commission President, Frans Andriessen, the Agricultural Commissioner, and Henning Christophersen, the Budget Commissioner, all of whom saw the issues in much the same way. This group constituted an *ad hoc* 'inner circle' of the Commission which developed an overall strategy for reform. This group of Commissioners and their Cabinets met on a regular basis to co-ordinate the development of the Commissioner's reform package.

Not at all surprisingly, from the perspective of public choice and organizational theory, consensus emerged on the general goals of action. The EC faced a severe crisis with imminent bankruptcy unless significant change occurred quickly. With survival at stake, individuals and organizations tend to subordinate their own goals to the collective interest. The focus on the broader goal of promoting the single European market as well as survival can be understood both in terms of enlightened self-interest and even of idealism.

The policy initiative, as expected, came at the senior administrator level where the individuals involved had a strong personal stake in preserving the CAP and in promoting EC organizational health. There are a number of reasons why the locus of decision shifted from the senior levels of DG-VI in the milk quota debate to the 'inner circle' for stabilizers. First, both the Commission President and Agriculture Commissioner were strong leaders with a desire to take charge. Delors had made the single European market something of a personal crusade and could not easily see this goal frustrated by agricultural stalemate. Andriessen had made an equally strong commitment to containing agricultural expenditures. Second, Claude Villain had retired as Director-General of DG-VI. His successor, Guy Legras, had been in office for a shorter period of time than had Andriessen, and so was not well positioned to challenge the authority of his Commissioner. Besides, the Commissioners and their Cabinets, with broader responsibilities and perspectives, and less weighed down by day-to-day management responsibilities and commitment to the existing standard operating procedures, were better placed than the established bureaucracy in the Directorates-General to lead.

The success of Delors, Andriessen and Christophersen in forming an 'inner circle' reflects both the severity of the crisis and the leadership capacity of the individuals involved. It also provides evidence of organizational innovativeness under stress, giving an indication of the EC's general vitality. A powerful incentive existed for such a group to form. The alliance of the President, the Agriculture Commissioner and Budget Commissioner was a natural one, given the nature of the crisis, and a powerful one. When this group agreed, other Commissioners could not easily demur, particularly since it represented most of the budgetary and agricultural expertise in the Commission and included the dossiers potentially most affected by reform. Agreement among the 'inner circle' would both speed the Commission process and minimize the need to make expensive 'side-payments' to win the support of other Commissioners. Moreover, they all shared a concern for fiscal soundness. Delors had been finance minister in France and Andriessen had held the same position in the Netherlands. With the general unwieldiness of a Commission swollen to 17 members with the admission of Spain and Portugal, the other Commissioners had an interest in deferring to the 'inner circle' to facilitate the quick action necessitated by the crisis.

Soon after the promulgation of COM 100, *ad hoc* working groups, consisting of Cabinet members and key personnel from the Directorates-General, were set up by the Commissioners to develop the agricultural, budget and structural elements of the Commission proposal. The efforts of these groups were generally co-ordinated by the 'inner circle', sometimes enlarged to include other Commissioners with relevant jurisdictions. Paradoxically, the agricultural discussions appear to have proceeded most easily, as this working group consisted of experts who shared a common perception of the problems of European agriculture. Everyone knew that agricultural expenditures and production had to be curbed. DG-VI appeared co-operative and made no effort to sabotage the process.

The decision to recommend stabilizers was reached through a process of elimination – another example of satisficing. A number of ideas were floated at the time. Large price cuts were unacceptable to a number of governments, particularly West Germany. The costs in terms of loss of support from farm groups appeared too great, with no counterbalancing gain in support from other groups. Mandatory production quotas, unacceptable to the UK and the Netherlands, seemed impossible to administer. Land extensification schemes, including set-asides, were expensive and did not seem all that efficacious in light of US experience. Besides, nobody in the Commission knew how to administer them. That left only stabilizers, really a variant of guarantee thresholds – a standard operating procedure – except with automatic penalties. This option did not excite the leaders of any country, but did not generate implacable opposition either.

It is not absolutely clear when the decision for stabilizers was reached. COM 100 proclaimed that reform of the CAP was essential if the EC was to have the necessary resources to carry out its new responsibilities. It further stated the need for progressive efforts to eliminate surpluses and check the steady increase in the budgetary burden. It called for a restrictive pricing policy, including more flexibility in guarantees and intervention mechanisms and a greater degree of producer co-responsibility. Somewhat ironically, given the final outcome, it urged that market forces be allowed greater play to avoid sinking deeper into 'a morass of administrative burdens', which would bring consumer resistance and loss of foreign markets (CEC 1987a, p. 10). Intervention was to be returned to its original safety net role of underpinning domestic markets for short-term price stability.

COM 100 made it clear that the 'inner circle's' fiscal soundness values prevailed along with the value of greater market orientation. The direction of Commission thinking became clearer with the release on 28 February 1987 of COM 101 (CEC, 1987b). This document observed that 'agricultural expenditures must be subject to discipline arrangements providing the instruments for genuine containment of expenditures' (CEC 1987b, p. 15). It argued that agricultural market costs must not grow faster than the Community's 'own resource' base. In the short run, action must be taken to ensure that annual budget allocations for agriculture are not exceeded. In the long run, production must be curbed. COM 101 proposed the introduction of budgetary stabilizers in all sectors either to achieve expenditure savings or to generate additional revenue, depending on the sector – with prompt action to avoid expenditure overrun (CEC, 1987b). The document recommended a requirement that the Council of Ministers act in a short time period – about three months.

Once consensus had been achieved in the 'inner circle' about the need for stabilizers, a decision was required over what would trigger penalties – production or finances. COM 101 had suggested automatic financial triggers (CEC, 1987b). Public choice and organizational process paradigms explain this preference on the part of the senior administrators. Financial triggers would work more effectively in guarding the budget against overexpenditure. They would also be easier to administer. However, the 'inner circle' rejected financial stabilizers as politically unacceptable, opting instead for production triggers. Though the Commission did not formally bargain with national governments and the farm lobby, extensive consultation took place, which influenced the stabilizer proposal's development. The Commission kept both governments and the farm lobby at arm's length from its planning process, but was ever mindful that its final proposal would have to achieve approval in the European Council.

The planners then had to face other issues. One such issue was how to balance the proposal so that there was something in it for both the northern countries of the EC and the southern ones. An even distribution of benefits and sacrifices seemed essential to ensure approval in the full Commission, where the Mediterranean nations now had a blocking minority, and where the North–South distribution was bound to be a central topic for debate. A second issue centred around how comprehensive the proposal would be.

The 'inner circle' opted for a package with stabilizers for all commodities. This would better balance the sacrifices and would prevent farmers from shifting their resources from a protected area to an unprotected one, so potentially creating new problems in the future. There was strong British and Dutch support for this position and no strong opposition from other member nations.

The stabilizers planning process was slowed because attention had to be given to a number of immediate issues associated with the 1988 price package, such as tightening milk quotas, adjusting green money and slackening beef protection. This illustrates a problem often missed in rational choice analysis, but understood by organizational process analysis – that decision-makers must often deal with multiple problems simultaneously, which limits their ability to deal with any one problem.

Responding to a mandate from the June 1987 Brussels summit to come up with a detailed plan to control spending, the full Commission approved and published an outline for action at the end of July 1987, just before the Commission's summer holiday ('Review of action taken to control the agricultural markets and outlook for the Common Agricultural Policy' (COM (87) 410)). The Commission plan called for both new financial resources and the institution of an automatically activated budgetary stabilizer system for the main farm commodity sectors. Increased financial resources and budgetary discipline appeared as two sides of a single coin. The plan aimed at cutting spending in each commodity sector whenever danger appeared of that year's production exceeding support targets.[9] The scheme allowed the Commission to take necessary action to keep spending below budget ceilings.

More specifically, the Commission planned to have a preset ceiling for expenditures in each of the commodity sectors. Continuous monitoring of production, currency values and international prices would indicate how close expenditures were to the ceilings. At preset points, support funds would be automatically 'cut off' or 'reduced'. A key point was that the stabilizer mechanism would operate in the year of threatened overspending, rather than delayed until after the spending had been exceeded – as with all other budget linked mechanisms in the past (*Agra Europe*, 31 July 1987, P/1). Little detail was provided about the actual methods to be employed for spending reduction. One of the few concrete figures mentioned was a maximum guaranteed quantity for cereals of 155 million tonnes. If production exceeded that level, the plan envisaged either price reductions or an increase in the co-responsibility levy, as well as restrictions in intervention, all along lines to be agreed by the Agriculture Council. If the amount of grain going into intervention stores exceeded a given amount, the Commission could suspend intervention buying and guarantee market stability by other means.

One general theme of the Commission's proposal is worth examining –

broad authority to the Commission to take the action necessary to deal with overproduction in the year that it occurred. This can be understood in a number of ways. First, it makes sense in terms of organizational theory. Organizations consistently seek to expand their authority and autonomy. But it can also be explained as a value maximizing response by the planners – they could justify giving the Commission discretionary power on the grounds that the Council could not act promptly or analytically. *Agra Europe* saw that the Commission was keen to prepare and apply specific measures within the next two months so as to be able to restrict expenditures on a record cereal harvest, then estimated at more than 170 million tonnes. DG-VI was left with the task of drawing up a detailed proposal. *Agra Europe* also noted that the Commission intended to present a report to the Council in the autumn on non-utilization of farm land, including set-aside, which could be applied to cutting cereal production.

The timing of the Commission's general proposal seems very interesting. Coming as it did just before the summer holidays in Europe, the proposal discouraged immediate 'shoot from the hip' reactions. This would allow the details to 'sink in' with more careful analysis of all the interlocking aspects before a considered reaction, which the planners clearly hoped would increase the possibility of acceptance. The Commission's timing was designed to maximize the probability of the proposal's success in the Council.

The Commission submitted its detailed recommendations on stabilizers to the Council in mid-September. In fleshing out its July plan, the Commission proposed a specific set of stabilizers for each commodity, triggered by levels of production (see *Agra Europe*, 9 September 1987, 18 September 1987, P/1 and 2; 25 September 1987, P/1, 3 and 5). For cereals, the proposed stabilizer mechanism consisted of three parts: a production ceiling (Maximum Guaranteed Quantity (MGQ)) to be fixed each year as part of the annual price package; a mechanism for reducing cereal prices in the event of the ceiling being exceeded, which included price cuts and an additional co-responsibility levy, which the Commission proposed applying in slices of 1 per cent with the first 1 per cent not incurring penalty; and adjustments in the intervention periods. For 1988–9, the Commission proposed an MGQ for cereals of 155 million tonnes, a limit on price reduction of 5 per cent and a limit on co-responsibility increase at 5 per cent (*Agra Europe*, 25 September 1987 P/1). The Commission intended to apply the new measures as soon as they could be approved.

4.2.7 The debate in the Council of Ministers

The Agriculture Council took up the Commission's stabilizer proposals on 23 September 1987 at its first meeting of the autumn. Interestingly, the proposals received a cautiously positive welcome (*Agra Europe*, 25

September 1987, P/2). All delegations agreed in principle on the necessity for action to keep agricultural spending within reasonable limits (agreement on this point was easy to achieve as the Council had already put forth documents making a general commitment to budget control (see *Agra Europe*, 25 September 1987, P/3)).

However, a major dispute developed, over organizational prerogatives as much as policy substance. The main stumbling block was the Commission's proposal to award itself greater executive powers on the justification that a more dynamic and flexible approach was needed for corrective measures in time to have the desired budgetary effect in any given year. The Commission argued that the current system, which required consultation with the ministers before any major changes in regulations, was too slow and ponderous to be effective. Several ministers argued in the Council that the Commission proposal would usurp their prerogatives. France and West Germany, supported by Ireland and Denmark, registered opposition to the principle of the Commission modifying Council decisions. Only the UK and Netherlands gave firm support to the Commission's proposals, with qualified backing from Italy and Portugal. The nations supporting Commission prerogatives tended to agree with the Commission's policy views, while those in opposition tended to disagree (*Agra Europe*, 25 September 1987, P/3).

Departing from the usual procedures, but repeating the pattern of the milk quotas debate in 1984, a special high-level group of senior national agriculture ministry officials was convened to do the groundwork necessary to facilitate the subsequent discussions. It examined the ramifications of the Commission's proposals for the various member nations' interests, identifying areas of agreement and disagreement. Most of this group's time was spent dealing with the increasingly threatening cereal situation. Originally forecast at 3.86 billion ECU, 1987 cereal market support expenditures were now expected to exceed 4.5 billion ECU, with estimates for 1988 running as high as 6 billion ECU (*Agra Europe*, 16 October 1987, P/1).

A number of contentious issues developed as the Council bargaining progressed during the autumn. First, although all delegations agreed that measures must be taken to keep agricultural spending within limits, considerable debate occurred over whether budgetary considerations or socio-structural ones should get priority. The UK and the Netherlands emphasized the importance of budgetary discipline, while France, West Germany and Belgium, supported by the Mediterranean members, warned that agricultural policy should not be centred around budgetary considerations. Paul de Keersmaker, the Belgian Agriculture Minister, argued that 'budgetary stability should not be achieved at the cost of social instability' (quoted in *Agra Europe*, 25 September 1987, P/3). He appealed to the Commission to permit a measure of flexibility in its policy, taking into account particular difficulties in different regions or sectors. But Andriessen, speaking for the Commission, took an uncompromising stance in defending the budget criterion.

The positions on this issue closely reflected the agricultural interests of the various member states. The UK and Netherlands had highly efficient agricultural sectors and could stand price cuts. Both nations, particularly the UK with its large net contribution to the EC budget, emphasized serious concern about the growth of agricultural spending. West Germany, though a net contributor, could not stand budget-induced price cuts. The Mediterranean nations, large recipients of social spending, had no reason to want this emphasis changed. Only the French position is difficult to explain. France had become a net contributor to the EC budget with a large component of efficient farmers and perhaps could absorb a price cut, but even a conservative government could not overcome a strong French tradition that agricultural policy should serve social purposes.

There was consensus in the Council about the untenability of the status quo and the necessity for change in the system. But no consensus had yet appeared about what should be done and when. One of the most critical divisions developed between those countries willing to accept the price cuts envisaged by the Commission's proposals (the UK, the Netherlands and, to a lesser degree, France) and those who found the requisite price cuts unacceptable (West Germany, Spain, Ireland, Greece and Luxembourg) (*Agra Europe*, 13 November 1987, P/v). West Germany, in particular, could not contemplate any price cuts for the cereal sector, where real prices had already declined considerably. A dispute developed between the UK and the Netherlands, on the one hand, arguing for direct price cuts, and France, on the other, advocating co-responsibility levies to help fund EC agricultural exports (largely from France) (*Agra Europe*, 23 October 1987, E/1).

Other issues abounded, with divisions closely following the lines of national agricultural interests. The Commission's proposals for MGQs came under question, particularly for cereals, where France and West Germany wanted to raise the MGQ to 165 million tonnes. Eleven states opposed the Commission's recommendation that the budgetary rules should be changed to prohibit shifting of funds from one commodity sector to another without permission of the 'budgetary authority' – the Council of Finance Ministers and the European Parliament (*Agra Europe*, 13 November 1987, P/v). A very contentious question developed over which should come first – approval of new revenue or stabilizers: France and West Germany thought revenues should be approved first, while the UK and Netherlands thought the reverse (*Agra Europe*, 20 November 1987, P/4). Differences also appeared between the Mediterranean nations, which wanted total financing of farm income supports to come from the EC, and the other members, who thought national governments should bear a share of the cost (*Agra Europe*, 16 October 1987, P/2).

Some nations tried to make their own proposals as alternatives to those of the Commission. West Germany, for instance, argued for quantitative controls on production, but this generated opposition by the majority of members on grounds that it would lead to anarchy and become a further step toward renationalization of the CAP (*Agra Europe*, 16 October 1987, P/1). Later, West Germany suggested set-asides as an alternative to price reductions. But the Commission was reluctant to develop this proposal, partly because it did not see set-asides as a very effective means of limiting production and partly because it did not know how to administer them. France suggested an overall quota for the whole arable sector – cereals, oilseeds and sugar – so as to ensure that price cuts from one sector did not divert production into another (*Agra Europe*, 16 October 1987, P/2). However, this proposal did not achieve general support either.

The failure of the French and West German proposals highlights an advantage the 'rules' give to the Commission in the Council of Ministers bargaining process. The Commission controls the agenda in that its proposal commands the floor unless an alternative develops unanimous support. This seldom happens in a body as heterogeneous as the Council and is becoming more unlikely as the EC expands.

Progress toward agreement on these various issues was impeded because none of the protagonist governments wanted to give in until it was sure that it had the best possible deal. The situation was still not critical in that the EC had funds allowing it to operate at least until mid-1988. This illustrates a general problem with decision-making through bargaining. Consensus on the necessity of action and even on what must be done does not always bring a quick agreement, even in time of crisis. While the goals may be clear, the distribution of sacrifices necessary to achieve them is seldom obvious. Individual actors have every incentive to string the process out to minimize their own sacrifices and to maximize those of other actors.

Another impeding factor was the inability of the Danish president of the Agriculture Council, Laurits Tornaes, to broker an agreement. He had just assumed office after a national election when the Council began its deliberations over the Commission proposal; it appeared that he was not well prepared to lead the Council to agreement.

Some of the differences were narrowed, but no general agreement on the agricultural stabilizers package was reached by the December summit in Copenhagen. The Council President's unaccepted final compromise proposal was forwarded first to the Council of Foreign Ministers, which could make little progress, at least in part because it lacked agricultural expertise, and then to the European Council.

The outlook for a successful summit thus appeared pessimistic, even with the non-agricultural elements of the reform package largely resolved. Consensus had been achieved on adding a fourth financial resource based on GNP. The members had clearly committed themselves to increase the funding for regional, social and structural programmes, though differences still existed about the size of the increase. They had also reached agreement on the principle of an emergency fund, primarily to compensate for fluctuations in the dollar.

The European Council met in Copenhagen on 5–6 December 1987 but could not reach agreement either on stabilizers or on other agricultural and non-agricultural elements of the reform package. Chancellor Helmut Kohl of West Germany is reported to have taken one look at the compromise plan on which the Danish presidency and teams of experts had laboured all night and exploded: 'It is not even a basis for negotiations' (*Financial Times*, 7 December 1987). Kohl's reaction apparently came after he could find no reference in the compromise to set-asides, which the West Germans had hoped to substitute for substantial price cuts. However, other issues besides set-asides remained unresolved. No agreement yet existed on the extent or automaticity of price cuts for the stabilizers, particularly for cereals and oilseeds. As a result, no agreement seemed possible on an overall spending limit for agriculture. The Dutch and British governments made it clear that they would not countenance any additional resources for the EC until agricultural spending was brought under control. Major differences remained about how much cash to make available for social and regional spending and about how to share the future financial burden.

The failure of the European Council meeting brings home again the limitations of summitry. Heads of government have a comprehensive overview and authority to make broad-ranging decisions. Yet, they are poorly equipped to resolve differences in complicated technical proposals. Intrinsically generalists, they almost never have time to become masters of technical detail.

4.2.8 From failure in Copenhagen to success in Brussels

The failure of the summit increased the immediacy of the EC's crisis (the Community did not even have an approved budget for 1988) and thus changed the political environment to demand a solution to the crisis. Once again the member governments were embarrassed, with aspersions cast on their competence to resolve EC problems. The Commission increased the pressure by taking the member states to the European Court for not producing a 1988 budget, and by threatening to cut off intervention if the Council did not agree on budget stabilizers in February (*Agra Europe*, 11 December 1987). Could anyone put an agreement together? The prospects did not appear promising at the time, because West Germany, most intransigent against price cuts for cereals, was assuming the Council presidency.[10]

The sceptics had forgotten a lesson of the 1984 milk quotas debate: that the Council presidency changes a nation's priorities. Chancellor Kohl, as

President of the European Council in a time of crisis for the EC, had to produce an agreement to protect his leadership credibility both at home and abroad. He thus had the incentive to make compromises on agricultural and other questions which might have been politically unacceptable at any other time. By suggesting an extra summit meeting to be held in Brussels, he increased his obligation to produce an agreement at that meeting. The West German government, obviously mindful of its commitments, worked diligently to piece together an acceptable compromise. This process started even before the Copenhagen summit.[11]

The West German government seems to have given the Ministry of Agriculture considerable leeway to resolve the agricultural disputes. In the Ministry, the key people were the minister, Kiechle, and his senior permanent official, State Secretary Walter Kittel. Kittel was especially well equipped to formulate an acceptable compromise because he had just returned to Bonn from Brussels where he had spent ten years as deputy chief of the West German mission to the EC. He could anticipate how each national delegation would react on specific compromise ideas and could judge overall political feasibility.

The West German strategy seemed to come out of a textbook on diplomacy. It recognized that West German interests could only be protected in the context of a general agreement, which meant sacrifices to build a winning coalition – a problem in balancing values rather than maximizing them. Apparently, this strategy contained a number of elements. First, it contemplated looking at the situation as it appeared to other member states. Second, it included calculations about how the dynamics of consensus-building would operate; as one official put it, 'a libretto had to be written'. Third, West Germany needed a partner. The British were ruled out because their position conflicted seriously with the German one. A French alliance had much more potential, leading to an effort to reconcile the bilateral differences between West Germany and France. Perhaps France could accept set-asides in return for German support of co-responsibility. Fourth, the opposition should be undercut. Perhaps an accommodation could be reached with the Dutch who, along with the British, had shown the greatest insistence on price cuts and budget discipline. Finally, when the patterns of a potentially feasible agreement had been shaped, Kiechle should make a grand tour of European capitals to build consensus. One official remarked that the operative question was how Bismarck and Caprivi would have acted in this situation.

A number of cereals issues proved difficult to resolve. The first centred around the level of the MGQ. The original Commission proposal had set the level at 155 million tonnes, but West Germany and France had held out for 165 million tonnes. The final compromise of the Danish presidency, accepted by the Commission, set the level at 158 million tonnes, now acceptable to West Germany, but not to France, which still insisted on 160 million tonnes (the final consensus figure). Second, the penalities for exceeding the MGQ needed specification. West Germany strongly opposed price cuts, but Dutch and British support depended on them. The Germans, to minimize the necessary price cut, made a strong pitch for set-asides, previously acceptable to the British and now acceptable to the French as the least restrictive form of production controls. The Commission reluctantly formulated a detailed set-aside proposal to facilitate agreement. This allowed the Germans to accept the possibility of limited price cuts. To the extent that price cuts were necessary, what form should they take? The UK and the Netherlands wanted direct price cuts, while the French argued for an increased co-responsibility levy. The Commission had originally opted to divide the cut between direct price cuts and co-responsibility, which now appeared as an acceptable compromise. What should be the limit on direct price cuts? The Commission by now had lowered its original figure to 3 per cent, but West Germany and France insisted on 2.5 per cent. The difference did not appear insurmountable.

An important oil-seeds stabilizer issue needed resolution. This concerned the price cut applied for each percentage point of production over the MGQ. West Germany held out for 0.4 per cent, but the Commission wanted 0.5 per cent. A compromise was reached of 0.45 per cent the first year and 0.5 per cent thereafter.

The German presidency scheduled a very busy calendar of meetings of the Agriculture Council in January in an attempt to piece together all the details of a comprehensive agreement. The effort did not produce complete success before the summit, but the differences had narrowed sufficiently for agricultural problems to appear solvable.

The summit convened in Brussels on 10 February, 1988. An apparent stalemate developed over the British refusal to allow an increase in revenues without stricter guarantees of agricultural spending controls than those provided by the final Agriculture Council presidency compromise. However, Mrs Thatcher was isolated, and she gave in to the majority position in return for a renewed rebate of the British budget contribution. She reportedly felt that she could get no better deal at the next summit at Hanover in June, and recognized that the Community would lose impetus in the meantime. This could imperil the '1992' programme, which Mrs Thatcher judged to be more important to the UK in the longer run (see especially the *Financial Times*, 15 February 1988).

In the final agreement, the MGQ for cereals was set at 160 million tonnes for the four marketing years from 1988–9 to 1991–2. The penalty fixed for exceeding that limit is a 3 per cent price cut for the year following the overproduction and non-refunding of a new 3 per cent co-responsibility levy (on top of the existing one of 3 per cent) collected in advance, in the year of production. For oilseeds, individual MGQs were set for rapeseed (4.5

million tonnes), sunflower (2.0 million tonnes), soya (1.3 million tonnes) and protein crops (3.5 million tonnes). Should production exceed the MGQ, support prices are to be reduced for the current season by 0.45 per cent for each 1 per cent in excess in 1988-9 and 0.5 per cent thereafter.

Events since the February agreement have tended to confirm the impression that it represented a more or less radical change in the position of agricultural policy in the EC. The price cuts for cereals and oilseeds came into effect. The Commission has continued its policy of price restraint with the 1988-9 and 1989-90 price packages. Following the February package, attention turned to the problems of the beef market, where high levels of intervention purchases were threatening the budget limit. After lengthy debate, the Council agreed on changes in the beef regime in January 1989 designed to weaken the intervention system and restore it to a safety-net role. In addition the Commission got Council approval for a policy of direct income payments, unrelated to production levels. This move towards decoupling is notionally linked to the need for adjustment to lower prices. It appears, however, that the scale and administration of these payments will be left to the individual countries. The payments are to be degressive, over a period of five years, and be limited to farmers with income levels below a certain threshold. It is too early to judge whether this instrument will be used extensively in the future.

The final agreement reached on the reform package in Brussels in February 1988 had all the markings of partisan mutual adjustment and government politics. It could not be interpreted as a package maximizing any single value, but rather reflected a compromise between different interests participating in the bargaining process. Elements were included that each of the participants could defend. West Germany got the credit for forging the agreement and could claim success for creating the set-aside and for minimizing the cuts in farmers' incomes. France could argue that the welfare of French farmers had been protected by the infusion of new funds into the CAP and that the potential damage of stabilizers had been limited. The UK and the Netherlands won limitations on agricultural spending plus price cuts for overproduction. The Mediterranean nations received large increases in regional, structural and social funds. The Commission attained new revenues to keep the EC solvent. It also got stabilizers, though not with the desired teeth and discretionary powers. All the participants benefited in that the movement towards the single European market could proceed smoothly.

The interplay between the structure of the bargaining process and the interests of the actors strongly influenced the values protected. The value of fiscal responsibility critical for the long-term health of the EC was well protected by the Commission, but was undercut by the division of authority between different Councils of Ministers. Agricultural values were strongly protected by the concentration of decision-making authority in the Council of Agriculture Ministers. On the other hand, the value of efficiency, receiving less than top priority from any of the participants in the process, was not well protected. Not surprisingly, there were few benefits for non-participants. The interests of consumers and other non-mobilized European groups received little attention. The interests of the EC's trading partners, including the USA, Cairns group and Third World nations, were largely ignored.

4.2.9 Stabilizers and the analytical framework

The analytical framework provides useful insights into the stabilizers debate. The long-term economic trends toward overproduction, stimulated by EC price support policy, generated a political and economic environment of financial crisis in 1987, analogous to the crisis of 1983–4. However, the commodities most seriously in surplus had shifted from dairy products in the earlier period to cereals and oilseeds in the latter, which now became targets for action. A new political development – the movement toward the single European market in 1992 – worked in support of agricultural policy change, because of the need to contain the growth of agricultural spending to make funding available for other priorities (such as increased structural support for the Mediterranean countries) and so to allow completion of the market. The atmosphere of crisis operated as it had in the milk quotas debate to weaken the influence of farm groups and to strengthen the position of the Commission.

The political environment in West Germany, where the government was threatened with the loss of its crucial agricultural constituency because of a continued decline in farm incomes (a consequence of the CAP), also worked to stimulate reform. The West German government knew from its experience in vetoing the 1985 price package that simple obstructionism would not serve West German interests in the longer run. A potentially more productive strategy was to go along with the need for change, but work to limit the damage to West German interests.

The structure of the decision process had a similar effect to that in the dairy quotas debate. Compartmentalization in the Commission and Council lengthened the bargaining, but the Commission and Council president had enough authority to catalyse a consensus over stabilizers. The practice of unanimity (as required by the Treaty of Rome in matters relating to budget resources) delayed action. This took the final decision to the European Council and allowed the West German government to scuttle the Copenhagen summit. However, it also allowed the British government to demand further CAP reform in return for agreeing to new budget revenues. Unanimity ensured a complicated package with balanced benefits and sacrifices. Once again, an outcome was reached with which all the member nations could live – thus protecting the legitimacy of the EC.

Public choice theory effectively explains the positions taken by the various farm organizations on stabilizers and the intensity of effort committed by these organizations. The position of the West German farm lobby was strengthened by its unity, coupled with the dependence of the West German government on the farm vote. Overall, the increasingly zero-sum game nature of agricultural politics worked to divide the farm lobby and complicate efforts to reach a united position. Public choice theory assists in explicating the positions of the various members of the Agriculture Council, who attempted first to balance national interests with farm group pressures, but who were ultimately forced to subordinate agricultural considerations to the greater interest of EC survival.

The organizational process paradigm and public choice theory provide good insight into the workings of the Commission in developing its proposal. Not surprisingly, the initiative for reform came from senior administrators – the Commissioner and his Cabinet. DG-VI could not effectively resist reform because of the untenability of existing policy. However, the final Commission proposal adapted the well-established standard operating procedure of guarantee thresholds into the Maximum Guarantee Quantity (MGQ). As organizational theory would have predicted, set-asides, which departed significantly from existing 'standard operating procedures', constituted the most difficult element of the final stabilizers package for the Commission. The formation of an *ad hoc* 'inner circle' in the Commission presents an interesting example of organizational innovativeness under stress. A threat to organizational survival creates strong incentives to change inadequate organizational procedures. Also, as predicted by organizational theory, the Commission proposal was developed through satisficing: options were considered sequentially, with adoption of the first feasible alternative which emerged.

4.3 SOME GENERALIZATIONS ABOUT THE DYNAMICS OF REFORM IN THE EC

A number of similarities appear between the policy debates over milk quotas and stabilizers which may suggest a pattern for successful reform debates in the future.

First, both debates became serious only when a major crisis had developed. In both cases, budget revenue exhaustion caused the crisis – unless action was taken, the EC would run out of funds and default on its commitments. The impetus to action was great – the Council either could make significant policy changes or jeopardize the EC's future. Since each member state has a strong stake in the EC's survival, each had an incentive to make the requisite sacrifices for reaching an agreement to deal with the crisis. Each could use the crisis as a justification for making sacrifices.

Second, the Commission reacted expeditiously in both crises and formulated a proposal which looked very much like the final agreement – only with tougher provisions. In the stabilizers debate, the Commission developed new procedures to facilitate policy development by setting up an 'inner circle'. This did not happen in the debate on milk quotas.

Third, in both cases, the Commission focused most attention on the commodities where costs were increasing most rapidly – dairy in the first instance and cereals and oilseeds in the second.

Fourth, before formulating its proposals, the Commission in both cases considered a number of options. Decisions were made through a process of elimination – satisficing. The primary test was not efficiency but acceptability. Would the proposed solution allow the EC to overcome its current crisis and win the approval of all member nations?

Fifth, the Commission coupled the proposed action in the primary commodity area with steps in other areas to create a reform package which provided balance between the members in the benefits awarded and sacrifices required. Once the package had been assembled, the Commission made every effort to keep it intact.

Sixth, both packages continued the historic trend of the CAP towards ever greater regulation. A shift toward deregulation was rejected.

Seventh, even though significant policy changes appeared inevitable from the beginning of both the milk quotas and stabilizers debates, the bargaining process still occupied the better part of a year before settlement and was completed only when EC bankruptcy loomed. Individual governments knew they would have to sacrifice parochial interests for the common good of EC survival but the distribution of necessary sacrifices was not clear. Each government had an incentive to hold out as long as possible in the hope that the others could be persuaded to accept a larger share of the burden. Vivid evidence is thus provided of the intrinsic inertia of bargaining processes.

Eighth, individual nations, with the exception of the UK and the Netherlands, represented agricultural interests almost to the exclusion of all other interests. No public group mobilized demanding that other interests should be given priority over agricultural ones.

Ninth, international pressures to reduce farm subsidies from the USA and other nations appear inconsequential. The budget created the only constraint to domestic agricultural interests – the growth of farm spending had to be contained. It was largely left to the agriculture ministers to decide among themselves how it was to be done. EC decision-making, as in all developed countries, was concerned almost exclusively with domestic priorities and interests.

Tenth, final agreement in both the dairy quotas and stabilizers debates required a failed summit. Summit failures highlight for the public the seriousness of the problem and generate political pressure to achieve a solution.

Eleventh, both final agreements required strong initiatives by Council presidents after summit failures. Fortuitously, the incoming presidency was held by the nation most obstructionist prior to summit failure. In both instances, the shifted priorities of the presidency led to a change in behaviour which contributed significantly to the final agreement.

Twelfth, both agreements started with a mutual accommodation between France and Germany, creating strong pressures for others to fall in line. The UK played a significant role in both debates, by insisting on fiscal responsibility as a precondition for the necessary increased funding. This influence, however, was limited by the necessity for the UK to negotiate a rebate on its budgetary contribution.

NOTES

1. The Fund is more commonly known by the acronym FEOGA, from its title in French, Fonds Européen de Garantie et d'Orientation Agricole.
2. Petit *et al.* (1988) provide a comprehensive treatment of the evolution of national positions and of the functioning of the EC policy process. The following assessment of the milk quota decision relies heavily on their work.
3. For a detailed discussion of the German perspective, see *ibid.*, pp. 53–62.
4. For a detailed discussion of the French perspective see *ibid.*, pp. 37–52.
5. For a detailed discussion of the Italian perspective, see *ibid.*, pp. 63–79.
6. For a detailed assessment of the Dutch position, see *ibid.*, pp. 80–96; for the British perspective, see *ibid.*, pp. 97–110.
7. The budget stabilizers were based on a maximum annual guaranteed quantity (MGQ). If production exceeds the MGQ, a penalty is imposed on the producers in the form of a price cut and/or increased co-responsibility levy for cereals and oilseeds, and the Commission is authorized to take other measures to alter the intervention arrangements to reduce costs.
8. The Cairns group was formed by a number of agricultural exporting countries, and includes Argentina, Australia, Brazil, Canada, Chile, Columbia, Hungary, Indonesia, Malaysia, New Zealand, the Philippines, Thailand and Uruguay.
9. For discussion of the Commission's original ideas, see *Agra Europe*, 26 June, 17 July, 31 July and 7 August 1987.
10. *Agra Europe*, in particular was very gloomy about the prospects for agreement under West German leadership. See the issue of 11 December 1987, p/ 1.
11. France and West Germany were attempting to work out a compromise plan immediately before the Copenhagen summit, but failed to reach agreement in time (see *Financial Times*, 5–6 December 1987).

PART III

AGRICULTURAL REFORM IN THE UNITED STATES

5 · THE UNITED STATES AGRICULTURAL POLICY PROCESS AND THE ENVIRONMENT FOR REFORM

5.1 INTRODUCTION

The United States shares with the European Community the qualities of pluralistic democracy. Both societies have highly developed groups representing divergent interests. These interest groups compete for influence with decision-makers, who themselves represent different constituencies. Political power is divided, so policy outcomes invariably reflect political bargaining. Both political systems have central governing bodies which sometimes come into conflict with the governments of member states. In both cases, agricultural policy-making falls principally under the jurisdiction of the central governing bodies. However, political integration has progressed much further in the USA than in the EC, with individual states having little influence in making US agricultural policy. There are other differences as well. The institutions which make agricultural policy in the USA, their interactions and the policy process differ greatly from the situation in the EC. The outside political inputs, though they share many similarities, impinge on the political process in different ways.

This chapter explicates the US agricultural policy process and how the question of reform has been dealt with. It begins by detailing the evolution of agricultural policy since the presidency of Franklin D. Roosevelt in the 1930s. It continues with a discussion of the agricultural policy environment in the 1980s and concludes with a description of the US agricultural policy process. Chapter 6 explores the values intrinsic to US agricultural policy and analyses the positions of various actors inside and outside the policy process. Chapter 7 examines in depth the political process leading up to passage of the omnibus Farm Bills in 1981 and 1985, and then makes an overall assessment of agricultural policy reform in the USA.

5.2 THE EVOLUTION OF US AGRICULTURAL POLICY

Agricultural policy in the USA has been in a state of flux for the past 50 years. At no period, except perhaps during the Second World War, has the policy been free of controversy and pressures for change. As a consequence, the concept of reform is perhaps less clear cut than in the case of the EC. But the fundamental problems that have arisen with the policy over the past few years have given rise to suggestions for radical changes akin to those heard in the EC and other developed countries. The process of reform is no less interesting because change is not unusual. The dominant position of the USA in many agricultural markets, as well as in other aspects of international affairs, gives a special importance to developments in US farm policy. Other countries may not always follow where the USA leads, but they cannot but be influenced by the path taken. Moreover, the close linkage between domestic policy reform and the current negotiations in the GATT make it particularly interesting to know the extent to which US domestic policy is flexible. If reform is not on the cards, the implications for the GATT process are striking.

US agricultural policy in the late 1980s is centred on a system of commodity programmes which have their origins in the Agricultural Adjustment Act of 1933. This piece of legislation, enacted in the midst of the Depression, when farm prices and incomes had collapsed, set the US government firmly on a course of regulating markets to support the prices of a few politically favoured 'basic' farm commodities.[1] The legislation created price supports enforced by supply controls (initially in the form of acreage allotments) to increase farm incomes to 100 per cent of parity, where parity referred to an index relating farm incomes to the purchasing power of farmers during 1910–14, a time when farm earnings were unusually high. Subsequent farm legislation, including the major statutes passed in 1939 and 1949, continued commodity price supports as the basis of US agricultural policy.

Price support policies worked fairly well during the Depression, the Second World War, and in the immediate post-war period, when world food supplies were tight because of the war's devastation. However, they began increasingly to fail in the late 1940s and 1950s, when they became prohibitively expensive because of the enormous surpluses produced. These surpluses stemmed partly from the production incentives of price support policies and partly from the revolution in farm technology (i.e. hybrid seeds, chemicals, farm equipment) which took place during that era. By 1960, a combination of price supports well above market-clearing levels, dramatic increases in crop yields, and the ineffectiveness or obsolescence of acreage limitations had generated record grain stockpiles, mostly under government ownership (Destler, 1980, p. 28). The US government spent about $1 billion in fiscal year 1961 just to store these and other commodities (Destler, 1980, p. 28).

The Kennedy and Johnson administrations first sought better control of farm programmes and farm programme costs by imposing very strict acreage limitations as part of a broad supply management approach.[2] After failing to gain wheat farmers' agreement to mandatory acreage limitations in a 1963 referendum, the US Department of Agriculture won congressional enactment of voluntary programmes where price supports were set lower and farmers received income support through direct payments. The 1965 Agriculture Act changed farm income support to a two-price system for wheat, feed grains and cotton.[3] Price support guarantees (loan rates) were dropped to market-clearing levels and higher domestic prices to farmers were maintained by marketing certificates (paid by consumers) in wheat, and through deficiency payments from the Treasury (paid by taxpayers) for feed grains and cotton. Wheat was also eventually shifted to deficiency payments. The deficiency payment was limited to a farmer's share of domestic utilization. It was not paid on the exported portion of farm production. To be eligible for farm programme payments a farmer had to accept the planting restrictions established by the Secretary of Agriculture in the planting regulations for the current year. The Secretary could adjust these restrictions to increase or decrease production, based on existing stocks, projected demand and projected production during the coming crop year under various programme and price assumptions. Before he could issue his annual programme regulations they had to be cleared with the Executive Office of the President, particularly the Bureau of the Budget (which became the Office of Management and Budget (OMB) in 1970).

The 1965 Agriculture Act can certainly be seen as a case of policy reform as the whole system of payments to farmers was changed. We have noted that large surpluses and high farm support costs were critical elements contributing to this reform. We have also observed how farmers strongly influenced the nature of change when wheat producers voted down the referendum to impose mandatory acreage restrictions. For the farm community, the 1965 farm bill represented a middle ground between two unacceptable alternatives: a thoroughgoing regime of production controls; and a complete dismantling of commodity programmes (Destler, 1980, p. 29). One advocate of stronger government regulation noted that the new programmes were a 'leaky and inefficient means of controlling production', but, he added, 'most farmers want it this way' (Cochrane, 1965, p. 147, quoted in Destler, 1980, p. 29). The new legislation preserved intact agricultural policy based on commodity programmes. Already, a strong commodity legislative lobby had developed, centred around such commodity groups as the National Association of Wheat Growers, the National Corn Growers Association and the National Cotton Council. The commodity lobby was in fact a creature of the farm legislation of the 1930s which created US commodity programmes (see Bonnen, 1987, pp. 6–7). This legislation produced highly valued special benefits (rents), which, in turn, produced concentrated interests and motivated those affected to organize to influence policy decisions. Public choice theory explains the process very well. Commodity organizations and other narrow interest groups gradually replaced general farm organizations as the principal vehicles for the political expression of farmer interest. As they grew stronger and stronger, they became increasingly able to influence the agenda of farm policy debate, which more and more focused on commodity policy. By 1965, the commodity lobby had become so strong that it would have been impossible to abolish farm commodity programmes.

The decreased general strength of the pro-agricultural forces in Congress constitutes another important factor in understanding the US agricultural reform in 1965 and subsequent legislation. This stemmed mostly from a decline in number of Congressmen representing agricultural districts, which, in turn, resulted from the general decline in the farm population. In the 1930s, at the inception of New Deal agricultural programmes, 25 per cent of the total US population lived on farms. The percentage had shrunk to 9 per cent by 1960 and below 5 per cent in the 1970s (Destler, 1980, p. 31). Fewer farmers, plus Congressional redistricting to conform more closely to the principle of 'one individual, one vote', resulted in a significant reduction in Congressional support for farm commodity programmes, particularly in the House of Representatives. 'Rural districts comprised 83 per cent of an absolute majority in the House in 1966; the percentage had dropped to 71 in 1969 and to 60 by 1973 (Barton, 1976, p. 144, quoted in Destler, 1980, p. 31). The decline in strength of the Congressional farm lobby contributed to the demand for limiting farm programme costs, a major impetus for the 1965 farm bill.

The 1965 Agriculture Act cut farm programme costs by creating incentives for reduced production and by creating an environment for increased exports. US agricultural price support programmes, beginning with the 1933 Agricultural Adjustment Act, had sacrificed potential export markets by setting US prices well above market clearing levels. Exports required expensive subsidies. Introducing the two-price system in 1965, with the lower price (loan rate) set at or near market clearing levels, provided a strong impetus for rapidly increasing agricultural exports and dependence on the international market. Trade dependence has provided a most important element in the agricultural reform debate of the late 1980s.

At first, deficiency payments were limited to a farmer's share of domestic utilization. They were not paid on the exported portion of farm production. This changed with the 1973 farm bill, enacted in the context of tight grain supplies and rapid export growth stemming in part from widespread famine and large-scale grain sales to the Soviet Union. This bill, to the delight of commodity groups, assured producers a target price for all their allowed production (including exports) through a deficiency payment representing the difference between the target price and the market price (or the price support loan guarantee, whichever was the higher). The target price was set well above world market prices in 1974-5.

The 1977 Food and Agriculture Act, passed in a booming period for US agriculture, continued the 1973 deficiency payment scheme. Some significant modifications in commodity policies were made. One of the most important of these changed the base for paid government set-asides from historic allotments to the much larger current year's acreage planted for harvest. Also, the Secretary of Agriculture was required to administer a farmer-owned wheat reserve and authorized to set up a similar programme for feed grains. The farmer-owned reserves aimed at providing a buffer stock to help stabilize producer prices which had been allowed to fluctuate with the end of the price support system and which had been highly volatile in the 1970s.

The 1970s were excellent years for farmers. Prices and incomes were high while government costs were low. In Congress, non-farm legislators paid little attention to farm issues. The commodity lobby, which, by now had fully adjusted to deficiency payments, safeguarded its interests. Campaign finance reform unintentionally strengthened the commodity groups.[4] Limitations on large political contributions provided the incentive for special-interest groups, including those representing commodities, to create thousands of well-funded political action committees (PACs). These PACs gained considerable influence over political candidates who, because of other reforms to enlarge participatory democracy, needed money to finance increasingly expensive media campaigns.[5]

5.3 THE AGRICULTURAL POLICY ENVIRONMENT IN THE 1980s

The agricultural policy environment has changed dramatically from global shortage in the 1970s to global surplus in the 1980s. A number of factors contributed to this change. First, the enormous investment made in Third World agriculture, which received its impetus from the 1974 World Food Conference, has begun to pay off, with significant increases in world food production. Second, the global weather situation had improved significantly after the widespread famine of the early 1970s. Third, agricultural production in industrial countries has continued to increase, partly because of government subsidies, and partly because of the continuing revolution in agricultural productivity. Fourth, the global debt crisis has had a significant negative effect on the abililty of poor nations to purchase food imports.

This change in environment has had a number of manifestations in the USA. Perhaps the most significant of these was the declining trend in US food exports which began after 1981 (see Figure 5.1). From a peak of $4 billion in 1981, exports fell to $26 billion in 1986. Weak foreign demand slowed export markets in the wake of the sharp increase in oil prices of 1979–80. High interest rates raised the debt-servicing burden to developing countries, and hit their ability to buy US agricultural exports. Aggressive export policies by other countries, particularly the European Community (see Chapter 2), exacerbated the situation. The US market share dropped, as other suppliers stepped up their efforts. In the early 1980s, Argentina captured a portion of the market for grains. This was in part a result of the US trade embargo on grain to the Soviet Union and in part due to Argentina's decision to remove some of the export tax on its primary industry. Brazil also entered the market as a major exporter, clashing with the USA in the citrus, vegetable oil and poultry markets. Above all, the dramatic rise in the value of the US dollar in the period 1980–5 hit agricultural exports (see Figure 5.2). Steady domestic expansion and favourable investment prospects encouraged an inflow of foreign currency. More important, high interest rates resulting from the determination of the Federal Reserve Board to defeat inflation, and the needs of the Treasury to sell bonds to pay for budget deficits, attracted a flood of overseas funds. The inflow drove the price of the dollar way above the level for sustaining the trade balance. US goods became priced out of world markets and foreign goods looked cheap to US consumers. Sectors such as agriculture which relied on world markets were hit badly.

When US exports fell in a situation of flat domestic demand, commodity prices also dropped. Since the prices farmers paid for their inputs rose at the same time, further pressure was placed on the agricultural 'terms of trade', as shown in Figure 5.3. For crop production, the ratio of prices received to price paid fell by 30 per cent over the period 1980–7.

This adverse price development took its toll on farm incomes. The income of farm households stagnated from 1980 to 1984. At the same time, the income level for all US households rose steadily (see Figure 5.4) with economic expansion. As a result, absolute incomes to farm households lagged behind the national average. Many farms, particularly the smaller and medium-sized units, relied more heavily on non-farm earnings to supplement farm income.

The fall in the price of crop products also contributed to a significant decline in the value of farm assets, as shown in Figure 5.5. Total value of assets held by the farm population started to decline in 1980, falling by 30 per cent over the next five years. Some recovery was noticeable in 1987, as farm prices stabilized. The fall in real estate values, particularly in the price of farmland, provided the chief reason for the decline in asset values. Figure 5.6 shows the dramatic drop in the value of farmland per acre, from over $800 in 1981 to $550 in 1987.

The combination of low incomes and low asset values sapped the capacity of farmers to repay large debts that many of them had incurred to help expand production in the boom years of the 1970s, often at very high interest rates. This led to a significant increase in farm foreclosures (see Figure 5.7).

The sudden decline in farmer prosperity was unprecedented since the

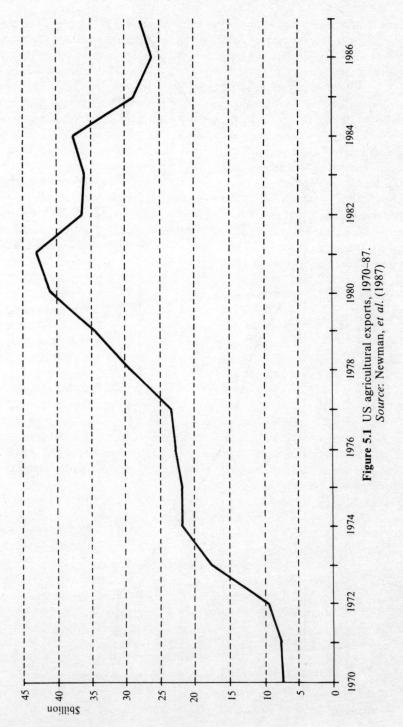

Figure 5.1 US agricultural exports, 1970–87.
Source: Newman, *et al.* (1987)

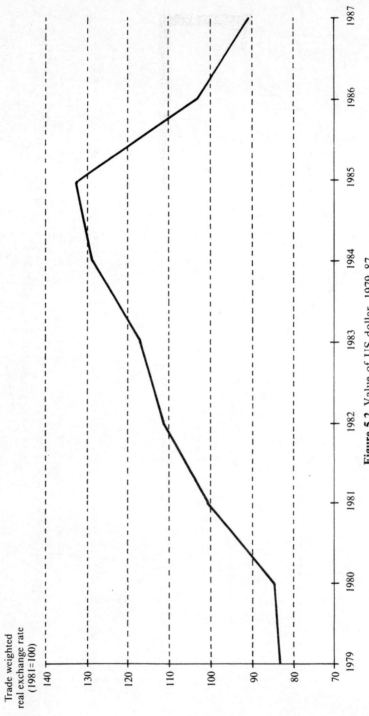

Figure 5.2 Value of US dollar, 1979–87.
Source: International Monetary Fund

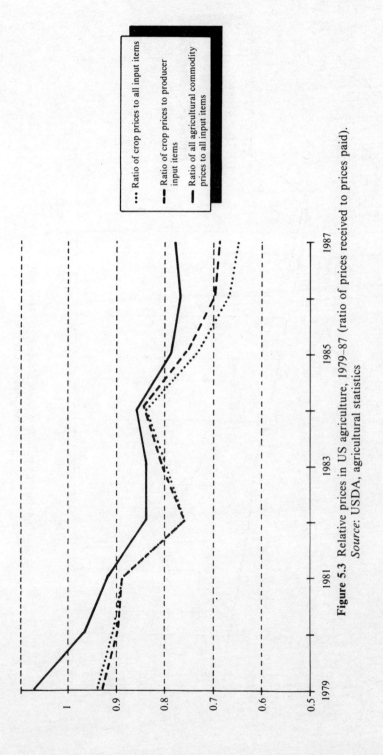

Figure 5.3 Relative prices in US agriculture, 1979–87 (ratio of prices received to prices paid).
Source: USDA, agricultural statistics

Legend:

··· Ratio of crop prices to all input items

▬▬ Ratio of crop prices to producer input items

▬ Ratio of all agricultural commodity prices to all input items

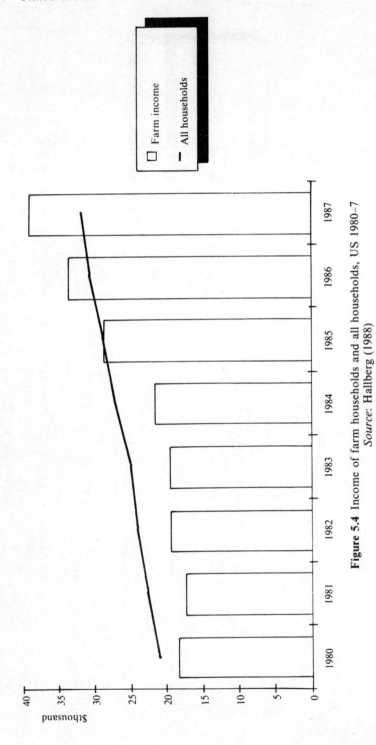

Figure 5.4 Income of farm households and all households, US 1980–7
Source: Hallberg (1988)

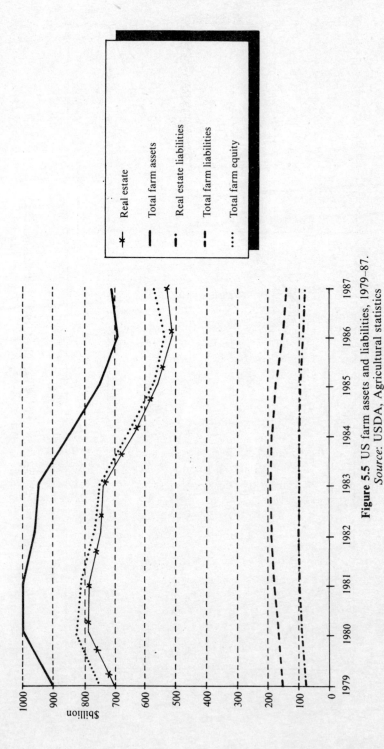

Figure 5.5 US farm assets and liabilities, 1979–87.
Source: USDA, Agricultural statistics

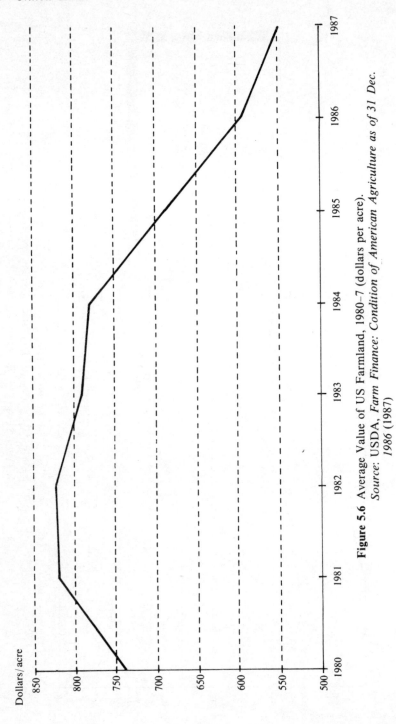

Figure 5.6 Average Value of US Farmland, 1980–7 (dollars per acre).
Source: USDA, Farm Finance: Condition of American Agriculture as of 31 Dec. 1986 (1987)

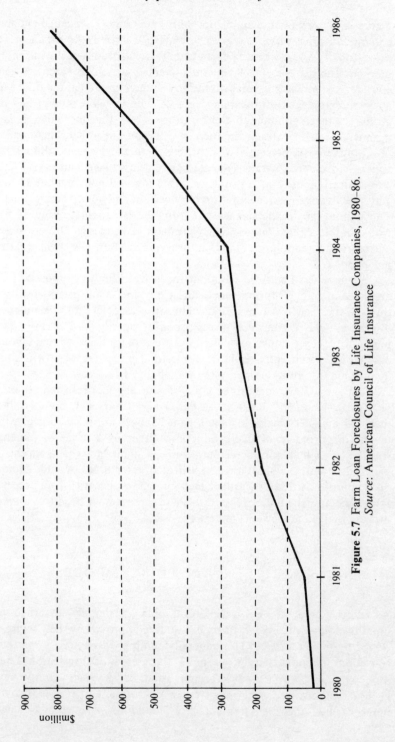

Figure 5.7 Farm Loan Foreclosures by Life Insurance Companies, 1980–86.
Source: American Council of Life Insurance

Depression years. It would probably not have happened under the commodity price support regime in existence until 1965, which preserved price stability and isolated farmers from the vicissitudes of the international market. The adverse farm economy created an environment which put considerable public pressures on the government for relief; the time was not auspicious for agricultural policy reform. The US government had mixed incentives in responding to the farm crisis. On the one hand, it had an incentive to help farmers in their plight. On the other, increased farm programme costs presented real problems to the Reagan administration, which had entered office dedicated to cutting taxes and spending. The administration also had a problem in that it could not calculate farm costs very well in advance in a situation of uncertain and volatile export demand. Throughout the decade, as farm programme costs rose (see Figure 5.8), one would have expected increasing government resistance to farmers' demands and increasing popularity of agricultural reform. But, as we will see, this did not happen.

US consumers had little economic incentive either to support or to resist agricultural reform during the 1980s. Consumer food prices rose steadily through the decade, but at a somewhat lower rate than for consumer goods in general. Only if consumer prices rise more rapidly than prices in general, might we expect consumers to be critical of policies which favour the agricultural community. Indeed, stable food prices create an environment favourable to public sympathy for the plight of farmers.

What would have constituted US agricultural policy reform in the surplus period of the 1980s? Reform, as defined in Chapter 1, could only have included measures involving significant changes in policy to deal with the underlying problem of overproduction, either as a series of incremental steps or as a single non-incremental shift. A significant change in the target price mechanism would have constituted reform, as would mandatory production controls or measures decoupling farm benefits from production. But to see how the policy reacted to these pressures we need to examine the process by which decisions are taken.

5.4 THE US AGRICULTURAL POLICY PROCESS

As indicated earlier, US agricultural policy is largely governed by an omnibus four- or five-year 'Farm bill' statute approved by the Congress and signed by the President.[6] This generally comprehensive legislation includes provisions on commodity programmes, farm credit, conservation, research, food stamps and PL-480 foreign food aid.[7] Such comprehensiveness has implications in terms of policy outcomes, and is at least partially induced by the requirements of building a winning coalition

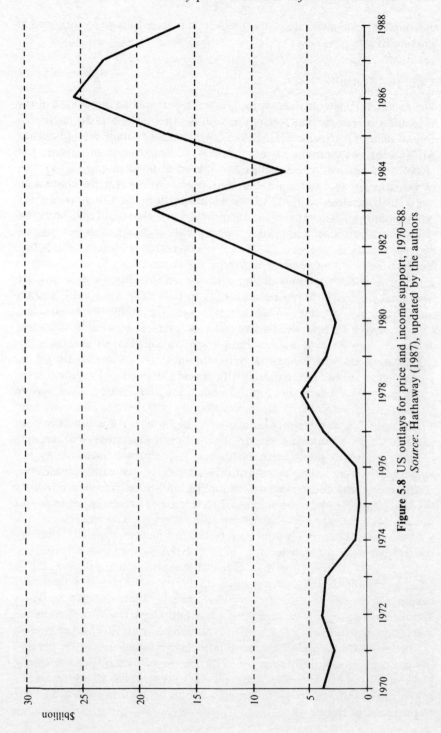

Figure 5.8 US outlays for price and income support, 1970–88.
Source: Hathaway (1987), updated by the authors

in Congress. In the decade of the 1980s, major farm bills were approved in 1981 and 1985.

5.4.1 The Executive

The farm bill review process typically starts a year or two in advance of the expiration of the current legislation with a series of papers from the US Department of Agriculture (USDA), Congressional committees and outside government, examining various aspects of current farm policy and recommending changes. Hearings are conducted to solicit the views of all parties having an interest in the legislation.[8] An enormous amount of material is generated for use by the administration and Congress. Taking into account policy feedback and the political and economic environments, USDA formulates an administration proposal for submission to Congress early in the legislative year in which the current farm statute expires (see Figure 5.9 for a schematic of the farm bill process). No formalized rules exist for how the Secretary of Agriculture puts together his proposal. He will usually assign primary responsibility to either the Assistant Secretary for Economics or the Under-Secretary for International Affairs and Commodity Programs, the two key offices for farm legislation, who will develop the proposal after consultation with various USDA agencies.

Two agencies with somewhat different incentives, subordinate to the Under-Secretary for International Affairs and Commodity Programs, have important input. The Agricultural Stabilization and Conservation Service (ASCS), which administers all the commodity programmes and has strong 'grass-roots' ties, is extremely influential.[9] The Foreign Agricultural Service (FAS), which administers export promotion progammes and collects foreign economic intelligence, has seen its influence increase as US agricultural trade has expanded. However, it has no 'grass-roots' constituency, and hence exercises less overall influence than ASCS. Before the USDA proposal can be submitted to Congress, it must be cleared with other Executive agencies having an interest in various aspects of the legislation and be formally approved by the President.[10] Typically, the only general Executive branch scrutiny of the USDA proposal comes from the White House staff and from the Office of Management and Budget (OMB), which goes over virtually every major item and exercises general influence in keeping proposed expenditures within administration guidelines. Other agencies such as the Department of State and Department of Commerce may attempt to influence parts of the bill which relate to their respective domains, but do not exercise general influence. Political developments and the political environment strongly influence the role each Cabinet agency plays. For example, the recent federal deficit problem has strengthened the role of the OMB. A foreign policy crisis would strengthen the hand of the Department of State.[11]

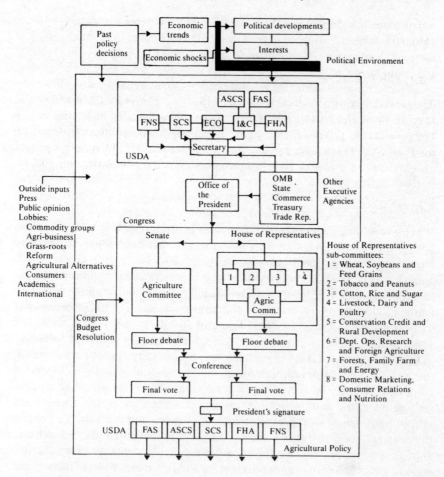

Abbreviations:
ASCS = Agricultural Stabilization and Conservation Service
FAS = Foreign Agricultural Service
FNS = Food and Nutrition Service
SCS = Soil Conservation Service
ECO = Economics
I&C = International and Commodity Programs
FHA = Farmers Home Administration

Figure 5.9 Bargaining process for US agricultural policy

The organizational process and government (bureaucratic) politics paradigms would lead us to expect the USDA proposal to recommend only marginal changes to existing programmes and would reflect accommodation between various USDA agencies, and, to a lesser extent, accommodation between USDA and other Cabinet departments. However, we need to take into account the fact that the Secretary of Agriculture, Deputy Secretary, under-secretaries, assistant secretaries and some other key officials are political appointees, responsive to the political priorities of the President. This leads to the further inference that USDA farm proposals also attempt to reconcile existing programmes with administration goals.

5.4.2 Congress

When the administration farm bill arrives in Congress, it is referred to the Senate and House Agriculture Committees which hold separate hearings (House hearings generally take place in the commodity sub-committees). Neither committee is bound to the administration's proposals in its considerations. Other proposals are usually considered, coming typically from individual Congressmen and commodity groups. For example, in 1985 94 bills were introduced in the House and 50 bills in the Senate, a total of 144 (Guither, 1986, p. 16). A wide variety of witnesses is invited to testify including general farm organizations, commodity groups, individual farmers, agri-business representatives, environmental groups, members of Congress, federal, state and local government representatives, academics from land grant and other institutions, consumer groups, hunger/relief groups and even a few representatives from foreign countries. In the Senate, the hearings generally take place before the full Committee on Agriculture, Nutrition and Forestry, while in the House they are held both by the full Agriculture Committee and by eight sub-committees, four of which are commodity-orientated.[12] In the next step of the process, the chairmen of the House and Senate Agriculture Committees introduce a comprehensive bill which becomes a vehicle for legislative mark-up. The mark-up or shaping of the final Congressional bills takes place in the full Senate Agriculture Committee and in the commodity sub-committees of the House Agriculture Committee. The House sub-committees report their recommendations to the full Agriculture Committee, which pieces together a composite bill.

The bills drafted by the agriculture committees are then submitted to the full House and Senate where they are debated, amended and, finally, approved. They often differ substantially from administration recommendations though they should (but do not always) stay within Congressional budget guidelines.[13] Senate and House agriculture bills typically differ from each other and the differences require reconciliation by a conference consisting of the Agricultural Committee chairmen and members of their committees which they select. The Conference Committee reports out a final bill not subject to amendment which must be voted up or down by each House or recommitted to the Conference Committee. The President may sign the bill, which then becomes law. Alternatively, he may veto it, which Congress then has a chance to override with affirmative votes in each House of two-thirds of those present and voting. Even though the administration seldom gets everything it wants in the final bill, it still has considerable influence, though the amount of influence varies, depending on such things as the interest the White House takes in the legislation, how strong and effective an advocate the Secretary of Agriculture is, and, whether the President's party controls Congress. The threat of a presidential veto is a powerful one. Also, Congress depends highly on USDA for the information and analysis it needs, though this dependence has declined with the growth in numbers and competence of Congressional staff resources. The increasing number and capabilities of lobbying groups in Washington, all of which provide their own information and analysis, has also worked to reduce congressional dependence on USDA.

The entire legislative process is a long and cumbersome one. It takes nearly a full year to complete. Typically, an omnibus farm bill is passed only in the final days of the legislative session when Congress is about to adjourn for Christmas, and when the prospect is a return to the provisions of the permanent 1948 farm legislation (including price supports) if no bill is passed. The process constitutes an excellent example of partisan mutual adjustment to which we referred in Chapter 1. The final bill is usually a finely crafted compromise balancing administration and Congressional priorities and a wide variety of farm and non-farm interests. The complex process involves hundreds of thousands of hours of effort on the part of USDA employees, Members of Congress, congressional staffers and lobbyists. As a result, the inertia is enormous, with a very great bias toward maintaining the status quo, allowing some adjustments at the margin. Many of those involved in the process are close to exhaustion at its conclusion. Serious debate of significant reforms in the absence of rare overwhelming consensus about necessary action would strain the system beyond its capacity. Hence, major changes are considered only under the most dire circumstances.

After a farm bill becomes law, it is administered by USDA. Each USDA agency has some leeway in the way it interprets and implements its part of the law. Implementation is strongly influenced by agency interests and standard operating procedures.

The omnibus farm bills provide only part of the picture of US farm policy at any given moment. Each farm bill gives the Secretary of Agriculture a certain amount of discretion in doing such things as setting target and loan rates and set-aside amounts. These powers allow him to respond to economic trends, economic shocks and political developments between farm bills. In addition, an agriculture appropriations bill must be approved annually to provide funds for administering the farm programmes. This involves another set of committees – the House and Senate Appropriations Committees and their agricultural sub-committees. These committees hold their own hearings and have considerable discretion in what they fund, though they must operate within the general guidelines of the omnibus agriculture bill and Congressional budget resolutions. Finally, Congress can and frequently does pass legislation in the period between the omnibus farm bills, either to modify basic legislation, or to cover some subject not included. There is a reluctance, however, to modify an omnibus farm bill in any significant way while it is in force because of the bargaining costs involved.

NOTES

1. For a very interesting discussion of the development of US commodity policies, see Bonnen (1987).
2. For details of actions taken by the Kennedy and Johnson administrations see Destler, (1980, pp. 28–30). For a more detailed discussion, see Cochrane and Ryan (1976, pp. 79–82).
3. For a summary of provisions of the 1965 Agriculture Act and subsequent major US farm legislation see Bonnen (1987, pp. 7–9).
4. For discussion of the political reforms of the 1970s *ibid.*, pp. 24–6.
5. We have discussed the impact of some of the other reforms in our discussion of Congressional actors and their positions in Section 5.4.
6. The Executive and Congress handle trade policy very differently from agricultural policy. In the Executive, trade policy has broad input from the Departments of State, Treasury, Commerce and Labor and the Office of the United States Trade Representative. The Foreign Agricultural Service (FAS) of USDA has major input when agricultural trade matters are involved. There are a series of co-ordinating committees. At the Cabinet level, the Trade Policy Committee (TPC) is chaired by the United States Trade Representative. Reporting to the TPC is the Trade Policy Review Group (TPRG) at the assistant secretary level. Below that, at the working level, is the Trade Policy Staff Committee. But, because the omnibus farm bill has always been considered domestic policy, the trade policy apparatus is pretty much excluded from the process, even though farm bills have enormous trade implications and have increasingly included provisions which directly address trade questions. In Congress, trade matters are handled by Foreign Affairs and Foreign Relations Committees, respectively, in House and Senate. Yet, the unwritten rules prevent these committees from examining commodity programmes. It will probably take a major change in the way farm policy is perceived to force inclusion of broad international relations interests into the farm bill process. Perhaps this will be a consequence of the current GATT negotiations.
7. PL-480 (Public Law 480), the US 'Food for Peace' programme, established in 1954 and continued to the present with some modifications, makes food aid available to developing nations. Originally designed primarily for surplus disposal, the emphasis has shifted over time to humanitarian and development aid.

8. For a detailed chronology of the 1985 Food Security Act see Guither (1986). For a similar chronology of the 1977 Agriculture Act, see Penn (1977).
9. For a discussion of the influence of ASCS and other USDA agencies, see Bonnen (1987, pp. 11–12).
10. The exact process through which inter-agency consultation takes place and by which presidential approval of farm legislation is obtained is determined by the wishes of each president. President Reagan organized his Cabinet into three policy councils covering national security, economic policy and domestic policy. Each of these is supported by inter-departmental working groups at under-secretary and assistant-secretary levels. Agricultural legislation had to be cleared through the Economic Policy Council, which was chaired by the Secretary of the Treasury, and included also the Secretaries of Commerce and State, the Chairman of the Council of Economic Advisors and the director of the OMB and other Cabinet members as appropriate.
11. Destler (1980) in analysing US food policy for the 1970s, has identified four important constituencies: farm policy; domestic economic policy; general foreign policy; and global welfare and development. He argues that the farm policy constituency generally prevails, but can be overcome by the domestic economic constituency in a time of domestic economic crisis and by the foreign policy constituency in a time of foreign policy crisis. It can even be overcome by the global welfare and development constituency when there is a question of mass starvation.
12. The House of Representatives commodities sub-committees are: Cotton, Rice and Sugar; Livestock, Dairy and Poultry; Tobacco and Peanuts; Wheat, Soybeans and Feed Grains.
13. All legislation passed by Congress, including farm legislation, is expected to stay within the guidelines of the Congressional budget resolution which is formulated by the House and Senate Budget Committees and approved by both Senate and House.

6 · VALUES AND POLICY POSITIONS IN UNITED STATES AGRICULTURAL POLICY REFORM

Any attempt at policy reform in democratic governments is strongly influenced by the prevailing values of society. This is as true for agriculture as for other areas. Hence, this chapter begins with a discussion of the values which have influenced the development of US farm policy. It then turns to an analysis of the interests, incentives and positions of the decision-makers and outside inputs. This discussion will provide an understanding of the parameters for agricultural policy reform in the USA.

6.1 VALUES INHERENT IN POLICY PROCESS

Bonnen (1987) has identified a number of deep-seated societal values pervading the US policy process which have their origins in the US historical experience. One of the strongest is *rugged individualism*, which comes from the early settlement period and expresses a strong belief in individual rights and responsibilities as against community or collective rights and responsibilities. Following from this is a belief in *laissez-faire* as opposed to government control of agriculture. Finally, *Jeffersonian agrarianism*, which holds that the strength of a democratic society depends on a strong, independent yeomanry has strong roots. Thus, the numbers and welfare of family farmers influence the strength of the nation. The first two values acted as strong forces keeping the government from intervening in commodity markets until the Depression of the 1930s, when they came in conflict with the third value, as the family farm was threatened.

A new value justifying government intervention in agricultural commodity markets emerged from this conflict without obliterating the old values. A belief developed that fundamental economic forces disadvantage agriculture in the market relative to non-agricultural sectors (Bonnen, 1987, p. 9). Some economists argued that, in an industrial nation, the terms of trade inevitably run against the farm sector and that, as a result, resources tend to earn less in farming than in the non-farm sectors. To avoid this, farmers should leave farming. Farmers perceived this as unfair. Bonnen

(1987, p. 9) notes that they viewed unequal returns given for an equal investment of labour and other resources as inconsistent with the concept of commutative justice. A distributive justice argument also developed and exercised influence in eliciting non-farm support for government intervention in agricultural markets (Bonnen, 1987, p. 9). Farmers, perceived to be much poorer than the average non-farm family, required government action to remove the inequity. A final justification for government intervention came from the general belief that agricultural markets were subject to far greater instability than non-agricultural markets, because of the highly inelastic demand and supply for farm products and the biological nature of the production process, with many perishable and semi-perishable products (Bonnen, 1987, p. 10).

The legacy for the policy process today is that policy-makers still do not feel comfortable with the idea of general government intervention in the farm economy and give a good deal of rhetorical support to the idea of the 'free market'. Commodity programmes, though, have a very strong value basis for support. Their advocates justify them on the grounds that they ensure distributive and commutative justice and preserve the independence of the American farmer and the survival of the family farm. What is not often considered is that most agricultural production today is not carried on by small family farms but rather by large operations (most of which are family-owned and -operated), which do not suffer from productivity disadvantages of the farmers of the 1930s. Current commodity programmes tend to create commutative and distributive injustice rather than justice in the sense that they benefit most those farmers already relatively well-off, but this is not widely perceived. Many poor farmers still live in the countryside. Most of the public and many member of Congress still believe that commodity programmes benefit these farmers in spite of the evidence to the contrary.

6.2 THE ACTORS AND THEIR POSITIONS

6.2.1 The Executive

As previously indicated, the US Department of Agriculture (USDA) plays the lead role in the development of farm policy and the Agricultural Stablization and Conservation Service (ASCS) exercises strong influence within USDA.[1] The ASCS role needs further amplification. ASCS is the focal point for lobbying efforts by commodity groups because it has responsibility for administering commodity programmes. As public choice and organizational process analysis would lead us to predict, ASCS and commodity groups have maintained close ties out of organizational self-interest, with commodity groups providing information and support for USDA programmes in return for the protection of their interests. ASCS has a politically powerful bureaucracy with a network of state and county offices, each with an elected committee of influential commercial farmers. These committees are influential in administrative and policy decisions. When threatened, ASCS has the ability to mobilize a formidable 'grass-roots' army of farmers and commodity groups to protect its interests *vis-à-vis* the Secretary of Agriculture, the Office of Management and Budget (OMB) and Congress (Bonnen, 1987, p. 11). It is very difficult for any other agency inside USDA to exercise this kind of influence. Thus, a severe obstacle to commodity policy reform exists inside USDA.

In the White House, no fixed structure exists to deal with domestic policy. Each President arranges policy-making as he sees fit. Two offices created by legislation tend to have permanency. Reference has already been made to one of these – which has exercised increasing influence on agricultural policy in the 1980s as agricultural spending has increased in the context of increased budget consciousness. OMB has responsibility for keeping all federal spending within budgetary guidelines and serves as a significant force for agricultural reform. The other statutory office is the President's Council of Economic Advisors (CEA), which has one Council member and one staff member assigned to agriculture. The Council's principal responsibility is for macro-economic policy, but it also analyses and participates in any area of policy with significant economic impact. In recent years the Council appears to have had little impact on agricultural policy decisions.

The President's Cabinet is currently organized into three policy councils: the National Security Council; the Council on Economic Policy; and the Council on Domestic Policy. All major economic policy questions, including agricultural policy, must be processed through the Council on Economic Policy which makes recommendations to the President. This Council includes the Departments of Treasury, Commerce, State and the OMB. It is chaired by the Secretary of the Treasury. As is evident from the membership, the Council on Economic Policy has no bias against reform of agricultural commodity policies. But, it is constrained by its dependence on USDA, which has much more expertise on agricultural questions.

6.2.2 The Legislature

Mention has already been made of the House and Senate Agriculture Committees, the House commodities sub-committees and of the agriculture sub-committees of the House and Senate Appropriations Committees. All of these are constituency committees with a vast majority of the members representing districts or states where agriculture is important. Moreover, in the House commodity sub-committees, the members overwhelmingly represent the districts in which the included commodities are produced. For example, in the recent one-hundredth Congress (1986–8), ten of the 14 members of the House Agriculture Sub-committee on Cotton, Rice and Sugar, including the chairman, represented districts which clearly had some interest in these commodities.[2] Other commodity sub-committees have comparable orientations. Public choice theory can explain this. Congressmen with agricultural constituencies can turn agriculture committee service into an election asset because they can deliver and protect benefits. The Agriculture Committee members, and, particularly, the commodity sub-committee members have a strong interest in protecting the vested rights (rents) provided by existing commodity programmes. The more prosperous farmers in their district, who have the greatest stake in commodity programmes, and who are generally better educated and more politically active, watch them closely. The increasing importance of raising money to finance election campaigns, and the money which commodity group Political Action Committees (PACs) contribute, act strongly to reinforce the commodity tie.

The Agricultural Committees, especially the commodity sub-committees, thus have a vested political interest in preventing commodity policy reform. Their operational rule of thumb is that any modification of existing programmes must 'hold harmless' impacts on prior property rights (Bonnen, 1987, p. 20).[3] The committee process does not appear at all conducive to efficient resource allocation. Each legislator tends to support commodity programme rewards for other Congressmen in return for their support of his commodity programmes. House sub-committee members support the recommendations of other sub-committees in the House Agriculture Committee in return for outside support of their own sub-committee's work. The welfare of farm groups is well protected in the process, but, the general public welfare is often not seriously considered.

The House and Senate Agriculture Committees do have to operate within certain constraints. They must, for instance, respond to problems with past farm legislation. Members must be aware that recommendations running too strongly against the general interest of Congress will be rejected. Agriculture Committee recommendations must provide rewards for other members of congress as well as for committee members. This partially accounts for the increasing comprehensiveness of farm bills. It now takes a very wide-ranging bill to generate a winning coalition. A need exists to pay enough attention to the administration's wishes to avoid a presidential veto. Congress must also avoid antagonizing the USDA bureaucracy which implements programmes and provides Congress with much information and support.

The sacrifices the House and Senate Agricultural Committees have had to make over the years to other interests seem relatively modest given the small and declining legislative base of farm interests. This can partially be explained by the strong support for farming from a public which still has very positive feelings about farmers. It can also be explained by the asymmetry of voting incentives for farm and non-farm district congressmen. On the one hand, farm district Congressmen gain recognition and votes by supporting commodity programmes. On the other hand, non-farm district congressmen gain little in opposing commodity legislation (food prices are low and the public is sympathetic to farmers). The accommodation process has been facilitated in the past by the increasing size of the budgetary pie. It will become difficult as the budget concerns increase. The Congressional budget resolution serves increasingly as a constraint. One problem in bringing the budget constraint to bear is the difficulty in assessing the cost of commodity programmes in a dynamic world trade environment.

Two general trends have acted to maintain Congress's commodity bias in agricultural policy. The first – an alliance between farm district Congressmen and those from urban areas – has had a paradoxical effect. As the number of farm legislators declined in the 1960s and 1970s, the ones who were left knew they needed some sort of alliance with a significant voting bloc to maintain their farm programmes. Urban Congressmen provided very natural allies as they needed support of their agenda, which included expanding food stamp programmes, in the 1960s and early 1970s, and increasing the minimum wage law in 1973 (Destler 1980, p. 33). Farm district Congressmen had an incentive to provide this support as the farm community would gain from increased food stamp distribution, which would increase domestic demand for agricultural products. As a quid pro quo, urban Congressmen would have to support continuation of commodity programmes. They could do so because commodity programmes had no readily observable effect in raising consumer food prices. The alliance was forged and it has worked well both to provide support for urban programmes and to maintain programmes for agriculture.

The second trend is the loss of leadership power in Congress accompanied by increased participatory democracy, which is part of a larger trend of loss of confidence in government stemming from Vietnam and Watergate.[4] A number of reforms legislated in the 1970s, including the creation of a very much larger number of sub-committees not subjected to the 'iron-first' rule of an authoritative chairman, had the purpose of opening the process up by more equally distributing power among 100 Senators and 435 Representatives. The net effect has been to increase greatly the fragmentation and chaos in Congress. For agriculture, the power of the commodity sub-committees has increased, which makes any reform even more difficult than it otherwise would have been. Bargaining costs to achieve consensus for change appear higher than ever before. Thus, the partisan mutual adjustment process deteriorates into maintenance of the status quo.

The Congressional process is so cumbersome, the interests so divergent, power so divided, and party discipline so weak, that constant danger exists of complete stalemate. Ameliorating this risk, farm state legislators, particularly those in the House, tend to put aside party differences in agricultural matters. Also, for agricultural legislation, one or two leaders trusted inside and outside the farm community, emerge in each chamber of Congress (not necessarily the agricultural committee chairmen) who fill roles as conciliators, 'honest brokers', compromisers and deal-makers. As we will see later, this function has been assumed in recent years by Representative Thomas Foley (Democrat, Washington), now Speaker of the House, and Senator Robert Dole (Republican, Kansas). These leaders seem motivated more to achieve action in Congress (which increases their prestige and power) than to cultivate a narrow constituency base.

6.3 OUTSIDE POLITICAL INPUTS

6.3.1 Lobbies

Commodity groups
In the first three decades of the twentieth century, the principal lobbies in farm issues were the general farm organizations, including the American Farm Bureau, the National Farmers Union, and the Grange.[5] But these groups lost influence as they became politicized and inflexible in their positions. They also became more and more irrelevant to the process as agricultural policy became commodity-dominated. The void was filled by the commodity groups which developed around the price support programmes established in 1933.[6] These groups had a very narrow focus, working to protect and enhance the special benefits to producers of a particular commodity through farm legislation. They became one base of a 'triangle of power' for agricultural policy (Bonnen, 1987, p. 16).[7] Each commodity group worked closely with allied interests in USDA and in Congress. The commodity groups became so strong that one seasoned observer could note:

> When the interest group leadership, the ASCS administrator of that commodity program and the House and Senate subcommittees with relevant jurisdiction agree, it matters not what the Secretary of Agriculture, or the President, or anyone else thinks about it. They are locked out of the policy process for that commodity by the 'triangle of power' and can influence the outcomes only with extra-ordinary political effort and cost (Bonnen, 1987, p. 16).

Farm legislation was formed by compromises between the various commodity 'triangles of power' where each would support the others' interests.

The development of commodity groups is well explained by public choice and organizational process theory. Specific benefits (rents) were created by commodity programmes, which the recipients then had an interest in organizing to protect. The commodity organizations, which developed in response, prospered when they developed politically effective machinery for maintaining and enhancing the benefits. They enhanced their base by providing their constituents with the information and advice necessary to mobilize support for future lobbying initiatives. In the process, the commodity groups developed norms consistent with their organizational interests, which limited their perceptions and analysis. They also developed self-interested standard operating procedures. The welfare of the commodity groups rapidly became as important as the welfare of their members. They thus came to pursue single-mindedly their commodity objectives. They used their ample resources to form mutual-interest alliances with groups in Congress and the Executive.

The narrow 'triangle of power' began to break down in the 1950s and 1960s as specialization of production led to increasing conflict among commodity groups and as the interests of farmers diverged commodity by commodity and region by region (Bonnen, 1987, p. 17). Also, conflict between agri-business and farm producer interests forced more and more decisions onto the Secretary of Agriculture and to the President. The 'triangle of power' eroded further as the complexity of the farm bills increased to include food stamps, environmental concerns and international trade. This increased complexity, along with the trend toward greater participatory democracy to which we have already referred, led to a vast proliferation of groups attempting to influence farm policy in the 1970s.

Grass-roots agricultural reformists

Browne (1988a, pp. 146–50) divides the new groups into two categories: the 'grass-roots agricultural reformists'; and the 'externalities/alternatives' lobby. The 'grass-roots agricultural reformers' are farm protest groups such as the American Agriculture Movement, which have emerged in response to the farm financial crisis of the late 1970s and 1980s. They have capitalized on the perception that the commodity groups only represent the largest of specialized producers rather than the 'family farm'. They have shown excellent mobilization skills with their protest-style lobbying and their ability to make demands on behalf of a widely accepted agrarian ethos or myth that hard-working farmers critically important to the nation's economy are financially threatened through little fault of their own by government policy (Browne, 1988a, pp. 146–7). But they have shown a paucity of new ideas, advocating such tired old war-horses as mandatory production controls and price support levels at 100 per cent of parity. The main accomplishment of these groups has been to create public sympathy for the plight of food producers, thus creating a political climate favourable to helping farmers out. While the 'grass-roots agricultural reformers' have been successful in raising public consciousness, they have not succeeded in negotiating specific policy proposals. They have few ties to agricultural policy-makers anywhere in government. They also are poorly financed and divided among themselves.

The 'externalities/alternatives' lobby

The 'externalities/alternatives' lobby consists of those groups who are interested in the negative consequences – or externalities – of agriculture and with alternatives to the present structure of farming (Browne, 1988a, pp. 147–9). They represent the needs and values of farm-workers, rural residents, consumers, the poor, environmentalists, and animals. These organizations suffer from a shortage of funds, limited staff resources, and the lack of a common philosophy – as public choice theory would predict, based on their diverse general interest constituencies. But, they do generate support because they are the only policy activists in agriculture who stand for non-farm and non-business values. They have succeeded in gaining attention in the policy process for food quality, proper animal care and land conservation. They are not well co-ordinated and do not have the resources to participate in all agricultural policy issues. They tend to ignore commodity programmes and to focus on emerging issues, where there is no well-organized opposition. A successful strategy has been to add provisions onto major pieces of farm legislation. Thus,

> The Food Research and Action Center focuses on food stamps, Bread for the World works on PL–480, Public Voice attacks the Dairy Program, the Humane Society of America emphasizes a farm bill provision to protect laboratory animals, and the Audubon Society and American Farmland promote new conservation provisions such as sodbuster and cross-compliance (Browne, 1988a, p. 148).

The commodity groups, though now joined by new actors in lobbying, still dominate the policy process (Browne, 1988a, pp. 146 and 148). They are strongest in Congress, but have significant influence within the Executive.[8] Their greatest strength is that they are defending price support and other programmes already in place. They also have considerable legitimacy in that they are recognized representatives of the farmers most directly affected by policy. Well financed, they have continued to cultivate close ties with USDA and the House and Senate Agricultural Committees. The commodity sub-committees depend on them for information and analysis. They play a major role in selling government programmes to the farm community. It would be unthinkable to make significant changes in policy without consulting them.

Commodity groups do have a number of weaknesses. First, they succeed only to the extent that trade-offs can be made between different commodity interests. This trade-off process has grown more difficult as agricultural policy has become more complex, including trade as well as domestic considerations. Commodity groups have divergent interests in a free domestic market and in free trade, which make it more difficult for them to work together. Policy complexity has also tended to divide individual commodity groups, necessitating a good deal of attention to internal cohesion. The increasing number of issues each commodity group must face makes policy formation difficult. Browne (1988a, p. 146) gives a good example of this problem in noting that,

> during the debates over the Food Security Act of 1985, the National Wheat Growers Association found itself having to establish positions on marketing loans, mandatory production controls, grain reserves, pesticide regulations, and tax reform, in addition to maintaining the wheat program.

Finally, increased budget consciousness is changing the nature of the relationship between commodity groups. Agricultural politics now tends toward a zero-sum game, where gains for one commodity group result in losses for another. This makes them much more wary of each other and less willing to co-operate automatically.

Agri-business

Agri-business would seem to have an advantage in the farm bill lobbying process with about 20 per cent of the nation's workforce involved in agriculture-related industry, representing 17.9 per cent of gross national production (Browne, 1988a, p. 148). It is extremely influential, but seldom exercises its full potential, probably because the stakes are usually not large.[9] Agricultural legislation generally has less-clear effects on the welfare of large diversified companies than it does on farmers and commodity groups. Individual corporations lobby for specific purposes, but do not always lobby very hard. Often they do not have to lobby very vigorously because of close ties with government officials. They also have every incentive to maintain low visibility as they have no need to raise funds and because visibility invites other groups to mobilize in response. Individual corporations frequently have divided interests, which hinders their ability to lobby forcefully. Cargill, for instance, is a grain marketer, soybean processor, poultry, egg and beef producer and seller of feed, seed and fertilizer (Stokes, 1985a, p. 636). Agri-business interests generally support a market farm economy and free trade; however, little co-ordination normally exists between industry lobbyists. This may be because the benefit does not justify the costs of co-ordinating the activities of large complex organizations, each of which has significant lobbying resources in its own right. The only time that agri-business appears to make a concerted effort is when an unusual threat exists to its collective interest, such as production controls. The effectiveness of agri-business lobbying is impeded because most lobbying decisions are made in corporate offices far removed from the political arena of Washington, DC (see Browne, 1986, pp. 126–8). As a result, agri-business lobbyists do not often have the necessary leeway to maximize their influence and cannot effectively co-ordinate their positions.

Consumers

There is a well-organized consumer lobby in Washington, DC including such organizations as the Consumer Federation of America, Community Nutrition Institute and the National Consumers Congress.[10] These organizations, loosely linked together, sometimes present joint testimony before the House and Senate Agricultural Committees during the farm bill debate. They generally support provisions which will steady domestic food prices, such as grain reserves, and which will improve the quality of food available on the market. They support nutrition research and the food stamp programme. They have not generally opposed deficiency payments commodity programmes which do not directly tax the consumer, accepting that these are necessary to stabilize food prices and farmers' income. They do oppose the milk and sugar price support programmes, arguing that these result in unnecessarily high prices for consumers. They advocate decentralization in production and direct income payments to farmers. The consumer lobby does have policy clout on food quality and safety issues, but it has not played a significant role in shaping commodity policy.

6.3.2 Other outside inputs

The media

The media has collectively become an important policy actor in the past several decades, as television has combined with the press as a potent force to influence policy outcomes.[11] This is as true for agriculture as for other policy areas. The media have largely taken over two important functions of political parties – access to voters and the setting of policy agendas. Media coverage, particularly television, has certain strong biases. It tends to sensationalize, oversimplify and personalize issues. It appeals to the emotions by conveying strong images and values. However, it is not effective in conveying policy complexity or in discussing policy options. The media tend to look at agricultural issues from the vantage point of the traditional agrarian ethos where the hard-working downtrodden farmer is trampled by government in his struggle to survive. Television has been particularly ineffective in explaining commodity policies and the options suggested for reform. The media have sometimes supported reform efforts when consumer interests are involved, advocating, for instance, significant changes in dairy and sugar programmes.

The media problem is at least in part a question of incentives. The farmer who is foreclosed is news; the farmer who prospers is not. Detailed discussions of commodity programmes, do not strike any emotional chords. Hence, it is hard to justify sending reporters out to do in-depth studies of farm legislation. Another part of the problem is that the available aggregate agricultural data cannot be used very easily to convey to the general public the fact that commodity programmes favour the few and do not really help farmers in general. Some of the collected data are misleading, such as average income figures for farmers – how many rich farmers are hiding behind average farm income? Other data do show disparities in benefits, but are often so abstract that they attract little public interest.

Public opinion
The general public appears highly sympathetic to farmers because of the deep-seated agrarian ethos already discussed and the rapid demographic transition off the land. As in Europe, a very large number of people are generally sensitive to the problems of farmers and supportive of government help for farmers. A nationwide public opinion poll conducted by the *New York Times* and CBS in February 1986, after the passage of the generous 1985 Food Security Act, found that 50 per cent of the public thought that federal spending for farm programmes should be increased (Robbins, 1986). Only 12 per cent favoured a decrease in spending. Five out of six Americans, the poll showed, 'think half or more of the nations farmers are facing "serious economic problems" ', while 55 per cent of the sample said they were willing to pay more taxes if an increase would help troubled farmers save their land. In comparison, just 46 per cent had said after the recent space shuttle disaster that they would be willing to pay more taxes to see the space shuttle continued.

The poll found a deep reservoir of goodwill in the general public for food producers, who, as many see it, also nurture what is best in the American character, and a willingness to give farmers special treatment (Robins, 1986; see also Clymer, 1986). Fifty-eight per cent of those questioned agreed that 'farm life is more honest and moral than life in the rest of the country', while 64 per cent felt that 'farmers are more hard-working than most other Americans', and 67 per cent said 'farmers have closer ties to their families than most other Americans do' (Robbins, 1986).[12] About half of those polled indicated that they would choose farm life if it was economically feasible. But, there was widespread disillusion about the future of small farms as a business. About 45 per cent thought such farms were outmoded, while 43 per cent disagreed. When respondents were asked whether farmers should be specially favoured or whether the government should 'treat farmers the way it treats other small businessmen', the margin was 52 per cent for and 42 per cent against giving farmers special treatment. When queried if special treatment should be given even 'if that means there will be less money to help people who are also having economic difficulties', the respondents split evenly, with 45 per cent favouring special farm aid and 44 per cent opposed.

Even though public support for farmers is both broad and deep, this support is based on some misconceptions about farming. For instance, 30 per cent of the respondents in the *New York Times*/CBS poll said they feared that widespread failures of small farmers would lead to food shortages and rising costs. The general knowledge of the actual structure of farming, commodity programmes and the distribution of farm programme benefits is not very great. There is little incentive to learn more. Food prices are stable and low, and expenditures for farm programmes, until recently, have been 'small change' compared to defence, education, health and other major government programmes. The public is not easily mobilized in support of agricultural reform.

Academics

Academics, particularly agricultural economists from land grant and other institutions of higher learning, supply input into the policy process. Their published writings, widely circulated in both USDA and among Congressional staff, do much to set the tenor of the policy debate. Academics have been influential in encouraging the international market orientation which characterizes US agricultural policy today. They have not been particularly influential in their attempts to reform commodity policies. Many policy officials were former academics and many former policy officials are currently academics. Academics play a major role in the data collection and analysis which precedes farm bill consideration. When Congressional hearings are held on the farm bill, several academic expert witnesses appear. The academic world has much discussed the problems with US commodity policies and has given serious consideration to a number of reform proposals including targeting, decoupling, and mandatory production controls. Academics do not have the power to force the policy process to consider reform proposals, but can influence the arguments when policy-makers place them on the agenda. They may also author proposals introduced by legislators.[13] Academics exercise influence to the extent that their arguments help policy-makers deal with pressing problems.

International

US omnibus farm bills, which basically define US agricultural policy, historically have been considered domestic legislation. Hence, political inputs from foreign countries have not appeared very important in the policy-making process. The success or failure of the current Uruguay Round of the GATT negotiations in influencing subsequent farm legislation will show whether this is changing. However, the international economic environment has become very influential in the 1970s and 1980s as agricultural trade has greatly increased and trade interdependence has grown. Decision-makers must now consider very seriously the international food trade situation when they design agricultural legislation as well as the trade consequences of that legislation. They must also consider the implications of actions which foreign nations have taken or might take to restrict or enhance agricultural trade.

Foreign reactions to US farm bills seemed rather muted before the 1980s because the trade implications were not always clear. Virtually every nation in the world views domestic agricultural policy as a sovereign right. To interfere in the US agricultural policy process would constitute an infringement on the domestic affairs of the USA and would invite reciprocal intervention. As the trade provisions of farm legislation have expanded and as the implications have become clearer, other nations have become much more vocal in their criticisms of US agricultural policy. This criticism has been much more directed to trade policy, the symptom, rather than to the commodity policies, the underlying cause of overproduction. Foreign criticism has weight in the foreign policy establishment, particularly the Department of State, charged with maintaining alliances and other considerations much more general than agricultural trade. However, the Department of State has no tradition of exercising general influence on the farm bill, certainly not on commodity programmes. USDA must listen to foreign criticism, too, but has been able to ignore most of it since the loudest critic, the European Community, has commodity policy problems at least as serious as those in the USA. In looking at food policy decisions for the 1970s, Destler (1980) concludes that foreign policy considerations play a major role in agricultural policy-making only during a foreign policy crisis. So far, no foreign policy crisis has had much impact on an omnibus farm bill.

A US domestic global welfare and development lobby has exercised influence in the development of the PL-480 foreign food aid, which is an important element of omnibus farm bills.[14] However, this lobby has never been very effective in influencing commodity policy formation. The public constituency of those favouring foreign aid in the USA is very small, and likely to be dominant only when starvation is the issue (Destler, 1980, Ch. 5). This is seldom the context of the farm bill debate. Even to the extent that starvation appears as an issue, commodity programmes are not easily linked to either the causes or the solution of the starvation problem.

NOTES

1. For a more complete discussion of the actors in the agricultural policy process, see Bonnen (1987, pp. 10–27).
2. The members of the sub-committee for the Democratic majority were: Huckaby (Louisiana, chairman); Espy (Mississippi); Jones (Tennessee); Stallings (Idaho); Harris (Alabama); Coelho (California); Stenholm (Texas); Tallon (South Carolina); and English (Oklahoma). The members for the Republican minority were: Strangeland (Minnesota); Emerson (Missouri); Lewis (Florida); Combost (Texas); Herger (Louisiana); and Holloway (Louisiana).
3. Bonnen holds that the same norm governs European commodity programmes.
4. For an incisive discussion of the impact of this trend on the entire agricultural policy process, seen Bonnen (1987, pp. 23–7).
5. For discussion on the development of agricultural lobbies, see Browne (1988a) and Bonnen (1987). For a more detailed treatment see Browne (1986).

6. Some of the commodity groups are the American Soybean Association; the National Association of Wheat Growers; the National Corn Growers Association; the National Cotton Council; and the National Milk Producers Federation.
7. For discussion of the 'triangle of power', see Talbot (1983, pp. 2–3).
8. The greater strength of commodity groups in Congress can be attributed to the greater dependence on campaign contributions and other support.
9. For a very detailed discussion of the agri-business lobby, see Browne (1988b).
10. This discussion is heavily indebted to Guither (1980, pp. 87–97).
11. For an incisive discussion of the policy impact of the media, see Bonnen (1987, pp. 27–30).
12. Thirty-nine per cent of those interviewed agreed with all three statements.
13. The best example of this is the Boschwitz–Boren bill to decouple agricultural subsidies from production. Many of the ideas for this bill originated in the Department of Agricultural Economics at the University of Minnesota. Cargill Inc. is reputed to have played a strong role in its development.
14. For a discussion of the global welfare and development lobby, see Destler (1980, pp. 26–35).

7 · UNITED STATES AGRICULTURAL POLICY REFORM, 1981-8

We now turn to case studies to examine the responsiveness of the policy process to reform initiatives. The 1981 and 1985 omnibus farm bills were chosen because they constitute the principal legislation governing agricultural programmes in the 1980s. The discussion will employ the analytical framework developed in Chapter 1.

7.1 THE 1981 FARM BILL

7.1.1 Economic trends and economic shocks

The economic situation in 1981 was not auspicious for commodity policy reform. The farm economy boomed, with record food exports in 1980 of $41.2 billion. Prospects for 1981 looked even better, in spite of a strengthening dollar. Government outlays for price and income support were only $2.7 billion for 1980 and did not threaten to increase greatly in 1981. Farm assets appeared at record levels and farm incomes were high. Yet, farmers seemed dissatisfied with their lot. After a rapid rise in the 1970s, their incomes had flattened out and even declined slightly.[1] They found that market prices for their commodities rose less rapidly than the prices they had to pay for fertilizer, credit, seed and machinery. Farm cash receipts and total production costs increased about 9 per cent in 1981, compared to a 5 per cent increase in cash receipts. Commodity prices were threatened by the prospect of a bumper crop in 1981.[2] Farmers blamed the government for their problems. They perceived better prices and higher exports had it not been for the 1980 embargo on grain sales to the Soviet Union. The dollar was strengthening, an economic shock, but it was not widely understood how this would affect agricultural trade. Inflation appeared at a very high level, at least in part because of the 1979 oil price rises. The cost of credit had become very high, with some commercial loans carrying 20 per cent interest (*Congressional Quarterly Almanac (CQA)*, 1981, p. 533). A farm debt problem was already developing. Overall, a situation presented itself where government had little incentive to change farm programmes and where farmers would lobby strongly to enhance the benefits they received.

7.1.2 Political developments

The political developments in the period preceding the 1981 farm bill allowed some possibility for agricultural policy reform. The number of farming district Congressmen had continued to decline in the 1970s as a result of the migration from the land. The rural–urban coalition appeared weakened, partly because of the congressional reforms of the 1970s, which reduced the power of committee chairmen, and increased participant democracy. The increased emphasis on sub-committees threatened to turn interests against each other. In 1981, for the first time, the farm bill would have to conform to the budget guidelines approved by Congress.

7.1.3 The political environment

The political environment in 1981 had elements both favourable and unfavourable to commodity policy reform. President Reagan and his Republican administration came into office with a strong commitment to lower taxes, cut spending and balance the federal budget. Reagan clearly wanted to reduce agricultural subsidies, but he had promised to help farmers out in the election campaign. The power in Congress was divided, with the Republicans controlling the Senate and Democrats maintaining their firm control of the House. The Republicans in Congress tended to support the President on reduced government spending, but many of them came from agricultural constituencies; as a result, they were unlikely to reduce farm spending. The Democrats did not share the Republican concern about the cost of domestic programmes. In fact, the party worked to maintain the urban–rural alliance, effective in the 1970s, where urban Congressmen supported commodity programmes in return for rural support for increased food stamps and other rural programmes. A new constraint appeared in the legislative process.

7.1.4 The Reagan administration proposals

The President submitted his proposals for the 1981 farm bill early in the legislative session. The administration had two main objectives (Sanderson, 1983, p. 4). The first of these consisted of cost containment. It wanted to keep the annual cost of farm commodity programmes around $1.5 to $2.0 billion. The principal target was the dairy programme, which, with price supports at 80 per cent of parity, threatened to escalate from $2 billion in fiscal 1981 to $3 billion in 1983. The administration wanted to reduce the annual budget outlays for dairy products to about $450 million per year. It also wanted to keep the costs of grain programmes below $1 billion.

The second objective was to eliminate programmes the administration thought had become obsolete (Sanderson, 1983, p. 4). For the grain sector,

Reagan proposed to do away with target prices and deficiency payments, relying on the farmer-owned reserve programme to support market prices. He also wanted to phase out the tobacco and peanuts programmes, which are government-sponsored producer cartels allocating production quotas. The administration also initially opposed the reintroduction of a loan programme for sugar.

One can infer from the Reagan proposals that the administration's ideology was more important than the pressures of the commodity groups in shaping the policy debate within the Executive. The policies, if implemented, would have significantly changed commodity programmes and hence incurred commodity group opposition. Ideology appears to have overcome bureaucracy. The permanent USDA staff had every reason to continue existing programmes and no incentive to bring about the proposed changes. David Stockman, the dynamic new director of the Office of Management and Budget (OMB), who had a well-known aversion to agricultural programmes, played a key role. Some influence may also have been exercised by agri-business which generally favours a free-market farm economy.

7.1.5 Congressional debate

The Congressional debate over the 1981 farm bill was long and contentious. Serious political conflict developed between the administration and Congress, between Senate and House, between Agricultural Committees and the urban coalition and within the Agricultural Committees. No leadership coalition developed to shepherd the bill through Congress. Even the commodity group alliance threatened to disintegrate at various stages of the debate, in part because of deliberate administration efforts to stir up long-standing rivalries between commodity groups. Also, the budget restraint forced the commodity groups to compete directly for shares of a smaller federal pie, thus shattering their vote-trading relationships.[3] The process came perilously close to producing no bill at all; and might have failed had it not been for the prospect of reverting to the outdated permanent 1949 farm legislation.[4] The final bill was approved only on 16 December 1981, just before adjournment. The Conference agreement passed in the House by a vote of only 205–203.

As the legislative session began, a conciliatory mood appeared in Senate and House. Both the new Senate Agricultural Committee chairman, Jesse Helms (Republican, North Carolina) and the House Agriculture Committee chairman E. 'Kika' de la Garza (Democrat, Texas) at first predicted that Committee members and their constituencies would be willing to make do with less. Helms noted: 'Farmers understand that unless this inflation is cured, they don't stand a chance no matter what kind of farm bill we pass' (*CQA*, 1981, p. 539).

However, when it became clear that the President was going to request extensive revisions to farm programmes, rebellion developed in both House and Senate Agriculture Committees. The administration's proposals were 'dead on arrival' when presented to the Agricultural Committees on 31 March and 1 April, 1981. Competing bills were introduced in the Senate by both Republicans (including Helms) and Democrats. Tensions mounted rapidly as House and Senate mark-up proceeded. Budget pressures sent farm interests scrambling to protect their programmes. An 'every-man-for-himself' atmosphere developed, threatening years of mutual accommodation in which lobbyists and members were inclined to look after each other's interests. 'It used to be that everybody could get their piece of the pie', complained one lobbyist, 'and, if the pie was too small, they [Congress] could just make it bigger' (*CQA*, 1981, p. 539). Commenting further, he lamented: 'There's not enough to go around.'

Senate Agriculture Committee
No serious consideration was given to commodity policy reforms in the Senate Agriculture Committee, not surprising given the strength of commodity interests in that forum. Rather, debate centred around shaving commodity programmes to meet budgetary guidelines, the kind of incrementalism which bureaucratic politics and partisan mutual adjustment paradigms would lead us to expect. Spending limits were achieved only with difficulty, even with a Republican majority. After disregarding most of the administration's requests, the Senate Agriculture Committee in its first week of voting tentatively added several billion dollars for programmes over the following four years.[5] It agreed by a 10–5 vote on 27 April to include a dairy price support plan favoured by industry, which would have provided 75 per cent of parity rather than the 70 per cent requested by the administration.[6] The following day, by a vote of 5–11, the committee rejected the administration proposal for discretionary powers to set wheat loan rates. *CQA* (1981, p. 541) reported that: 'More than once, Senator Helms warned members that they would have to "march back down the hill" – that is reduce the cost of programs before reporting a bill. "We've already broken the bank," Helms said on one occasion.' However, Helms sat quietly while the Committee approved tobacco and peanut programmes which did not contain requested administration changes.

The Senate Agriculture Committee came somewhat closer to fiscal reality after a series of 'closed door' sessions held between Senate majority leader, Howard Baker (Tennessee); Senate Budget Chairman, Pete Domenici (New Mexico); and Deputy Secretary of Agriculture, Richard Lyng. It finally approved measures calculated to be only $50 to $150 million over budget limits. On Senator Dole's initiative, cuts were made in corn and wheat loan rates and fixed rates rather than indexing were set for rice loans. However, the administration was denied discretionary authority to set target price and loan rates. The Committee approved an expensive new sugar support programme which the administration did not want. Dairy supports came under the most serious attack because of the surplus situation. After an extensive debate, the Committee approved a plan which authorized the Secretary of Agriculture to set price supports between 75 and 90 per cent of parity but giving him discretion to lower the support level to 70 per cent when costs or quantities got too high. The Committee also got into the area of foreign trade when it approved measures requiring Congressional consent to agricuiltural trade embargoes and farmer compensation.

Senate floor debate
The agenda for debate on the Senate floor was significantly wider than in the Agriculture Committee. Commodity programmes came under serious challenge, but all survived intact in the final Senate bill, partially for political reasons that had nothing to do with agriculture. Senate floor action was delayed while Congress approved Reagan's budget and tax bills. In vote bargaining over these measures, the administration dropped its opposition to the sugar and peanut programmes to gain necessary votes from southern Senators (*CQA*, 1981, p. 542). When the Senate did take up the farm bill, sugar, peanut and tobacco programmes all came under substantial attack, but they survived because of the administration's reversal. Senators Richard Lugar (Republican, Indiana), Mark Hatfield (Republican, Oregon) and Dan Quayle (Republican, Indiana) attempted to crack the 'feudal' tobacco and peanuts programmes open so that any farmer could grow these lucrative crops (*CQA*, 1981, p. 542). Senators Paul Tsongas (Democrat, Massachusetts) and Dan Quayle tried to kill or drastically reduce the sugar programme on grounds that it would largely benefit wealthy corporations and add hundreds of millions of dollars to food bills. Part of the opposition to peanut and tobacco programmes can be attributed to an anti-regulation mood, but part stemmed from anti-Helms sentiment (*CQA*, 1981, p. 539). Helms had alienated many members of Congress with his outspoken views on such issues as abortion, mandatory bussing, desegregation and excessive spending on food stamps. The divisions among farm groups were quite obvious during the voting, when some dairy and wheat state Senators voted against killing an amendment by Lugar to dismantle the peanut programme (*CQA*, 1981, p. 542).

Bowing to the threat of a presidential veto, the final bill approved by the Senate on 14 September 1981 conformed more closely to administration wishes than the Committee action and was less generous to farmers. Target prices for wheat, rice, cotton and feed grains were significantly reduced. Dairy supports were also cut back further. Senator Robert Dole played a leading role in achieving final consensus. *CQA*, 1981, p. 541, noted that he made his case by frequently reminding colleagues 'there's no money to shovel out of the Treasury' for more generous farm programmes.

House Agriculture Committee

The House Agriculture Committee was even more generous to commodity groups than its Senate counterpart. It began mark-up on 30 April and reported out a 'budget-busting' farm bill on 19 May. Target prices and loan rates were raised for feed grains, rice and cotton. Dairy price supports were authorized at 75 to 90 per cent of parity. The peanut price supports were increased and the quota lowered. A sugar price programme was authorized at 44 per cent of parity or about 19.6 cents per pound for 1982. The Committee did feel pressures to control costs, but resisted them, at least in part because of confusion and exasperation about the budget process (*CQA*, 1981, p. 543).

House floor debate

An extended debate took place on the House floor. The final accommodation between urban and rural interests, achieved only with difficulty, significantly cut the Agriculture Committee expenditures recommendations. The floor debate did not get started until 2 October, which caused Congress to miss the 30 September date when the 1977 farm bill expired. This forced emergency action to prevent return to the provisions of the 1947 permanent farm legislation. The delay was part of a successful bargaining strategy to get administration approval of a $700 million increase in food stamps in return for a compromise package of amendments cutting the cost of the over-budget committee bill.

Assembling the compromise package of amendments was in itself an interesting process. It involved very delicate vote trading arrangements among regional commodity interests and urban food stamp advocates. The frayed farm coalition regrouped to help piece this compromise together. Its strength was shown in the initial 7 October vote approving the package by 414–14. Representative Fred Richmond (Democrat, New York), a member of the Agricultural Committee and a strong advocate of food stamps was reported to have said: 'I want to support sugar . . . tobacco, rice, cotton, dairy, every one of these other commodities' (*CQA*, 1981, p. 544).

The principal element of the compromise was a $1 billion cut in proposed dairy subsidies offered by Representative Berkley Bedell (Democrat, Iowa), which gradually lowered parity supports to 70 per cent in 1984–5, unless federal purchases were less than 3.5 billion pounds of milk, in which case support would be fixed at 75 per cent of parity. Other cuts were made in the Agriculture Committee's recommendations for target prices and loan rates for feed grains, rice and cotton.

When floor debate did begin, the sugar, peanut and tobacco programmes came under attack. By a vote of 213–190, the Representatives voted to cancel the new price support programme for sugar. Sponsors Peter A. Peyser (Democrat, New York) and Margaret Heckler (Republican, Massachusetts) 'declared that creating a new program for sugar growers was unthinkable while the elderly, poor and students were forced by budget cuts to lose federal benefits' (*CQA*, 1981, p. 545). The House also voted to cancel the acreage allotment and poundage quota system which for years had prohibited all but a select group of farmers from growing peanuts for market, though it did vote to retain peanut price support loans. The tobacco programme barely survived a strong challenge, primarily because of a well-organized drive by the self-styled 'tobacco boys' – legislators from North Carolina and other southern tobacco states – which was supported by the House leadership (*CQA*, 1981, p. 545). Some of the opposition to all of these programmes stemmed from personal and political animosity. Northern Democrats were angry with their southern colleagues for supporting President Reagan's budget and tax measures. Some also wanted to get back at Senator Helms for his social views and for protecting peanuts and tobacco while insisting on cuts in dairy and other farm programmes. The House debate required seven full days of often acrimonious discussions. The bill was finally passed on 22 October.

The Conference
The House and Senate conference participants began formulating the final bill on 5 November after being strongly urged by the President to accept the provisions of the less expensive Senate bill. The final product was closer to the Senate bill than to the House bill, but still risked veto because it would have cost hundreds of millions of dollars more than the President wanted. House rebellion was also courted when conference participants voted to keep the Senate's sugar price support programme, maintaining prices at 17.0 cents per pound for the 1982 crop, with annual 0.25 cents per pound price increases thereafter. The differences between the House and Senate dairy provisions were compromised, setting minimum dairy price supports for the next four years in dollars rather than the inflation-related parity index. The minimum support for 1982 would be at the current $13.10 per hundredweight with increases for the next three years to $13.25, $14.00 and $14.60. The conference participants continued the tobacco programme which had survived a strong challenge in both chambers, and overruled the House in continuing the peanut programme.

A major dispute developed over grain supports. House-approved wheat and feed grains subsidies would have cost $4 billion more than those approved by the Senate, which was a matter of great concern to the administration. House Democratic Whip (and former House Agriculture Committee chairman) Thomas Foley (Democrat, Washington) appeared willing to compromise the differences, but wanted benefits indexed, which the administration opposed. Finally, a compromise was worked out between Foley and Senator Dole which dropped indexing and fixed wheat loans at $3.55 per bushel for crop years 1982–5, with corn loans set at $2.55 per bushel and other feed grains set in relation to corn. Wheat target prices were set at $4.05 per bushel for 1982, with increases in 1983–5 to $4.30, $4.45 and $4.65, respectively. Corn target prices were set at $2.70 per bushel for 1982, with upward increases to $2.86, $3.03 and $3.18, respectively, in 1983–5. The administration was not given very much discretion to vary these price support levels.

The final bill was signed by the President on 22 December. It was calculated to cost $428 million more over four years than the version approved by the Senate. The partisan mutual adjustment process had come close to breaking down, but had finally worked out a compromise that seemed acceptable to all. The President did not get commodity programme reform, but he did get concessions from Congress to limit predicted cost. The House was unable to cut sugar and peanut programmes, though it was able to get the Senate to go along with more spending on dairy and grain programmes. The commodity groups achieved their minimum objectives in that all the programmes survived, though most had to settle for less than they wanted. The urban coalition received increased funding for food stamps though it had to accept higher dairy and other price supports than it would have liked. The President might have achieved more had he not initially proposed an end to both target prices and loan rates, which was unacceptable to Congress. He might also have achieved significant action to cut tobacco, peanut and sugar programmes, so closely divided was sentiment in Congress, had he not had to abandon his opposition to these programmes in order to get southern support for his budget and tax programmes.

It would appear that a number of factors influenced the final outcome. The administration's emphasis on cost containment and the Congressional budget process served to constrain the spending impulses of the House and Senate Agriculture Committees. However, this effect was greatly overshadowed by the overestimation of future inflation and the false expectation of continued strong export markets, which exerted pressure to increase price support levels. These miscalculations caused the actual cost of the 1981 farm bill to be billions more than anticipated. They also caused all the wrong supply signals to be sent. Congress's refusal to grant the administration leeway in adjusting price support levels allowed the expenditure situation to get totally out of control. Actual budget costs of farm programmes prior to and during 1981 did not appear as a factor, except for dairy, where high expenditures provided an impetus for support-level cuts. Both commodity groups and the urban coalition exercised influence; they worked together to maintain each others' programmes and to stifle reform. Strong input came from farmers who saw their situation deteriorating. Foreign political and economic inputs, on the other hand, did not seem important. Continued high levels of foreign trade were assumed and little attention was paid to the appreciating dollar, which would soon contribute to export decline.

A note should be added about the sugar programme included in the 1981 farm bill. This was a new programme, not the renewal of an existing one. In 1974, after 40 years of routinely supporting sugar legislation, Congress ended sugar supports when sugar prices reached unprecedented levels.[7] As sugar prices declined again in the late 1970s, policy-makers were subjected to increasing pressure from sugar growers to renew support. Import fees supporting domestic prices were limited to 50 per cent *ad valorem*, and hence were less effective at low world price levels. Congress and the administration succumbed to this pressure in 1981. The key factor was President Reagan reversing his stance to gain southern support for his budget and tax programmes. The new plan became narrowly acceptable only because it promised to add no new budget cost to agriculture programmes. The government would be prevented from spending money and accumulating stocks under the non-recourse loans by controlling imports. At first, it was thought that this could be done through import fees and tariffs. But by 1982 the administration found it necessary to impose formal quotas, based on a country's average sugar exports to the USA for five of the seven years from 1975 to 1981, to maintain the price level set in the legislation (Mahler, 1986, p. 8). These quotas have been progressively reduced because the high support price has engendered greatly enhanced domestic production and substitution of corn sweeteners for sugar in the domestic market. The quota for 1988 was only 750,000 tons, down from 3,174,000 tons in 1983. It will probably soon be reduced to zero and the USA may eventually have to dump its sugar surplus on the international market. This has obviously had a very adverse affect on US sugar suppliers, mostly poor Third World countries which have a real comparative advantage in production. There is little evidence that consideration of the consequences for these suppliers received any consideration in the 1981 farm bill debate.

7.1.6 Assessment

The government politics and partisan mutual adjustment paradigms seem to explain very well the outcome of the 1981 farm bill legislative debate. Bargaining occurred between players with divergent interests and perspectives and the outcome represented a political resultant, which was inefficient in its allocation of resources but reasonably acceptable to participants in the process. It was not an outcome that anyone would have planned, or one which would have been possible had budget limits been taken more seriously. As public choice theory would have predicted, the commodity interests, which had a large stake, dominated the process. They committed significant resources and were able to take advantage of their close ties with the agricultural committees which write legislation. They managed to save their basic programmes, though they faced serious challenges and had to make significant concessions to urban interests and to the President. The President had to give up his plans to reform commodity programmes in order to gain farm votes for his budget and tax programmes. He had to be content with congressional concessions on spending levels. As the government politics paradigm would suggest, analysis in the Congressional process was very limited. The range of options considered seemed very narrow. The final outcome represented only incremental change from the 1977 farm bill.

7.2 DEVELOPMENTS BETWEEN THE 1981 AND 1985 FARM BILLS

7.2.1 The Payment-in-Kind programme

The farm economy deteriorated very significantly in 1982, necessitating drastic action. Farm production peaked while the export market soured. Yields rose to record levels for the second year in a row and exports declined from a record $43.5 billion in 1981 to $40.5 billion in 1982. As a result, government commodity stocks grew to a level of 150 million tonnes, enough to meet the nation's domestic demands for a full year. Storage costs added significant increases to farm programme expenditures which rose to an unprecedented level of $12 billion in 1982. At the same time, farm income dropped sharply and farmland values began to decline.

President Reagan announced the Payment-in-Kind (PIK) programme as a response to the developing farm crisis on 11 January 1983.[8] This programme would provide payment to farmers of wheat, corn, cotton and rice (all crops in surplus) not to plant these crops in 1983. The administration hoped that up to 50 per cent of the nation's farmland would be idled. This programme seemed attractive in that it would allow the administration to save on budget costs for storage, get rid of the surplus, and cut production, which would eventually increase prices and raise farm income. Congress delayed action on the plan, but the administration implemented it on its own initiative and Congress acquiesced.

This programme can in no sense be considered agricultural policy reform, but rather a stopgap measure which did not attack the underlying problem of overproduction. It did temporarily make federal expenditures appear smaller, but there were huge hidden costs in the value of the government commodities given away. Large farmers benefited inordinately because the $50,000 maximum in cash payments was waived. The administration justified waiving the maximum as the only way of gaining the participation of the large farmers who produce most of the surplus. The programme offered little relief to the middle-sized farmers who were hurting most and threatened many rural businesses by cutting deeply into sales of fertilizer, farm equipment and other farm-related products.

7.2.2 The dairy diversion programme

Agriculture suffered another adverse year in 1983. Federal expenditures for price support and other farm subsidy programmes reached an extraordinarily high level, variously estimated at between $19 billion and $22 billion, not including the $9.7 billion used to pay farmers under the administration's PIK programme (*CQA*, 1983, pp. 373–80). Exports fell back again, to a level of $34.5 billion, while land values continued to decline. The administration still had a problem with dairy production running about 112 per cent of consumption and the resulting continued build-up of the dairy surplus. In 1982, Congress had passed legislation which made a levy of $1.00 per hundred pounds (administered in two 50 cent steps) directly on dairy farms' milk production in an effort to limit the burgeoning surplus, but this had not succeeded in its goal. Something had to be done about the dairy surplus and about the large dairy contribution to continued high farm programme costs.

The politically powerful dairy lobby, which had contributed over $2 million in Congressional campaign contributions over the previous two years, knew some action would be taken, but wanted to minimize the damage to its interests.[9] The dairy industry was extremely unhappy with the assessments, which it regarded as a tax on production with no compensation to enhance consumer demand. However, at first it appeared divided among itself about what to do. Most producers wanted a paid diversion, but about 15 per cent from the South-east and southern California preferred a significant price cut (Petit, 1985, p. 43). The dairy interests were brought together in support of a paid diversion by their friends in Congress who warned them that they would not get favourable treatment in the legislature. if they were divided. The administration, which had just overcome its ideological opposition to paying farmers not to produce by instituting the PIK programme, was willing to support a dairy diversion programme bill, if this could be combined with a target price freeze, which it wanted to prevent future surpluses in wheat, feed grains, cotton and rice.

Once Congress started considering this initiative, the administration lost control of the situation. Neither House nor Senate was willing to go along with the target price freeze given the poor situation of the farm economy, so the Congressional leadership dropped this part of the proposal. Instead, to maximize the chances for passage, they linked the paid milk diversion to a bill favoured by the tobacco lobby to preserve tobacco supports. The combined coalition of the dairy lobby and the tobacco lobby was sufficiently strong to prevail. The power of this coalition became evident in the debate. It easily killed a plan by Representative Barber Conable (Republican, New York) to substitute a significant milk price support cut for the diversion. The dairy lobby overcame strong opposition from beef, pork and chicken producers who were afraid that their prices would be depressed, and from Pizza Hut Inc., Taco Bell Inc., the milk chocolate makers (Hershey, in particular) supermarket chains and convenience store operators who were afraid that market prices for milk would be increased (Petit, 1985, p. 43).[10] Other commodity lobbies supported the dairy-tobacco coalition, hoping to gain support for their programmes in the 1985 farm bill. The press did not support the division. Editorials in the *New York Times*, *Wall Street Journal* and *Washington Post*, strongly implied that the bill was a 'rip-off' by the dairy lobby at the expense of the public interest (Petit, 1985, p. 45). However, the press did not get involved until late in the policy debate and could not mobilize public opinion against the diversion. The majority and minority whips supported the diversion bill and one of them, Thomas S. Foley (Democrat, Washington) helped shepherd the measure through the House Agriculture Committee.

A bill was passed providing for a 15-month paid milk diversion, with producers paid at the rate of $10 per hundred pounds for reducing their milk production by between 5 and 30 per cent (at the same time lowering price supports from $13.10 to $12.60 per hundredweight and repealing the second 50 cent assessment levied in 1982). The Reagan administration had a serious dilemma. A veto would have endangered the re-election chances of two Republican administration stalwarts in the 1984 election – Senators Jesse Helms (North Carolina) and Rudy Boschwitz (Minnesota) – and might have increased farmer antagonism to President Reagan himself in his 1984 re-election campaign. Under these circumstances the President signed the bill.

Public choice theory, government politics and partisan mutual adjustment paradigms provide a good explanation for what happened. The dairy cost and surplus problem required action. The dairy lobby and its Congressional friends satisficed (in the sense that they were looking for an acceptable solution, not necessarily the best one) and came up with the paid diversion. The leading actors engaged in 'crisis-coping', thinking only how they could deal with the problem of the moment and at the same time maintain their positions. Economic analysis played a minimum role in this process and medium- and long-term consequences were completely ignored. A winning coalition of dairy and tobacco forces mobilized in Congress and became strong enough to carry the day. The outcome was a bargaining resultant, but one that favoured the interests which had the largest stake in the outcome.

The dairy diversion no more constituted agricultural reform than the PIK programme. Both programmes were expensive stopgaps, which do not attack the long-term problem of overproduction. All they did was postpone more fundamental change.

7.3   THE 1985 FOOD SECURITY ACT

7.3.1   Economic trends and economic shocks

The economic trends at the beginning of 1985 appeared much more favourable to agricultural commodity policy reform than the economic trends at the beginning of 1981. Most important, the cost of price and income supports had skyrocketed. Total government payments for the four-year period were $63.3 billion, compared to $27.7 billion for the period from 1978 to 1981 (Guither, 1986, p. 7). Productivity had continued to increase and stocks were at very high levels even with the PIK and dairy diversion programmes and a drought leading to a poor harvest in 1983. Exports had plummeted from a peak of $43.8 billion in 1983 to $31.2 billion in fiscal year 1984 because of the strong dollar and high loan rates (see Chapter 5, Figure 5.1). At the same time as US exports declined – an economic shock – European Community exports increased, as the EC pursued an aggressive policy of export expansion. Thus, a strong incentive existed to make US exports more competitive by moving more to a market agricultural economy.

On the other hand, the economic situation of the American farmer had worsened, making it difficult to pursue reforms which might ask the food producer to make substantial sacrifices. About 214,000 farms, out of 1.7 million, experienced financial stress because of high debt and an inability to generate enough cash to pay their bills (Guither, 1986, p. 6). The index of prices received by farmers declined from 139 in 1981 to 135 by December 1984 (1977 = 100). The index of farm real estate values fell from 158 in February 1981 in 128 by April 1985 (1977 = 100).

7.3.2   Political developments

A resurgence of rural populism appeared which Runge and Halbach (1987, pp. 155–61) have linked to growing instability in international markets, deflationary price movements and financial stress in agriculture (a political force at least in part emerging from economic factors). This populism would have farmers determine their own destiny and would isolate agriculture from the vagaries of international markets. It exercised very significant influence in getting the producer referendum for mandatory supply controls on the congressional agenda. As we shall see, this initiative came close to succeeding.

The precipitous decline in exports galvanized a strong political commitment to regain export share even if this included direct export subsidies. The catalytic event which broke the dam of administration resistance to export subsidies and which made export promotion a primary objective of the 1985 farm bill was Cargill's well-publicized threat in 1984 to import cheap grain from Argentina into the USA.

7.3.3 The political environment

The political environment had aspects both favourable and unfavourable to reform. On the positive side, the trade tensions with the EC argued strongly for reform. Increased concern about the budget deficit and the need to get government spending under control provided another favourable factor. President Reagan had just been re-elected with an overwhelming mandate and could make significant change without personal political cost. On the negative side, the downtrodden farmer received strong sympathy, catalysed by the media, particularly television. Consumer demand for reform did not develop because food costs remained relatively stable. Finally, the President could not push too strongly for agricultural reform, because control of the Senate was at stake. Republicans had only precarious control of the Senate, holding a 53-47 majority. Twenty-two Republican seats were up for election in 1986, including seven in the Midwest farm belt. The Democrats, of course, maintained an overwhelming majority in the House of Representatives.

7.3.4 Preparations for the Farm Bill debate

The increased salience of farm issues was emphasized by the actions taken in preparation for the Congressional debate. As early as 19 May 1983, Senator Roger Jepson (Republican, Iowa) convened a series of hearings on the general topic 'Toward the Next Generation of Farm Policy'. He declared that 'farm programs implemented in 1981, 1982 and 1983 have been costly and have proven to be ineffective in reversing the deterioration of the farm sector' (quoted in Guither, 1986, p. 7). Another series of hearings was held by 'Kika' de la Garza, chairman of the House Agriculture Committee. At one of these, former Secretary of Agriculture Bob Bergland observed that the homogeneity of American agriculture had broken down into rich, middle-class and poor farmers and that only the middle-class group really needed help. Yet the government's income and price programmes had been based on the concept that they helped all farmers. 'Year in and year out, we debate target price levels, while the realities in agriculture scream out for an entirely new approach' (quoted Guither, 1986, p. 8).

The Senate Agriculture Committee did not hold hearings but solicited written statements from farmers, farm organization leaders, agri-business groups and agricultural economists. The USDA held a series of six listening sessions across the country at which 240 people presented papers. In Washington, the Economic Research Service issued a series of reports dealing with the record of commodity programmes in the past. It became clear from the preliminary discussions that a strong impetus existed to change current commodity programmes and to do something to help the distressed farm economy – goals which were somewhat in conflict.

The farm issue rose to the top of the political agenda almost immediately after President Reagan's second inauguration, when several hundred state legislators and 15 Midwest Governors descended on Washington to obtain more federal aid for farmers (Guither, 1986, p. 13). Galvanized to action, Congress approved an emergency farm credit bill which the President vetoed because of the cost. This increased the impetus to do something to help farmers out of the worst agricultural depression since the 1930s.

7.3.5 The Reagan proposals

The administration's farm bill proposal was announced by the Secretary of Agriculture, William Block, on 22 February 1984. It included provisions to make US agricultural policy more market-orientated by lowering loan rates and by phasing down target prices and basing them on the market price (Guither, 1986, p. 14). Other provisions would have lowered limits on direct payments, phased out the dairy support programme and banned benefits to farmers who converted erodible land to crop production.

The decision-making process leading up to the administration's proposal is not completely clear. In preparation, the various agencies within USDA prepared some recommendations which were forwarded to the Assistant Secretary of Agriculture for Economics, William Lesher, who had been entrusted with responsibility for formulating the administration proposal. Even though the Agricultural Stabilization and Conservation Service (ASCS) exercised influence, Lesher maintained control. It would appear that Lesher and his deputy, Randy Russell, drafted the proposal themselves without extensive intra-USDA negotiations. However, with the budget constraint perceived as very important, they had to consult with the OMB, whose director, David Stockman, had considerable hostility toward agricultural programmes. OMB's budget recommendations implied deep cuts for agriculture, forcing Secretary Block to go cap-in-hand to Stockman to get some of the cuts reinstated. It is not clear how much analysis Lesher and Russell completed. They had two goals: to make US agriculture more trade competitive; and to reduce costs (*CQA*, 1985, p. 527).

The market economy orientation in the 1985 recommendations was similar to the administration's position during the 1981 farm bill debate and reflected the President's ideology. The loss of exports and increased farm programme costs had strengthened the administration's resolve. Once again, the influence of the commodity groups within the administration did not appear strong. Otherwise, it seems unlikely that the President would have had the temerity to advocate abolition of the dairy programme.

7.3.6 The Congressional debate

The general reaction in Congress

The President's proposal appeared 'dead on arrival' in Congress, just as its predecessor had been in 1981 (Guither, 1986, p. 2). It was not seriously debated in either House or Senate, though the administration did have an influence in shaping the final outcome. The resignation of William Lesher, the author of the Reagan farm proposals, at the beginning of the Congressional debate, created a vacuum which hindered the administration's lobbying efforts. It took his successor, Bob Thomson, some time to fill the void. A bipartisan consensus developed to lower loan rates to make US exports more competitive. However, Democrats and Republicans differed with each other and with the administration on target prices. Democrats, who saw the farm crisis as an important political issue in the forthcoming Congressional election, favoured freezing target prices for the life of the farm bill. Republicans, who in general were more budget-conscious, favoured slowly cutting target prices, though this stance was not supported by farm-state Republicans. The Senate, of course, was controlled by Republicans, and the House by Democrats.

The House and Senate Agriculture Committees were overwhelmed with alternative farm bill proposals submitted mostly by members of Congress and lobby groups. Ninety-four were submitted in the House and 50 in the Senate (Guither, 1986, p. 29). Some of these were extremely comprehensive, others had only limited coverage. There was so much to consider that even the Committee staffs had trouble keeping track of all the options. The situation was worse for the legislators who had to divide their time between agriculture and other Congressional business. As one former Senate Agriculture Committee staff member put it:

> What we on the Committee staff did at that time was to lay out each of the many proposals on spreadsheets with provisions for a given item side by side. There were so many details that the staff could barely handle things. The Senators, with so many demands on their time could not cope. In order to get their attention, the staff had to break proposals down into single-page options representing fundamental choices. (John Campbell, personal communication, 1988)

The Committees were also overwhelmed with different points of view. Three hundred and thirty-six testified before the House Agriculture Committee and its sub-committees, while 262 appeared before the Senate Agriculture Committee (Guither, 1986, p. 17). Government politics and partisan mutual adjustment paradigms suggest the need to simplify policy options to reduce the bargaining costs involved in trying to reach consensus. This is exactly what the Senate and House Agriculture committees did for the 1985 farm bill. Both Committees worked wherever possible to preserve the structure of existing programmes, looking for ways to cut costs.[11] However, something had to be done about target prices and loan rates. Both Committees spent considerable time trying to reach consensus on proposed changes to the deficiency payments system. Debate tended to focus around three options: maintaining some variant of the current system with lowered loan rates; initiating marketing loans; and conducting a referendum on mandatory supply controls.

Senate Agriculture Committee

The Senate Agriculture Committee initially reacted negatively to the Reagan farm bill proposal. The chairman, Senator Helms, announced his own farm bill only a few days afterwards, saying he didn't want to criticize the administration bill and that he would keep an open mind (Guither, 1986, p. 15). The Committee conducted 16 days of hearings in March and April, listening to a broad spectrum of witnesses, including general farm organizations, commodity groups, agri-business, environmentalists, consumer groups, government officials and academics. Producer groups, in general, and commodity groups, in particular, tended to dominate the hearings. There were 38 witnesses from general farm organizations along with 48 others from commodity groups (Guither, 1986, p. 38). The general farm organizations generally expressed their philosophical positions in their testimony (Guither, 1986, Ch. 3). For instance, the American Farm Bureau Federation favoured a market-orientated policy backed up by target prices as an income supplement. The American Agriculture Movement favoured mandatory production controls. The testimony of the commodity groups was narrowly focused on preserving the current programmes. The American wheat growers, for instance, called for target prices to be maintained at $4.38 per bushel, the continuation of the current loan rate at $3.30 per bushel, set-asides if stocks get too large, a long-term conservation reserve, and a marketing loan programme.

In the Senate, mark-up took place in the full Agriculture Committee, with the exception of the food stamps and commodity distribution title, where hearings were held in sub-committees and recommendations made to the full Committee. The mark-up involved consideration of nine major farm bills and numerous other less comprehensive ones. The Helms bill served as the mark-up vehicle. Progress came slowly in the nearly evenly divided body, which had nine Republican and eight Democrat members. The Committee's approach to price support constituted the most difficult issue. Three alternative proposals were considered:

1. The Harkin bill (Senate bill 1083), calling for a farmer referendum on mandatory acreage controls, high loan rates and set-asides increasing with size.
2. The Andrews–Cochran–Melcher proposal to eliminate target prices and replace them with a loan adjusted to budget guidelines and marketing loans.

3. The Dole–Zorinsky compromise proposal setting target prices the same as 1985 at first, then shifting to a percentage of the loan rate; with loan rates of $3.00 for wheat and $2.40 for corn for 1986 and as a percentage of market prices thereafter; with marketing loans, acreage reduction and paid diversions; and an option of mandatory production controls for wheat, subject to referendum (see *CQA*, 1987, pp. 532–4; Guither, 1986, pp. 51–2).

The Senate Agriculture Committee mark-up proceedings got off to a good start, on 14 May, with agreement to require export subsidies. However, stalemate soon occurred with an 8–8 vote on the broad concept of setting farm price supports between 75 per cent and 85 per cent of existing rates (*CQA*, 1985, p. 533). The vote hinged on lowering target prices and loan rates or just loan rates. It showed the general lack of consensus on Capitol Hill and among farm groups about how to restructure the deficiency payment system. The Committee then moved on to mandatory quotas and marketing loans which were defeated. It also considered the Boschwitz–Boren bill which would have provided generous cash payments to farmers as part of a 'transition' to market-orientated farming (see Paarlberg, 1988, pp. 119–21). This innovative proposal did not receive approval because it was 'too expensive'; had arrived too late in a process already overwhelmed; and according to one participant 'was too much of a departure . . . people didn't know enough . . . there was too much uncertainty about the consequences' to attract the necessary support.

The Committee still had not reached agreement when it adjourned for its July recess. When it returned, it first approved tough 'sod-buster' (ploughing fragile grasslands) provisions and then tentatively accepted the Dole–Zorinsky compromise. But the Dole–Zorinsky compromise was undercut by two Republican farm state defections and the Committee sent on to the Senate floor a bill which would have frozen target prices for four years.[12]

Senate floor debate
Senate floor debate began on 25 October, more than a full month after the Senate Agriculture Committee had reported out its bill. The consensus-building process on the floor moved extremely slowly and consumed over four weeks. The process was dominated by Senator Dole, the Senate majority leader, who played the role of broker–dealmaker. A number of important issues required resolution. One such issue was a target price freeze. The administration strongly opposed a freeze and had substantial bipartisan support outside of grain-producing states. After much discussion, and the addition of a number of 'sweeteners' into the bill by Senator Dole, the Senate agreed to freeze target prices for two years and allow slight annual reductions afterwards.[13] Dairy policy also received a good deal of attention with a strong move to reduce milk price supports beginning on 1 January 1986. The vote was close, but the forces for holding the price

support steady prevailed by three votes. The sugar policy came under attack from Senator Bradley (Democrat, New Jersey), but this effort failed on a 60–32 vote, with a very strong effort in opposition made by the sugar-producing interests and the corn sweetener industry. Senator Pressler (Republican, South Dakota) attempted to set up a three-tier target price schedule for wheat and feed grains, giving highest prices to small producers, but this amendment failed. Senator Boschwitz (Republican, Minnesota) wanted to establish a general marketing loan for wheat, feed grains, cotton and rice, but it failed by a vote of 48–42.[14] Boschwitz and Boren also brought their decoupling proposal to a floor vote and it failed narrowly.

The commodity groups exercised considerable influence in the Senate debate (Guither, 1986, p. 89). In addition to the strong impact of the combined sugar producer and corn sweetener lobby on sugar policy, the wheat and corn groups achieved a two-year target price freeze, the milk producers prevented a target price drop (though they were unable to gain acceptance of their paid diversion programme), and the rice producers got a marketing loan. The peanut and tobacco programmes did not even come up in the Senate debate.

House Agriculture Committee
The House Agriculture Committee considered the entire farm bill first in sub-committees, each of which conducted their own hearings (during February, March and April), and wrote up their own sections of the Committee bill. The Wheat, Soybeans and Feed Grains Sub-committee, under the chairmanship of Congressman (and Majority Whip) Tom Foley, had the most difficult task in its deliberations as its programmes were the most controversial, most costly and involved the most states and producers (Guither, 1986, p. 39).

No commodity programme was seriously challenged in either sub-committee or committee. Support levels constituted the principal issues. Congressman Foley came up with a general proposal in his sub-committee which survived the full Committee to set loan rates between 75 and 85 per cent of average domestic price over a five-year period (Guither, 1986, p. 42). But the loan rate could not be lowered by more than 5 per cent in any one year unless the market price had not risen above the loan rate by at least 5 per cent, in which case the Secretary of Agriculture could reduce the loan rate by an additional 20 per cent. This proposal also required that wheat producers idle 30 per cent of their cropland and that feed grain producers idle 20 per cent. Considerable sentiment appeared for mandatory production controls and the marketing loan. There was some support for targeting benefits through different levels of target prices for different classes of producers.

The final Committee bill did not make major changes in existing programmes. The Foley proposal for loan rates was adopted for wheat and feed grains and target prices for these commodities were frozen for two years. Strong 'sod-buster' and 'swamp-buster' provisions were inserted, along with provisions to create a 40 million acre paid conservation reserve. At the last minute, the Committee accepted a proposal by Representative Berkley Bedell (Democrat, Iowa) for a referendum on 'voluntary' production controls (*CQA*, 1985, p. 530). The industry favoured paid dairy diversion and herd buy-out was accepted over a simple price cut. The sugar and peanuts programmes were preserved intact. The Secretary of Agriculture was given considerable authority to lower the loan rates for cotton and rice to make them competitive on the export market. The Committee authorized funds for export enhancement.

House floor debate
The full House debated the farm bill between 26 September and 8 October. Most of the Committee recommendations survived, though there were some interesting challenges, both by those who wanted to spend more and others who wanted to spend less. An attempt to lower the sugar price support failed after one hour of debate, so strong was the sugar and corn sweetener lobby. An attempt to kill the dairy diversion programme also failed. Two-tiered target prices were narrowly rejected. A proposal to lower target prices generally did not pass. The referendum on mandatory acreage controls came up again and was only defeated after heavy lobbying by the administration and agriculture organizations. (CQA, 1985, p. 531).

Unsuccessful efforts were made to change tobacco and peanut programmes significantly. Generous food stamps provisions were included to ensure the support of urban representatives. Commodity groups exercised strong influence in the House debate and worked closely together to influence the outcome.

House–Senate conference
The Senate and House conference members met between 5 December and 14 December to shape the final farm bill, which became known as the Food Security Act of 1985. The administration, concerned about increased farm expenditures implied by both House and Senate bills, lobbied strongly to keep costs down. In a letter to conference participants, the new OMB director, James Miller, argued against a target price freeze lasting more than one year and asked for authority to make 5 per cent annual reductions thereafter. He also asked for a milk price cut with no assessments or dairy diversion programmes. Finally, he argued for executive discretion in limiting farm programme outlays to $50 billion over the fiscal year 1986–88 period (Gurither, 1986, p. 101–2). During the conference, Secretary of Agriculture Block was usually close by to influence the deliberations. The President himself met with the conference leadership to discuss what was acceptable.

The conference made a pretty even compromise between the Senate and

House bills. The Senate bill was more closely followed for wheat, cotton, rice and sugar while the House bill was more closely followed on dairy, wool, peanuts and soybeans. Final feed grains and trade provisions reflected about equally the influence of each chamber. More specifically, target prices were frozen for two years, with reductions of 2, 3 and 5 per cent in subsequent years, at the discretion of the Secretary of Agriculture. Loan rates were generally reduced and set in the future according to formula, with increased discretion given to the Secretary of Agriculture. Tough 'sod-buster' and 'swamp-buster' provisions survived, as did mandatory set-asides and the paid conservation reserve. A new and little-noticed decoupling provision was inserted to freeze the bases and yields for deficiency payments based on 1980–5 averages as a cost control measure (Guither, 1986, p. 114). The Secretary of Agriculture received the authority to supplement foreign sales with negotiable PIK certificates for cotton and rice should the loan rate not be competitive. A whole-herd buy-out was approved for dairy and the paid diversion was eliminated. Milk prices would be reduced by stages. Sugar, tobacco and peanuts programmes were continued basically unchanged.

7.3.7 Assessment

The final 1985 Food Security Act was approved on 18 December. The vote was much more strongly affirmative than the 1981 farm bill, with a margin of 55–38 in the Senate and 325–96 in the House. Even though more options, such as targeting and mandatory acreage controls, had been debated than in 1981, passage was smoother and existing programmes survived with smaller challenges. The commodity lobbies seemed more united than in 1981 and even more influential as a result. The perceived crisis in farming played a major role in limiting the congressional attacks on farm programmes. In the Senate, the large number of Republican legislators up for re-election in 1986 also played a role in sustaining existing programmes. The media galvanized public support for farmers with a series of features on the 'farm crisis' which generally gave the viewer the impression that all farmers were going out of business (Bonnen, 1987, p. 30). Three movies based on the theme of agrarian troubles received wide public attention: '*Places in the Heart*', '*The River*', and '*Country*'. The testimony of the three movie heroines, Sally Fields, Sissy Spacek and Jessica Lange before a Congressional committee, along with Jane Fonda, was a national media event. Some role in limiting the opposition may also have been played by the temporarily reduced farm costs for 1984, as a result of the 1983 drought.

The 1985 Food Security Act reflected the same qualities of bargaining described by government politics and partisan mutal adjustment paradigms as the 1981 farm bill had done before. However, in 1985, the process worked more smoothly because the commodity groups seemed more united and the farm programme opponents muted their attacks. The final bill reflected the national consensus that farm programmes should be more market-orientated to reduce costs and to increase exports. There were elements in the bill which satisfied the administration, congress, commodity groups and the urban coalition. But no group got all it wanted. Intensity of interest was important, as evidenced by the commodity groups' success. General public misinformation about the nature of the farm crisis and about the way commodity programmes operated worked to sustain narrow commodity interests. The budget pressures, though they were stronger than in 1981, were still not influential enough to cause significant overhaul of any commodity programmes. However, they were strong enough to induce a first step toward decoupling and reform of the deficiency payments system with the freezing of eligible bases and yields.

As indicated earlier, administration efforts to restrain agricultural spending were weakened by Assistant Secretary William Lesher's resignation at the beginning of the legislative debate. While Secretary Block lobbied forcefully for administration proposals, USDA influence was often overshadowed by the team of Lesher and former Under-Secretary Richard Lyng, who consulted privately with Congressional leaders, particularly Bob Dole. Though Congress wrote the final Food Security Act, a working group from the various USDA agencies (particularly the offices of budget, economic analysis and the Economic Research Service) exercised influence at all stages of the legislative process in setting parameters of acceptability for the administration. This group had considerable leeway in that it did not have to work every new idea through the bowels of the bureaucracy. It fought to get the largest reductions in target prices and loan rates. It had a strong antipathy toward any acreage reductions, reflecting in part the influence of agri-business. It wanted to restore supply–demand balance. In its arguments to Congress, this group stressed how government programmes did not benefit mainstream farmers; that only 15 per cent of the payments were going to those most seriously distressed. With considerable help from agri-business, it was instrumental in beating back the Harkin–Gephardt threat of supply controls.

7.4 US AGRICULTURAL REFORM EVALUATED

There has been some reform in US agricultural policy in the 1980s. Nothing was changed in the 1981 farm bill which one could regard as reform. The PIK programme and the paid dairy diversion also do not fulfil the conditions of working to remove the underlying incentives toward overproduction or to promote greater equity in farm programme benefits. However, the freezing of the bases and yields for deficiency payments in the 1985 Food Security Act provided a significant step toward decoupling farm benefits from production and hence constitutes reform. The creation of the 40 million acre conservation reserve and the tough 'sod-buster' and 'swamp-buster' provisions also can be considered as reform in that they deal with overproduction in more than a passing way. The provisions lowering loan rates to market clearing levels seem consistent with reform, but the maintenance of high target prices is not. The evidence presented in this chapter provides insights about why there has been some reform, and why there has not been more.

What seems most striking is how biased the US agricultural policy process is toward maintaining the status quo or – at most – moving very incrementally. Looking at the situation first through the lenses of the government politics paradigm, one sees power deeply divided, requiring a new proposal to go through a large number of steps before it becomes law, each involving bargaining among diverse interests. Enormous bargaining costs are incurred in trying to build winning coalitions for change all the way through the process. The situation is exacerbated by the comprehensiveness of the final farm bill, reflecting a delicate balance of interests. Any major change in policy threatens this balance. One element of this balance – urban support of farm programmes in return for farm support of food stamps – has become especially important. Farm interests were able to maintain a strong urban base to stave off reform efforts in both 1981 and 1985 by supporting more generous funding for food stamps.

Another factor retarding change is that the participants in the critically important initial bargaining steps in the House and Senate Agriculture Committees, where the farm bill is formulated, tend to come largely from agricultural constituencies which have a vested interest in present policies. As explained by public choice theory, the members of Congress with the greatest electoral incentive to serve on the Agricultural Committees are those from agricultural districts. These legislators have strong reasons to maintain current commodity programmes. Public choice theory also provides insights about why non-agricultural Members of Congress have little electoral incentive to vote against current commodity programmes. There are no votes to be gained by opposing farmers because of the agrarian ethos and stable low food prices. Farm district members carry the day, because they are better positioned and have strong feelings about the outcome, and because there is no very strong countervailing force.

The rules for bargaining also work to maintain the status quo and to frustrate reform. The constitutional separation of power between the US executive and legislative branches of government has allowed Congress to ignore two presidential farm bill proposals which contained significant elements of reform. The openness of the process, while maximizing access by inviting information and even farm bill proposals from the outside, tends to contribute to decisional overload, which obstructs reform. During the 1985 farm bill debate, the Agricultural Committees, overwhelmed with lobbyists and different proposals, could not give adequate attention to promising new ideas such as the Boschwitz–Boren decoupling plan.

The organizational process paradigm also is useful for explaining the resistance to change in the policy process. The House and Senate Agriculture Committees and particularly the House sub-committess have very parochial perspectives, which make them unable to deal very effectively with the broader national interest. They tend to 'crisis-cope' and react to the immediate political and economic situation. They do not easily make decisions based on the analysis of national interest and are not particularly good at looking ahead. A great deal of satisficing goes on in the Congressional Agriculture Committees. That is to say, they do not consider many alternatives and look merely for an acceptable solution, not necessarily the best one. The options normally considered are variants of the present standard operating procedures (SOPs). Adapting SOPs has the advantage of minimizing uncertainty, which organizations abhor.

The outside political inputs have been heavily tilted against agricultural policy reform and this is well explained by public choice theory. The lobbies with the largest stake which are thus the best financed and most active are the commodity groups and agri-business which have a strong interest in preserving the benefits (rents) provided by present programmes. Consumer, environmental and agricultural alternatives lobbies are more diverse and have a lesser stake, and hence are less effective. The media's incentives to sensationalize, oversimplify and personalize have led to coverage of agricultural issues not particularly conducive to reform.

The political environment has not appeared very favourable to reform either. At the time of the 1981 farm bill debate, farm programme costs and surpluses did not seem much of an issue. The main concern was to help farmers out of their cost–price squeeze. By 1985, surpluses, farm programme costs and declining exports did exert significant pressures for reform. But, of course, these pressures were counterbalanced by strong political pressures to help the farmer out of a major debt crisis.

The reform which did take place in 1985 occurred primarily because of vastly increased agricultural spending since 1980, while the federal budget deficit increased. This put the farm lobby on the defensive, forcing it to adjust to protect its more important interests. It also strengthened the hand of the administration which was ideologically unsympathetic to farm programmes. The administration was able to transcend the USDA bureaucracy and prepare a farm bill proposal which would have dramatically changed agricultural policy. Unfortunately, the administration overplayed its hand and submitted a bill outside the acceptable political parameters in Congress, causing the policy initiative to shift to the less reform-minded Congress.

Overall, the analytical framework developed in Chapter 1 has proved effective in explaining the outcome of the 1981 and 1985 farm bills. Its greatest limitation lies in explaining the Reagan Administration Farm Bill proposals which went to Congress in 1981 and 1985. We had expected the administration proposals to reflect a compromise between the USDA bureaucracy and the political appointees of the President. In fact, both bills sent to Congress by the administration represented triumphs for the Reagan political appointees and ideology in that they proposed a free market economy for agriculture with the elimination of target prices and loan rates. The administration imposed its will because it could isolate the USDA bureaucracy from farm bill formulation. The administration position can perhaps be explained in terms of public choice; the political threat presented by the farm lobby in presidential elections is so small that little incentive exists to sacrifice ideology for farmer support. However, one cannot easily explain why the administration ignored the political climate in Congress, only for its proposals to be 'dead on arrival'. Perhaps the administration postured as part of a confrontational bargaining strategy designed to elicit concessions from Congress. It is not self-evident, though, that the administration strategy got farm bills more favourable to Reagan's wishes than if legislation more acceptable to Congress had been proposed.

7.5 DEVELOPMENTS SINCE THE 1985 FOOD SECURITY ACT

The provisions of the 1985 Food Security Act have remained largely intact at the time of writing (March 1988). The Conservation Reserve has removed millions of acres from production. The freezing of bases and yields has worked to prevent growth in the production of agricultural commodities. However, it has had an unintended effect of preventing acreage shift to profitable soybean production as farmers plant corn (maize) to preserve their allotted bases. Target prices were cut by 2 per cent for 1988, as specified in the Act. They were cut by an additional 1.4 per cent by the executive-legislative reconciliation reached in November 1987 to prevent the across-the-board government spending cuts mandated by the Gramm-Rudman-Hollings Act (*CQA*, 1987, p. 398). They will be cut by an additional 3 per cent in 1989 and 5 per cent in 1990.

Some additional measures towards decoupling have been added since the 1985 Food Security Act. For instance, in the fiscal 1988 Reconciliation Bill, Congress approved a '0-92' programme, for 1988 and 1989 allowing wheat and feed grain producers to receive 92 per cent of projected income subsidies on land taken out of production (*CQ Weekly Report* (*CQWR*), 9 January 1988, p. 73). Previously, farmers had to plant 50 per cent of their base acreage to be eligible for deficiency payments.

To deal with the still serious debt problem, President Bush, in his first budget (final year 1990), has called for a $1.4 billion cut in commodity programmes. Two proposals are reported to be under serious consideration in the OMB: cutting target prices 5 per cent per year; and lowering base acreage by 15 per cent (*CQWR*, 4 March 1989, p. 444). The second proposal has the advantage of allowing farmers to plant certain alternative crops on land removed from their base, which would allow them to recover some of their lost income support payments, and to respond better to market conditions. There seems to be a division in the new administration between the new Director of the OMB, Richard Darman, who wants commodity programmes overhauled in 1989 as part of a comprehensive budget package, and the New Secretary of Agriculture, Clayton Yeutter, who has suggested that Congress might want to extend the 1985 Food Security Act for a year 'with few if any changes' until after a trade agreement (*CQWR*, 4 March 1989, p. 444). Yeutter has suggested that, alternatively, Congress could 'do a full-scale farm bill next year for four years with the expectation that there will have to be modifications in a very major way a year later (*CQWR*, 4 March 1989, p. 444). This division is not surprising from the perspective of our analytical framework.

Considerable sentiment exists in the Senate, where nine of the 19 members of the Agriculture Committee are up for re-election in 1990, to delay reconsideration of the 1985 Food Security Act. This sentiment is not widely shared in the House, where members have to run for election every two years. Another political dynamic is at work in that some Congressional agricultural leaders want to avoid extending the current law until 1991. They believe that going to the floor twice in two years squanders agriculture's scant political capital (*CQWR*, 4 March 1989, p. 444). Consensus does exist among the forces supportive of agriculture in both Senate and House and among the farm lobby to oppose any action to reconsider commodity programmes in 1989. These groups have every reason to fear that agricultural interests will fare far less well if farm policy is examined in a budget debate rather than in a farm bill debate where the agricultural committees would have the policy initiative.

7.6 THE 1990 FARM BILL AND THE PROSPECTS FOR REFORM

The outlook for far-reaching reform in the farm bill debate, whether in 1990 or 1991, does not look especially promising at the time of writing. The economic trends do not look very favourable. Commodity programme costs have declined dramatically, partly because of the 1988 drought. At the same time, exports have increased largely because of export subsidies and the sharp decline in the value of the dollar. Stocks are also down, mainly because of the drought, but also because of the success of the conservation reserve and other programmes removing land from production and because of increased exports. The declining cost of farm programmes removes much of the pressure for agricultural policy reform caused by the continuing US budget deficit. However, the improved economic situation of farmers reduces the public sympathy evident during the 1985 farm bill debate.

There is a strong probability that current commodity programmes will be retained in the next farm bill with some changes at the margin to allow agriculture to 'do its share' in dealing with the budget deficit. There may be some further steps in the direction of decoupling payments from production. It will be easier to expand this trend than it was to begin it, because SOPs are now in place. However, there appears to be little demand for radical policy change. In the absence of such a demand, business will proceed pretty much 'as usual' in the next farm bill debate for the House and State Agriculture Committees, which, as we have seen, have a strong interest in maintaining the status quo. The provisions of the 1985 Food Security Act have the distinct advantage in that they represent a mid-position between the two policy extremes of the free market and mandatory supply controls, both of which have very strong opponents.

The incentives for agricultural policy reform could be further reduced if the higher market prices associated with the 1988 drought continue through 1990. On the other hand, favourable weather could produce bumper crops, especially with the reduction of set-aside requirements, and dramatically increase farm programme costs. Such increases, by raising the spectre of the zero-sum game between agricultural interests and other claimants to government largess, would change the political calculus, to the advantage of the forces advocating reform. Commodity groups would tend to turn on each other, weakening their overall political power, while the voting majority in Congress would have a much stronger incentive to cut agricultural programmes. The hand of the OMB in restricting agricultural expenditures would be strengthened and other Cabinet agencies might increase the surveillance of USDA. Increased budgetary pressure would do other things. For instance, it would provide a 'blame shift' for a farm district Congressman to vote for reform. He or she will then have the excuse available 'we had to do something, I did the best I could'. It also could change the psychological predisposition of farm interests. Much more incentive would exist to go along with reform in the hope of influencing its direction, rather than to risk losing everything.

An agreement in the GATT negotiations might also change the political calculus to increase the probability of reform. Such an accord would bring groups supportive of trade liberalization into the commodity policy debate, where they would be pitted against commodity interests. It would also take the policy initiative away from the Agriculture Committees in that they would have to respond to an agreement formulated by others. These Committees, should they try to prevent changes in commodity programmes, could find themselves in the unenviable position of being blamed for sabotaging a beneficial trade agreement. With the bargaining context changed from agricultural policy to trade policy, the agricultural committees would also have to share legislative authority with other committees less favourable to farm interests.

A number of suggestions emerge from the experience of the 1981 and 1985 farm bills about how to go about achieving reform in the future. First, it seems necessary to have proposals fully developed well in advance of the farm bill debate. Once debate starts, the process becomes so overwhelmed that it cannot really consider any new ideas. Second, the chances of a reform proposal succeeding are vastly increased with some support from the farm community and agri-business. These interests are so well placed in the process as to necessitate cultivation of their support. Third, emphasis should be placed not so much on highly visible target prices, but on less visible things such as freezing bases and yields. The commodity groups will mobilize their full powers to prevent change on the visible things, particularly target price cuts which threaten their legitimacy. They may not do so on things that are not so obvious. Fourth, it would be very helpful to link reform proposals to the conservation rationale. A strong conservation constituency exists in the media, general public and Congress. Clearly, this link had importance for achieving approval for the conservation reserve, and the 'sod-buster' and 'swamp-buster' provisions. Finally, a need exists for much better public education. The public needs to be much better informed about where farm programme benefits are going now, which will require much better data on who gets government largess and how much.

NOTES

1. Income per farm for 1981 was expected to average approximately $24,000, nearly $1,000 less than 1979. Of the 1981 figure, only $7,950 was earned on the farm, with the remainder gleaned from outside jobs and other non-farm sources of income (*Congressional Quarterly Almanac* (*CQA*), 1981, p. 533).
2. Farm production was in fact up by 14 per cent in 1981.
3. David Stockman admitted that dividing the commodity lobby was a deliberate administration tactic to block budget-busting farm demands (*CQA*, 1985, p. 535).
4. The 1949 Agricultural Act set the price support level for basic commodities at 90 per cent of parity for 1950 and between 80 per cent and 90 per cent of parity for 1981 (see Cochrane and Ryan, 1976, p. 75).
5. The following discussion on Senate committee and floor action is indebted to *CQA*, 1981, pp. 541-3.
6. The dairy lobby was simmering because of spring congressional action cancelling a scheduled upward readjustment rate due to an enormous surplus. Under the current 80 per cent of parity level, the government expected to acquire more than 13 billion pounds of butter, cheese and dry milk. That was more than 10 per cent of total dairy production, and, according to USDA, more than the government could store (see *CQA*, 1981, p. 541).

7. For a discussion of the development of US sugar policy, see Mahler (1986).
8. See *CQA* 1982, pp. 351–2 and 361–2, for discussion of the PIK programmes.
9. For an excellent discussion of the political process leading up to the approval of the milk diversion, see Petit (1985, pp. 38–57).
10. Petit (1985, pp. 47–8) argues that the beef, poultry and pork producers were ineffective because they were slow to organize in opposition to the diversion. Most members of Congress had made up their minds by the time they were approached by the meat producers.
11. The budget constraint could have been more effective if Congress had been able to pass a budget resolution before August, when the Agriculture Committee's work was almost done.
12. The two defections were Senators Andrews (Republican, North Dakota), who had generally supported the Democrats in maintaining target prices, and McConnell (Republican, Kentucky), who voted with the Democrats to remove a budget hold on another bill to maintain tobacco supports, placed by Senators Boren (Democrat, Oklahoma) and Pryor (Democrat, Arkansas). It was ironic in that Senator Dole was the author of the tobacco plan.
13. Dole got some fiscally conservative Democrats to go along by including cost-saving devices to take land out of production. He brought rice producers along with three new provisions, including one to increase the land taken out of production. He won sugar producers with a plan to lower the cost of sugar imported into the country. He gave corn belt Senators a guaranteed income subsidy regardless of how market prices turned. Soybean farmers got a flat $40 per acre, and sunflower producers got $35 per acre.
14. Marketing loans imply that the farmer sells his product for whatever price he can get on the market, with the government making up the difference between the market price and the loan rate. Marketing loans are thinly disguised export subsidies.

PART IV

INTERNATIONAL ASPECTS OF AGRICULTURAL POLICY REFORM

8 · INTERNATIONAL POLICY REFORM AND THE TRADING SYSTEM

8.1 INTRODUCTION

Reform of domestic agricultural policies in the USA and the European Community is intimately linked to another aspect of policy change. Impetus has developed in recent years to reform the international trading system for agricultural products. This has reached its peak in the current Uruguay Round of GATT negotiations, which started in September 1986 and is due to finish at the end of 1990. The push for reform of the trade system reflects a growing dissatisfaction with the performance of the world market for agricultural products, adding to the cost of domestic farm programmes. Minor disputes in farm trade have threatened to escalate into major trade conflicts reaching far beyond agriculture, and the resulting effect on US–EC and US–Japan bilateral relationships has hindered other aspects of foreign policy.

The experience of both the EC and the USA in reforming their agricultural policies has been heavily conditioned by these developments in international markets. The trading system and its performance have influenced the political and economic environment in which domestic policy is set. This is particularly true of the behaviour of world prices. Much of domestic policy has been premised on the unstable and 'unrealistic' level of world prices for agricultural goods. Importers impose variable levies to keep a stable domestic price level, or organize trade through state purchasing agencies which achieve similar objectives. Exporters typically use purchasing agencies to guarantee a market for domestic producers, and then find various ways of bridging the gap between the domestic floor price and that on international markets. The more world market prices are depressed, the more determined are importers to defend domestic producers and the more energetic the exporters become in finding ways to sell abroad. What has now become obvious is that such domestic policies in the agricultural sector of the major trading countries play the dominant role in determining the level and stability of international prices in temperate zone and competitive tropical agricultural products. Prices are depressed as a result of aggressive dumping of surpluses, and by the denial of import access as profitable commercial markets are closed to bolster internal farm programmes.

Levels of protection for agricultural products rose markedly over the period 1983–6, largely as a result of falling world prices. Moreover, the high leve! ~f agricultural protection embodied in domestic programmes became widely publicized as a consequence of studies by the OECD (1987; updated in OECD, 1988) and the US Department of Agriculture (USDA 1987; updated in USDA 1988a). Figure 8.1 shows the development of the aggregate level of protection, as measured by the USDA's calculation of the producer subsidy equivalent (PSE), since the early 1980s. The PSE gives an indication of the producer subsidy necessary to have replaced the mix of policy instruments actually used. For non-agricultural products, tariff protection is generally in the order of 7–12 per cent in the OECD countries. Adding in various domestic subsidies could give a PSE for non-farm goods of perhaps 10–15 per cent. For agriculture, in the major OECD countries, the level of implied producer subsidy is generally much higher, reaching nearly 80 per cent in Japan but exceeding 40 per cent in both the USA and the EC. This gap between the levels of agricultural and non-agricultural protection has helped to focus attention on agricultural trade issues. As a result, it has become widely accepted that reform of the agricultural trading system requires major changes in the domestic farm policies of the major trading countries.

The EC and the USA share a strong interest in properly functioning international markets for farm commodities, just as the rest of the world shares an interest in the reform of US and EC internal agricultural policies. Agreement between the USA and the EC is an essential condition for the success of international trade policy reform. Bilateral trade frictions are also less likely to emerge in a world of effective GATT trade rules and respected dispute settlement procedures. Trade reform therefore has a broader constituency than domestic reform but is strongly linked to it. The process of trade reform is therefore worth examining both in its own right, as an important dimension of international agricultural policy, and as a process parallel to that of domestic reform.

Concern about the deterioration of the international trade system is not new. Agricultural trade has been characterized by unstable prices and government intervention for decades – if not centuries. Attempts to regularize this important part of trade have been made within the GATT on several occasions in the past, but without success. What is largely new is the explicit link between the domestic and international reform process. Governments increasingly recognize domestic policy changes as necessary for improving the trading system. For the first time these domestic programmes have been placed on the international negotiating table. Similarly, the strengthening of GATT rules on agricultural trade is clearly premised on domestic policy adjustments. At the domestic political level, support for internal reform may hinge on the existence of parallel changes in other countries.

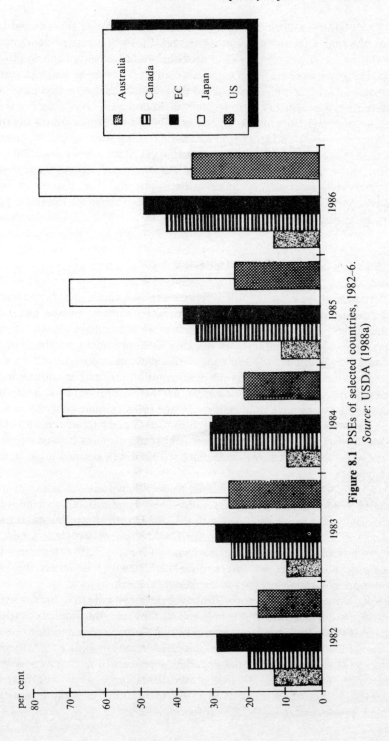

Figure 8.1 PSEs of selected countries, 1982–6.
Source: USDA (1988a)

This chapter will explore some of the links between the domestic and international reform processes. Although it does not attempt a detailed analysis of decision-making on agricultural matters within the GATT, the chapter discusses the international context in which national reform decisions are taken. The first part of the chapter describes the nature of the international pressures on domestic reform and past attempts to deal with the issues of agricultural trade. This is followed by some exploration of the current attempts to reform the agricultural trading system, and the positions of the USA and the EC in those negotiations. The chapter concludes with some suggestions on the relevance of the analytical structure of previous chapters to the issue of international reform. The extent to which international reform is necessary for the achievement of domestic policy change is discussed in the next chapter.

8.2 INTERNATIONAL REFORM

International agricultural policy reform can be examined with the aid of a framework not unlike that used in earlier chapters for the analysis of domestic policy change. Longer-term economic trends influence the world market for farm products, as do shorter-term shocks to the economic system. Economic trends and shocks also play an important role in setting the political agenda for international negotiations, and in influencing the negotiating positions and strategies of the various international policy actors. Decisions have to be made on trade rules; bargains have to be struck on market access and the use of subsidies; standards and health-related trade restrictions have to be agreed; and trade disputes between countries have to be settled. All this takes place within a well-defined organizational framework.

It is tempting to treat international trade policy positions as extensions of domestic agricultural policy decisions – the same officials and politicians performing the same functions with the same motivations, but taking some decisions in Geneva rather than in Washington or Brussels. Under this interpretation, international trade policy is merely an extension of the domestic policy process. International agreements will reflect the lowest common denominator consensus between national positions influenced primarily by domestic factors. Countries certainly will strive for consistency between domestic and trade policy decisions and the implementation of international agreements commonly relies on implementation through national policy. In that sense the distinction is blurred. Moreoever, countries use the international negotiating process to pursue national ends, and some nations are sufficiently influential to be able to impose their agendas on international meetings. But the national and the international policy processes are essentially different.

The differences between domestic and trade policy reform processes show up in many ways. First, the objectives are different. Domestic reform seeks the improvement of the workings of domestic farm policy, regardless of the impact on other countries. External influences may be taken into account indirectly, in that they help shape economic trends, economic shocks, political developments and the political environment in which decisions are taken, but they are not central to the reform decision. Trade policy reform seeks the improvement of the trading system and, hence, is strongly influenced by international factors. It can be consistent with outcomes unacceptable to the domestic interests. The extent to which domestic interests constrain trade policy will vary from country to country, but trade policy objectives will often conflict with domestic priorities.

Besides the different objectives, domestic and trade reform involve different constituencies, different bureaucracies, different political alignments, and different bargaining processes. The main constituencies involved in domestic reform are the farm population and the taxpayers. For reasons discussed in earlier chapters, consumer interests rarely play a major role in farm policy decisions. Trade reform is of direct interest to the non-agricultural sector, primarily the food industry and the non-farm manufacturing interests, and to the export-orientated part of the farm sector. Resistance to trade reform springs mainly from those that might be hurt by imports under more liberal market access. Consumers should also favour trade reform, but their pressure groups seem as silent on this issue as on domestic reform.

The difference in constituencies is mirrored in the bureaucratic process. Agricultural ministries take the lead in domestic reform under pressure from other departments such as national treasuries, but have a more subsidiary role in trade talks, except where export interests dictate an active stance. Trade departments take the lead in trade talks, defining the agenda and the posture but relying on specialist departments for detailed positions on issues.

The way in which trade policy is handled within the bureaucracy differs from country to country. In the USA, the main responsibility for trade matters lies with the office of the US Trade Representative: in the EC, a sub-committee of the Foreign Ministers Council, called the '113 Committee' after the article of the Treaty of Rome which covers foreign trade, deals with trade negotiations on behalf of the Community. Individual member states have ministries of external trade, which provide the support for the 113 Committee. How these trade ministries relate to their agricultural counterparts is crucial to the formation of policy.

Finally, since international trade is regulated by a set of rules established by the GATT, policy reform implies international negotiations leading to agreement to change the rules. The bargaining process for international negotiations is different from that in domestic politics. Though some nations clearly have more influence than others, none is strong enough to impose its will on the international system. The principle of national sovereignty implies that changes in trading rules cannot be forced on a nation without its consent. Hence, international agreements to change the rules must reflect a high degree of consensus which, in turn, requires a willingness to compromise on the part of national negotiators. The broader interest in reforming the rules may imply sacrificing narrow domestic agricultural interests – though past experience suggests that this effect is rarely strong.

8.3 PRESSURES ON THE POLICY PROCESS

Economic trends and shocks, together with political developments, set the scene for domestic policy reform. The same can be said for reform of the international trading system. In many cases these are the same pressures; in others they differ from purely national influences. To explore these influences it is useful to consider the functions of a trading regime. In purely economic terms, trade allows a country, and hence individuals within that country, to improve their well-being. Individuals can buy foreign goods when they are cheaper than those available from domestic firms and they can sell into more profitable markets overseas. In addition, flows of capital can seek out the best investment prospects, rather than being limited to national borders. Impediments to such free flows of goods and capital – and increasingly to services – reduce the potential benefits of trade.

Trade does bring with it certain problems. Not least among these is the instability either inherent or induced in international markets. Fluctuating world market prices for agricultural products are an example of such potentially harmful instability. Exchange rates that bounce around at the apparent whim of the international financial markets are another source of problems. Dumping by governments attempting to shift a domestic problem of oversupply onto international markets provides a constant hazard. Sudden closure of a market abroad can also bring severe problems to the firms that have supplied that market. For all these reasons and more, governments treat trade with a measure of caution: it is an indispensable part of economic life but needs to be kept under control.

The degree and nature of this control is the essence of the 'trading system'. The present system includes broad agreements not to intervene in trade; to refrain from taxing goods as they cross borders; to deregulate capital flows; and to avoid any discrimination between domestic and foreign goods. But the system also includes agreements to regulate trade; to define import quotas; to grant preferences to certain countries; to respect minimum prices; to control exchange rates within agreed bands; to countervail against dumping; and to impose standards and quality controls on trade flows. The trading system is a mixture of freedom and control in much the same way that domestic economies blend private enterprise and public regulation.

The economic pressures to improve the trading system arise when the balance between the elements of the system is lost. In agriculture the overregulation of trade had denied many countries the advantage of international specialization. This negative impact on growth and living standards is felt by people outside agriculture. Consumers are denied access to reasonably priced food, and non-agricultural sectors are priced out of their markets by higher input and factor costs. Exchange rates are distorted, and countries with the resources to produce foodstuffs at reasonable prices cannot earn the foreign exchange to buy industrial goods from other countries. The broad trend since the early 1960s has been towards an opening up of international markets and an increase in trade flows. The situation in agriculture has slowed that process.

It was suggested in Chapter 1 that economic trends have their greatest impact on decisions if they are in line with political developments. In this case, the economic and the political tides are moving in the same direction. Deregulation at home has been accompanied by freer international trade. The same arguments for a more market-orientated domestic economy spill over onto the international agenda. Many countries have developed an aim to be 'internationally competitive', and that seems to require opening the domestic economy to imports as well as internal restructuring.

This prevailing political mood clashes directly with the desire to control the level of agricultural incomes and those of the rural population. The inherent conflict of interest among countries in international agricultural markets will continue as long as governments remain directly involved in managing the markets for domestic producers. Ultimately the issue is the reconciliation of domestic policies with the requirements of an international trading system which has brought widespread benefits to the world economy – and indeed to world agriculture. The same issue has haunted previous attempts at multilateral discussion of agricultural trade. To what extent can national agricultural policies be discussed directly, as opposed to being held sacrosanct? The Uruguay Round constitutes a bold move to change the rules. It removes the presumption that domestic policy considerations could dictate trade policies even when those policies fall out of line with GATT procedures. This would imply a willingness to bring national policies into accord with the needs of trade relations. Such a move would have been unthinkable only a few years ago.

In this quest for global responsibility in domestic policy-making, the USA and the EC have particularly important roles to play. Though other countries such as Japan, Canada and Australia will be deeply involved in the process, it is difficult to see any outcome which does not effectively reconcile the interests of Europe and the USA. The USA and EC must agree on the agenda and the pace of any negotiations on agricultural trade and domestic policy. It is this agreement which is at present proving elusive.

8.4 GROUP AND NATIONAL INTERESTS

National agricultural sectors are linked primarily by world markets, including the market for farm products, agricultural inputs and new technology. The most direct way in which one country's policy can influence another's is by changing the price level on world markets and thus the profit from exports or the cost of imports. If reform implies a reduction in domestic levels of protection, then the a priori presumption would be a cut-back in production and an expansion of consumption. This would imply a reduction in exports or an increase in imports, both leading to higher world prices. For foreign farmers dependent upon world price levels, these higher prices would be beneficial, whether they were selling to domestic consumers in competition with imports or shipping products into export markets. More often, farmers would feel the benefit less directly. In so far as government policy acts to support domestic market prices, the impact would show up first in programme costs. Higher prices would reduce export subsidy expenditures and cut levy receipts. Those markets protected by import quotas would find the quota rents reduced, with the incidence of the reduction depending upon the method of allocation or sale of the quota rights.

The impact of higher world prices is likely to be felt most directly by exporting country governments concerned by the cost of export subsidies. In effect, they receive a gratuitous decrease in their own protection levels through the actions of others. The political cost of domestic reform may be reduced, though the economic benefit from reform also declines. Importing countries would also find the prospect of domestic reform less daunting, so long as the rise in the world price is not strong enough to raise fears of shortage. This complementarity among reforms in various countries can act as a powerful political argument for co-ordination of policy change.

The other side of the same coin is that a rise in world prices takes some of the pressure off domestic policy in other countries. Reform may be easier, but it also seems less urgent. The budget cost of farm programmes is an administrative embarrassment when on the increase. Agricultural ministries may have to seek supplementary appropriations during a fiscal year, or argue for increases from one year to the next. The focus of all other departments is brought to bear on the profligate ministry, and everyone becomes an expert at cutting the programmes. By contrast, when world prices give agricultural budgets a break, the interest in farm policy quickly wanes.

Awareness of the interdependencies among farm policies – through the impact on world prices – has increased in recent years. Various studies have appeared which model world markets for several countries and commodities. These studies include specific parameters for domestic policy behaviour and for the links between world market prices and domestic price response. All of these studies point to an increase in world prices as protection in the industrial countries is reduced.[1] The magnitude of this price impact differs from one study to the next, depending upon such imponderables as the Soviet and Chinese response to changes in world market prices, as well as on more researchable issues, such as whether US set-asides really control supply.

Despite these differences, the overall picture is reasonably uncontroversial. World prices for sugar, dairy products, beef and rice are severely depressed by the actions of developed countries, by 30–50 per cent. For cereals the picture is less clear, since a part of the demand for cereals reflects high levels of support for dairy and beef production. Without that demand, cereal markets would weaken. Nevertheless, world cereal prices would probably rise if support were removed from both arable and livestock enterprises, along with cereal-based products such as flour. By contrast, those animal feed products such as soybean meal, corn gluten meal and cassava pellets that depend for their attractiveness as feed ingredients on high domestic cereal prices could face a falling demand. World prices could be reduced considerably for some of these products.

One can explain this notion of depressed world prices in terms of domestic policies. Some part of each country's price support goes towards offsetting the impact of the policy of others. And some part of one's own policy impact acts to depress the prices for farmers abroad – or increase the burden on foreign governments and foreign consumers as they maintain their farmers' incomes. The recent cross-commodity, cross-country models can indicate the magnitude of these impacts. One such set of estimates is shown in Table 8.1. The first column shows the proportion of the transfers under farm price support programmes which are 'needed' to offset the impact on world prices of the other listed countries. For the USA, Canada and the EC, about one-half of the support goes to offset the impact of other countries' policies. In addition, the EC and the USA each depress world prices for their own exports: a further part of price support is 'wasted' in this way. Australia and New Zealand would need transfers several times the present levels to offset the impact of other countries' policies; by contrast, Japan does not seem on these results adversely affected by the policies of others. The proportion of transfers to farmers which corresponds to potential losses by other farmers is shown in the second column of Table 8.1. Under this measure the policies of Australia, New Zealand, and Europe have a higher impact on others (as a proportion of domestic transfers) than do those of the USA and Japan.

It is clear that agricultural protection and price support have become

Table 8.1   External effects of price support transfers, selected countries, 1986–7 (percentage of transfers to producers).

	Offset by policies in other countries*	Loss of income by farmers abroad†
USA	43.0	39.2
Canada	73.8	60.1
EC	37.5	42.0
Other Western Europe	27.5	36.5
Australia and New Zealand	512.8	76.9
Japan	5.8	17.3

Source: Author's calculations based on Roningen and Dixit (1987).
*Percentage of transfer to producers in home country which is necessary to offset the policies in the other countries listed.
†Percentage of transfer to producer in home country which represents a loss to producers (or consumers and governments) in other countries listed.

trapped in a cycle of subsidy and counter-subsidy, with each policy premised on the existence of similar measures in other countries, but no country satisfied with the outcome. Under such circumstances one would expect that no country could afford to make a unilateral policy change in the direction of reducing protection. Given the political sensitivity of sharp reductions in farm income, policy reform needs a broad basis of support. Exposing one's farmers to depressed world prices could risk losing some of that support. By the same token, a reduction in protection in other countries would reduce this downside risk and make it easier to garner political support for changes in farm policies. As a consequence, the political argument for co-operation and co-ordination rests on a mutual dislike of the present situation and the need to act together.

The economic argument for co-ordination appears less clear-cut. Protection in one country depresses world prices and imposes costs on exporting countries, while benefiting importing countries. For these exporters to counter with their own protection, further depressing the price, is of doubtful economic advantage: in effect they keep up domestic prices at the expense of taxpayers and consumers, with much of the benefit going to the recipients of the subsidized exports. This means that exporters could gain in economic terms by unilaterally reducing export subsidies, and thus reducing the economic costs of their policy. If other exporters (or importers) could be persuaded to remove their protection at the same time, this would yield a further economic advantage, but such action would not be necessary to the achievement of economic gain. Unilateral reduction of support in each country is likely to bring the major benefits to the exporters. Importers, moreover, have rather little economic incentive to see other countries (both importers and exporters) reduce protection. Support for farmers overseas improves the terms of trade of those countries that must import feed and foodstuffs.

The economics of policy reform would therefore support independent action, even if such action is consistent with ongoing diplomatic and commercial pressures for the reduction in overseas protection. Except in the matter of world market stability, where co-ordinated action may prove necessary to achieve agreed goals, the economic case for domestic policy reform stands or falls on a country-by-country basis. The argument for international co-ordination is rooted in the politics of domestic policy reform.

8.5 THE GATT AND AGRICULTURAL TRADE

The institution most concerned with the conditions under which goods are traded internationally is the General Agreement on Tariffs and Trade (GATT). Set up after the Second World War, the GATT provides a set of rules which the 'contracting parties' agree to observe, and acts as a forum for the negotiation of changes in trade barriers. The basic propositions embodied in the GATT are plainly liberal in intention, emphasizing the mutual benefits of freer trade, outlawing export subsidies and quota restrictions, and encouraging mutual reductions in consolidated tariffs. The GATT preaches non-discrimination among member states through the extension to all other contracting parties of the market access granted to 'most favoured' nations – subject to defined exceptions for customs unions and developing countries. It allows for the settlement of disputes, for compensation and for trade sanctions against violators of the Agreement. Though originally orientated largely towards industrial countries of the OECD bloc, its membership has now expanded to include many developing countries and some centrally planned economies. Seven rounds of negotiations have been successfully completed since the inception of the GATT, which have led effectively to a low-tariff system for manufactured products in developed-country markets.

From the start, agriculture proved a problem area for the GATT system of more liberal trade. Agricultural policies were largely excluded from the Agreement's strictures against non-tariff restrictions on trade (Article 11), as a response to the feeling, particular in the USA, that domestic policy measures should not be subject to international limitations.[2] Primary products were also excluded from the general prohibition of export subsidies (Article 16). Although other parts of the Agreement do require that governments manage their domestic agricultural policies so as not to harm the legitimate interests of others, and oblige governments to consult on agricultural trade problems, these provisions have rarely been applied. Waivers were frequently sought to exempt particular policy actions from the GATT code. Most notable among these derogations was the waiver granted to the USA in 1955 which effectively removed the major elements of US agricultural policy from international scrutiny. More recently, the tacit acceptance by most countries of the Common Agricultural Policy of the EC has reinforced the notion of the primacy of domestic policy in international trade discussions.

One measure of agricultural trade problems is the number of complaints brought before the GATT in this area. Since 1976, there have been 17 occasions when a GATT panel has been appointed to look into an agricultural trade complaint, out of a total of 32 GATT cases over this period. Eleven of these 17 complaints involved objections against the EC, and included products ranging from pasta and wheat flour to poultry, citrus, beef, apples, sugar and animal feed. There are two main reasons why the EC is so often cited by trading partners: the widespread use of export subsidies (refunds) targeted by market and relatively unconstrained by spending curbs; and a switch from deficit to surplus in many products unaccompanied by a reduction in support prices to take account of that change. As a consequence, EC export (and import) policies have been under attack for two decades. The impact on non-agricultural trade relations has been a constant concern.

8.5.1 The legacy of past policies

The ineffectiveness of the GATT in dealing with illiberal elements of national agricultural policy has not prevented the incorporation of agricultural discussions in the various GATT rounds of trade negotiations. Though many of the important agricultural trade issues were not on the agenda, a modest degree of liberalization has been achieved through the reduction of tariffs and the establishment of tariff-free quotas for certain products. A number of tariffs on (at the time) minor traded goods were 'bound' in the Dillon Round of trade talks in the early 1960s, when the newly formed European Community negotiated the necessary changes in member state duties on imports from third countries. Many of these commodities, such as soybeans, protein meals and cassava, later became big-ticket items on international trade – to the discomfort of EC policy-makers.

In the Kennedy Round, later in the 1960s, a major divergence of views emerged about the nature of agricultural trade policy, with the USA arguing for a return to the GATT notion of a market-orientated trading system, and the EC generally favouring managed markets through commodity agreements. The EC proposed a temporary binding of support levels (relative to negotiated reference prices), but this was rejected by the USA as perpetuating protectionist policies in importing countries. Finally, an 'agricultural component' of the Kennedy Round was agreed, which included in particular an International Grains Arrangement (IGA) (1967), a modified version of earlier International Wheat Agreements. The stabilization provisions of the IGA had a short life, as surplus grain production pushed prices below the established minimum, and countries proved unwilling to hold domestic output in check.

In the next round of talks, usually known as the Tokyo Round, which was concluded in 1979, agriculture again appeared on the agenda. The underlying issue was still the extent to which agricultural trade should be subject to the same rules as trade in manufactured goods. Should markets be free or managed? Should domestic policies be the subject for negotiations? Should export subsidies be banned or otherwise controlled? Should quantitative trade barriers be phased out? And should importers be able to shield their markets from disruption? Disagreements on these fundamental issues persisted through the Tokyo Round, and prevented any substantial progress towards liberalization. Some quantitative restrictions were relaxed, two commodity agreements were concluded (for dairy products and for meat), neither endowed with instruments to stabilize markets, and an attempt was made to incorporate a code of conduct for export subsidies.

This last development, the attempt to bring agriculture within a set of rules governing export subsidies and countervailing duties, held out some promise. The Subsidies Code obliges countries to avoid export subsidies which lead to an 'inequitable' share in world markets or which undercut prices. However, the implementation of that code, through the repeated challenge within the GATT of certain practices (such as the EC's export refunds), has not been successful. Interpretation of such concepts as an 'equitable' market share leads inevitably to trade conflicts and can render meaningless the spirit of the original agreement.

Whether the GATT can improve its effectiveness in dealing with agricultural issues is likely to be put to the test in the current GATT round of negotiations, the Uruguay Round, which includes agriculture as a centrepiece. How far this initiative can proceed depends upon whether the parties concerned, particularly the EC and the USA, have confidence in the GATT mechanism for resolving trade issues in agriculture.

8.5.2 Preparation for the Uruguay Round of trade talks

The process of preparing both technically and politically for a reform of agricultural trade has been under way for some years. In November 1982, the GATT Council established a Committee of Trade in Agriculture (CTA) to look into the ways in which agricultural trade could be better handled within the GATT framework. Many of its proposals, tabled in November 1984, addressed the issue of the way in which existing GATT articles and codes could be applied more effectively. Particular attention was given to the implementation of Article XI, which allows quantitative restrictions on agricultural imports under certain circumstances, and Article XV, which condones export subsidies for primary products.

Meanwhile a parallel activity was going on in the Organization for Economic Co-operation and Development (OECD). Agricultural policies in OECD members have been studied by the Secretariat in the past and have been discussed in the Agriculture Committee. But unlike macro-economic policy, where such discussions of national policies have led to a degree of co-ordination, OECD discussions of agricultural policies have rarely gone beyond the descriptive. The OECD ministerial meeting in May 1982 gave the Secretariat a mandate to undertake

> an analysis of the approaches and methods for a balanced and gradual reduction in the protection of agriculture . . . an examination of relevant national policies and measures which have a significant impact on agricultural trade . . . [and] an analysis of the most appropriate methods for improving the functioning of the world agricultural market (OECD, 1987).

This initiative, known as the Trade Mandate, was to be supervised jointly by the committee on Agriculture and the Trade Committee. The Joint Committee reported to the Ministerial Council of the OECD the results of its study in May 1987.

The OECD interpreted the Mandate in an appropriately broad way, and looked at the whole range of domestic agricultural policies. Building on a quantitative measure of farm support used previously in the UN Food and Agriculture Organization, the OECD calculated Producer Subsidy Equivalents (and Consumer Subsidy Equivalents) for several member countries. Though countries with high levels of protection were less than enthusiastic with this attempt to quantify the effect of support policies, the Mandate Report represented a milestone in the discussion of agricultural trade. In what constituted an important political development, details of national policies were openly discussed for the first time in a quantitative framework, and trade impacts examined in an even-handed way. Subsequent decisions to update the calculations have suggested that countries find them useful as information for improved policy decisions.[3]

8.5.3 The Uruguay Round

The GATT effort culminated in the launching of the Uruguay Round in September 1986. The Punta del Este Declaration opened up the way for negotiations on all agricultural programmes that influence trade in farm products. The section on agriculture called for 'greater liberalization' and 'more operationally effective GATT rules and disciplines' regarding 'measures affecting import access and export competition'. It was made clear that the measures referred to included domestic policies as well as border measures. The inclusion of domestic support policies represented a new departure which recognized that domestic policy reform provides the key to progress in agricultural trade relations.

In May 1987, the OECD ministers confirmed their commitment to these negotiations but went further in advocating changes in domestic programmes towards a greater market orientation. The ministers called for concerted efforts to reform domestic farm policies with the long-run aim of allowing market forces to determine production patterns. Although short-term palliatives such as supply controls were accepted as useful, and adjustment assistance was considered desirable, the emphasis was on liberalization. Income objectives were to be dealt with in ways that did not distort trade patterns or impose undue costs on other countries. A high-level push to this process came from the Tokyo summit in 1986 and the Venice summit in 1987. The Toronto summit in 1988 confirmed the importance of progress in this area of international co-operation.

Even with the importance of this technical groundwork and with the significance of the political commitment, the most notable feature of the present negotiations has been a series of remarkable proposals tabled by the major participants. Countries were invited to submit, by the end of 1987, their ideas for the conduct of the negotiations and their proposals for the implementation of the aims of the Punta del Este Declaration, but the responses were more far-reaching than most observers would have expected. The USA responded first, by tabling a proposal in July 1987: the Cairns group and the EC followed with their own proposals in October 1987, together with a separate paper by Canada.[4] By February 1988, the Nordic countries and Japan had tabled papers outlining their respective positions, and a group of food-importing developing countries had held discussions to co-ordinate their ideas. The substance of the most significant of these proposals is indicated in Table 8.2

Seeking the 'high ground' in the debate, the USA made a radical proposal for the elimination of 'all policies which distort [agricultural] trade'. All such measures would be phased out over ten years following the Uruguay Round, i.e. by the year 2000. The US proposal would exempt certain domestic programmes considered to have only small effects on production and trade, such as domestic food programmes and international food aid, and farmer income supplements not linked to a farm's level of production. Progress towards liberalization would be measured by monitoring the changes in domestic support programmes with an aggregate indicator such as the PSE developed in the OECD. The proposal suggested credit for any policies introduced since the Punta del Este agreement that have contributed to reducing the imbalance on world markets. On the short term, the USA was silent, but the proposal recognized that GATT rules would need strengthening 'to reflect the trading environment that will exist at the end of the transition period'.

Table 8.2   Main elements in six GATT negotating proposals

United States (July 1987)
- – Eliminate trade-distorting subsidies over a period of 10 years
- – Remove all barriers to market access over a period of 10 years
- – Use a PSE-type measure for monitoring progress in liberalization

Cairns group (October 1987) (a)
- – Freeze present level of subsidies which distort trade
- – Reduce support by an agreed target amount over a period of 10 years
- – Introduce a new set of GATT rules for agriculture which would eliminate present 'exceptions' and prohibit trade-distorting subsidies
- – Use a PSE-type measure for monitoring progress

European Community (October 1987)
- – Take short-run co-ordinated action to stabilize major temperate-zone markets
- – Undertake balanced and significant cut in levels of support over an agreed period
- – Improve GATT rules to prevent backsliding
- – Use a 'PSE-type measure adjusted for supply control

Canada (October 1987) (b)
- – Eliminate all trade-distorting subsidies over an agreed period
- – Set interim target for, say, five years
- – Phase out of waivers and binding of access
- – Use a PSE-type measure with credit for supply control and omitting trade-neutral policies

Nordic Countries (December 1987)
- – Bind and reduce export and domestic subsidies
- – Reduce barriers to market access
- – Use a PSE-type measure as qualified in the Canadian proposal

Japan (February 1988)
- – Freeze present export subsidies
- – Phase out export subsidies over time and reduce trade-distoring effects of domestic subsidies
- – Negotiate improvements in market access
- – Use of a PSE-type measure is not needed

(a) Members of Cairns group are Argentina, Australia, Brazil, Canada, Chile, Columbia, Hungary, Indonesia, Malaysia, New Zealand, the Philippines, Thailand and Uruguay.
(b) Canada also endorsed the Cairns group proposal.

The emergence of the Cairns group in the run-up to the Punta del Este meeting, and its subsequent formulation of a proposal which falls somewhere between the EC and US positions, has been one of the most interesting developments in this round. The Cairns group proposal offered a similar view of steady reductions in protection over a ten-year period, but suggested a three-stage agenda. The first stage included a freeze in present subsidies which distort trade. The Canadian paper followed the lines of the Cairns group paper that introduced the notion of a five-year 'first phase' to the liberalization process, and was more explicit about the composition of the aggregate measure, for which the Canadians coined the name 'Trade Distortion Equivalent'. In the longer run, a new set of GATT rules would be developed which in effect removed present exceptions for agriculture. This would be followed by the phased reduction of these subsidies, using a PSE-type aggregate measure of support.

Like that of the Cairns group, the EC proposal emphasized the need for short-run actions, and was specific in calls for measures to firm up cereal, sugar and dairy prices. Like the US proposal, that of the EC endorsed the notion of an aggregate measure of support based on the OECD work, though modified to take account of supply control policies and exchange rate variations. The EC position included provision for a substantial decline in support levels, but did not endorse the notion of a zero target in support.

In contrast, to the exporters, the Nordic countries and Japan tabled more cautious proposals. Each included liberal elements, but carefully placed the onus on exporting countries to reduce subsidies and restore discipline in world markets. The Japanese proposal appeared unique in not endorsing the notion of an aggregate measure of support.

The trade negotiations continued in Geneva during 1988. The Agriculture Group met seven times during the year to try to reach agreement on the framework for negotiations.[5] In addition, two working groups were set up to look more closely at the issues of support measurement and health regulations. A group of developing countries produced a paper which spelled out the concerns of food-importing countries that world prices could rise as a result of trade liberalization in agricultural markets.[6] The additional papers tabled by the major protagonists proved just as important. In April, the Cairns group presented the results of its own meeting which had been held in Bariloche in February 1988. This meeting proposed a short-term programme of action to include both a freeze and a two-year phased reduction in support as a 'down-payment' on longer-term reform. The down-payment would ensure that changes to policy would be made during the negotiations rather than waiting until after their completion *News of the Uruguay Round (NUR)*, no. 16, 31 May 1988; Australian Bureau of Agricultural and Resource Economics 1988).

At the June meeting of the Agricultural Group, the EC presented papers which developed its earlier position. The EC elaborated on its 'short-term' measures in markets considered to be particularly distorted. Among the proposals was one to freeze PSEs (modified somewhat from the OECD version) at their 1984 level – a date which would have given full credit to the EC for CAP reforms and taken as a reference a period when the dollar was unusually strong. By the July meeting, the Cairns group had refined its down-payment proposal, and suggested 10 per cent reductions in support for the years 1989 and 1990 (*NUR*, no. 18, 2 August 1988). Unfortunately, a split developed in the ranks of the Cairns group, with Canada unable to go along with an Australian communication detailing these reductions – on the grounds that Canadian dairy policy would be jeopardized.

The meeting of the Agriculture Group in October saw three significant developments. The Japanese negotiators gave their approval to the use of an aggregate measure of support – at least on an experimental basis. The USA abandoned the simplicity of its July 1987 proposal by contemplating a freeze on support and protection for 1989 and 1990, providing that agreement could be reached at the Montreal Mid-term Review (December 1988) on the longer-term elimination of support. The new US paper also introduced a notion that had surfaced in the GATT committee on Trade and Agriculture and the US 1985 farm bill of converting non-tariff measures to tariffs (*NUR*, no. 20, 4 November 1988).

The USA and the EC appear to share an area of common ground upon which to build a lasting reform of their domestic farm policies. The common elements include a long-term commitment to a reduction in protection; an across-the-board approach to negotiating support reductions; a serious attempt to strengthen the rules governing agricultural trade; and, a commitment to the principle of multilateral processes and policy co-ordination. The long-term commitment to reducing agricultural protection constitutes a useful starting point. It is not, however, of much value without a mechanism for implementing such a commitment. In this respect the apparent acceptance by major GATT participants of the idea of an across-the-board approach to trade negotiations in agriculture provided a positive development.

The lack of constructive dialogue between the EC and the USA constituted the most serious problem faced by negotiators in 1988. The EC labelled the US 'zero-option' proposal unrealistic, but did not respond with any more realistic objective for support reduction. Instead, it emphasized the short-run measures in its own proposal, and avoided any early commitment to a target for reduction in support. It appeared to be more concerned to achieve international recognition for the first, already accomplished, painful steps towards reform of the CAP. US actions taken in the two years following Punta del Este, including an expansion of export subsidies (the Export Enhancement Programme) and a relaxation of set-aside requirements (ostensibly as a reaction to the 1988 drought) were seen as aggressive in contrast to the EC's attempts to take control of cereal production. Moreover, the EC seemed to have had little interest in negotiating with an outgoing administration and appeared willing to wait to see what changes the November 1988 presidential election would bring.

All this was seen on the other side of the Atlantic as typical European prevarication. The USA laid down the challenge to trading partners to make a bold move, only to be met with a proposal for short-term market management and harmonization of protection (implying import barriers on soybeans and corn gluten). The USA in 1988 showed no willingness to compromise. It insisted on the principle of total elimination of trade-distorting subsidies, even though this was seen as a direct threat to the existence of the CAP, and hence quite unacceptable to the EC. The Bush administration, taking office in 1989, bowed to the reality of the EC opposition, and agreed to water down the objective to one of 'progressive reductions' of support. The final two years of the Uruguay Round negotiations will tell how substantial such reductions prove to be.

8.6 LINKS BETWEEN TRADE NEGOTIATIONS AND DOMESTIC POLICY

The exchange of papers by negotiators in the GATT Round may appear somewhat divorced from the 'realities' of farm politics in Washington or in Brussels. Could a US administration possibly negotiate in Geneva a plan to eliminate the greater part of its domestic farm programmes, given its great difficulty in getting minor cuts in those same programmes through Congress? And can one really believe that the EC Commission can accept a multi-year binding and reduction in CAP support under the GATT when it has clearly been unable on its own to control spending on farm policies? At first glance, the political relevance of the GATT negotiations seems suspect. Trade negotiators have to act out the charade, but they know that at the end of the day it is domestic politics that will prevail. The history of agriculture in the GATT suggests that this view of trade negotiations is not too far from the truth.

The other side of the coin is also worth a moment's consideration. Suppose that US and EC governments have a strong preference for an open, multilateral trading system in which trade disputes are handled by a strengthened GATT, and a dislike for trade frictions over farm products which threaten to divert attention from more important matters. Assume that a major rationale for farm support has been to protect domestic farmers from the 'unfair' practices of foreign governments; and that reductions in such support will erode market shares. Under these conditions it might be possible to have the trade 'tail' wag the domestic 'dog'. Put in these terms, the GATT proposals do not seem necessarily out of touch with political (domestic) reality.

The US proposal for an elimination of all trade-distorting support is premised on a belief that US agriculture would be competitive in a free-trade environment. Given a 'level playing-field', the American farmer can use superior technology, large farm size, climatic advantage and sophisticated management skills to sell on world markets. Protective policies in other countries distort such competition at present, and so should be removed. There may be some short-run problems as US price support is removed, but in the long run a stronger agricultural sector will emerge. This view is apparently behind the tacit support given to the administration by the major farm groups.[7] The support of these groups seems to rest on the notion of *complete* elimination of subsidies – the aspect often thought to be the most politically naive.[8] In other words, partial liberalization would still leave foreign governments able to block US exports and to subsidize goods destined for US markets. Suspicion of the devious foreigner, devising yet new ways to circumvent international agreement, is not confined to agriculture. But the weakness of the GATT mechanism, the complexity of farm policies, the difficulties in measuring incentive effects, and the fact that it may be much easier to enforce a complete than a partial ban, suggest that this view may be partly justified in this case.

The EC proposal of October 1987 was less dramatic than that of the USA, but it too looked out of line with domestic farm politics. Nevertheless, the position was approved 'as a basis for negotiations' by the Council of Ministers, including the agriculture ministers from members states that spend weeks every year arguing against the mere suggestion of price cuts in the annual price negotiations. It is possible that this, too, was done with the expectation that no progress could be made: a shallow gesture to avoid annoying the USA. But it is more likely that the EC proposal was a conscious attempt by the Commission to impose on the domestic political process some constraints from outside the narrow agricultural arena. The agriculture ministers felt unable to oppose the general will to have a successful Uruguay Round, and were prepared to go along with the possibility of some external constraints on their action rather than risk being blamed for heightened trade tensions.

The conflict between domestic and international forces shaping farm policy may soon reach a head. The notion of short-term action and down-payments on longer-term reform put the trade talks in the same time-frame as domestic policy decisions. The Bush administration will soon have to make clear its intentions with respect to domestic legislation. There will be the usual conflicts among proponents of different types of agricultural programme. In the context of the 1990 farm bill, acceptance of the 'down-payment' could be enough to allow the new administration to restrain those who wish to see either more inward-looking or more aggressive farm policies. The EC is also at a critical point in time with respect to domestic policy. If agreement could be reached on a co-ordinated attempt to improve the trade situation, then this might well prove effective in supporting the EC domestic reform process. A specific pact to reduce protection levels, such as envisaged in the US and Cairns group proposals, would 'lock in' the Commission's overall reform plans against backsliding by the Council of Ministers. The 'blame' for such reform could be shifted to the GATT – the price Europe has to pay to keep the multilateral trading system intact. The drift away from the most trade-disruptive policies (such as open-ended export subsidies) would be reinforced and more cost-effective (partially decoupled) alternatives adopted.

The mid-term review in December 1988, however inconvenient its timing in terms of elections, could have been the place for broad agreement on aims; in the event, the lack of any agreement on agriculture at Montreal slowed the Uruguay Round to the pace of previous GATT negotiations and lost the momentum of 1987. The outcome was to leave to the GATT Director-General the task of finding a compromise before a new deadline of April 1989. In the event a formula was found to keep the discussions going; it is not so clear that real progress has been made on resolving the underlying conflicts between the EC and the USA.[9]

One development in 1988 could not have been foreseen. As is often the case in farm politics, the weather took a decisive hand in the proceedings. A severe drought in 1988 across much of the USA reduced corn and soybean crops as well as the availability of hay and forage. Stocks fell sharply and world prices rose. Budget costs of farm support fell both in the EC and more particularly in the USA. Though the underlying imbalance between capacity and commercial demand did not change significantly with one year's drought, some signs emerged that the long depression in world markets was ending. In particular, imports into developing countries began to rise after the long period of debt-induced stagnation. As a result, short-term measures which seemed so pressing in 1987 appeared somewhat less necessary two years later. Whether the economic situation has changed enough to alter perceptions about the seriousness of the problem in the longer run remains to be seen.

8.7 INTERNATIONAL REFORM AND THE ANALYTICAL FRAMEWORK

The analytical framework developed in Chapter 1 provides insights into the failure to date of the Uruguay Round to achieve agreement on reforms of trade policy and domestic agricultural policy and gives some indication of the future prospects for success.

The public choice paradigm focuses on the incentives provided to individual actors by self-interest. The Uruguay Round offers the prospect of the negotiators bringing agricultural policy into conformity with the general principles of the GATT. It also brings trade and foreign policy actors who have an interest in reform into the agricultural policy process. However, it does little to change the incentives of domestic policy actors who must approve any international agreement. Negotiating outcomes requiring the USA and EC to reduce their domestic agricultural subsidies would have to achieve the support of the House and Senate Agricultural committees and the council of Agriculture Ministers. Members of these bodies have very strong links with the farm lobby whose legitimacy, as indicated in other chapters, is based on the continuance of commodity price support policies; they are unlikely to accept subsidy cuts unless no other alternative exists.

The US 'zero' option can be seen as a Reagan administration attempt to overcome this opposition by offering the prospect of increased income to US farmers through increased exports to newly open markets. Moreover, the zero option had the advantage that it did not favour one commodity interest over another. However, commodity groups could claim little credit for any increase in farm income generated by international acceptance of the US proposal. It is true that the US proposal did achieve some support in the House and Senate Agricultural Committees and from the US farm lobby, but this support may have been tactical in that the zero option provided an excellent initial bargaining position. It also had the advantage of shifting any blame for the failure of the Uruguay Round to the EC, in so far as the Community could not have accepted the Reagan proposal. The inflexibility of the US negotiating position could indicate an administration realization that it faced great difficulty selling anything less than complete elimination of subsidies to domestic agricultural groups fearful that partial liberalization would favour some commodity interests over others (see Stokes, 1989, p. 287).

The EC proposal can also be understood in terms of public choice. Its vagueness on the magnitude of the reduction of domestic agricultural subsidies may reflect a realization by the commission that the farm lobby and the Council of Agriculture Ministers would strongly resist any internationally negotiated cuts in domestic subsidies. The EC negotiating inflexibility provides further evidence of the political difficulties created in the community by subsidy reductions imposed from outside.

The organizational process paradigm helps explain the slowness of the Uruguay Round negotiations. The Uruguay Round has increased the number of actors involved in the agricultural policy and further divides responsibility. Co-ordination between the various actors in the USA and Europe takes a great deal of time, adding a strong element of inertia. It is not simply that several organizations have to co-ordinate their activities. Even more important, new standard operating procedures for co-ordination must be developed – not easily accomplished among organizations jealous of their prerogatives; and suspicious of any changes which introduce new uncertainties into the policy process. There are elements in both DG-VI and USDA whose authority is sufficiently threatened by the GATT negotiations that they have strong incentives to resist agreement. Co-ordination is further complicated by the tendency of different organizations to see different faces of an issue. Trade bureaucracies perceive international agricultural trade negotiations very differently from agricultural bureaucracies. Organizations usually do not accept more than incremental policy change except in reaction to crisis. The reduction of the budget pressures on agriculture caused by the increased EC revenues and by the US drought has removed some of the impetus for policy change and may have taken the issue out of the 'crisis' category.

The government politics paradigm allows us to focus on the changes in the agricultural policy bargaining process brought about by the Uruguay Round. In one sense the new action channels would appear to favour the forces pressing for agricultural reform and to ensure more progress towards reform. However, there are now more bargaining interactions, which increases the bargaining costs of achieving change. The complexity of the domestic bargaining processes in the USA and EC severely restricts the flexibility of international negotiators who can change their positions only when there is consensus in the domestic process. Expanding the bargaining arena to include international negotiations allows new opportunities for misperception and miscommunication, which can present severe obstacles to agricultural policy reform.

The failure of US and EC negotiators to grasp one insight of the partisan mutual adjustment paradigm may help to explain the failure of the Montreal Mid-term Review in December 1988. In bargaining between individuals representing different interests, it is often possible to achieve agreement over means even when there is no consensus over ends. The US insistence on international acceptance of the goal of eliminating agricultural subsidies may well have prevented pragmatic agreement on reform measures which different nations could have seen as consistent with quite different objectives.

The various paradigms taken together would indicate that crisis is just as important for achieving reform internationally as it is for reform in the domestic arena. Even though the input of forces favourable to reform has been enhanced, policy inertia has in no way been reduced. This inertia can only be overcome when there is consensus that the current policy is untenable, and this is likely only in time of crisis. The crisis in agricultural spending which existed at the beginning of the Uruguay Round served as a strong impetus for progress in the negotiations. Progress slowed markedly as the budget crisis eased. It will probably increase again in a year or two, if the weather is good and the upward trend in world agricultural production returns.

NOTES

1. The most accessible of these studies are Tyers and Anderson (1987; Parikh *et al.* (1988); OECD (1987); Roningen and Dixit (1987); and the Commission of the EC (1988).
2. For a fuller discussion of the treatment of agriculture in the GATT see Hathaway (1987).
3. For a fuller discussion of the OECD work see Sanderson, Warley and Josling (forthcoming).
4. Although a member of the Cairns group, the Canadian government decided to produce its own proposals in case the Cairns group could not agree on a position.

5. A brief account of the progress of the negotiating group is found in the GATT publication, *News of the Uruguay Round of Multilateral Trade Negotiations (NUR)*.
6. The signatories to this proposal were Egypt, Jamaica, Mexico, Morocco and Peru (*NUR*, no. 19, 5 October 1988).
7. It is sometimes suggested that farm organizations put such a low priority on success in the GATT Round that they do not think it worth objecting to the US proposal. If so, there exists the possibility for considerable backtracking in the event of an agreement on long-term liberalization.
8. The zero option was in part a conscious political stance designed to gain support from US farm organizations. Not only were these groups concerned about foreign governments taking advantage of partial liberalization, but also they were afraid that limited improvements would favour one commodity group over another (see Stokes, 1989, p. 287).
9. The agreement in April 1989, formally the conclusion of the Mid-term Review, laid out a detailed work programme for the final two years of negotiation. It did not, however, resolve the key issue of the format for the agricultural negotiations. Countries have until the end of 1989 to present their ideas on this issue (*NUR*, no. 27, 24 April 1989).

9 · AGRICULTURAL REFORM IN THE UNITED STATES AND THE EUROPEAN COMMUNITY COMPARED

9.1 INTRODUCTION

The ongoing agricultural policy reforms in the EC and in the USA each provide an interesting example of policy change in a democratic society. Comparing the two experiences can add further clarity to the picture. The differences between the economic trends, economic shocks, political developments and group interests on the two sides of the Atlantic may help to explain the different reform paths taken. Similarly, the differences in the structure of the decision-making process may account for alternatives chosen along the way.

This chapter explores some of these similarities and differences in the light of the previous discussion of EC and US reform. It also raises the question about what lessons one should draw from the analysis of the reform process in the EC and the USA. This is focused around four issues: the pace of policy change; the role of crises in decision-making; the links between national reform and international negotiations; and the prospects for new policy instruments and directions in the future.

9.2 ECONOMIC SIMILARITIES AND DIFFERENCES

EC and US farmers are subject to much the same broad economic pressures. The domestic market for basic foodstuffs grows at a snail's pace, as affluent consumers spend income on other items. Even where demand for a food product is buoyant, the return to the farmer is often only a small part of the consumer cost. Foreign markets have increasingly become an integral part of the outlet for farm produce. At the same time the flow of technology from the public and private sectors continues, allowing costs to be reduced and output increased. When overseas markets are expanding then problems seem solvable. Farmers adjust to market opportunities and policy-makers sleep at nights. When world markets stagnate, pressures build up for the policies and hence for farmers.

This fact of life has been apparent in the USA for some time. The EC has only recently joined the ranks of those dependent upon foreign agricultural markets. Twenty years ago it was still the case that the EC was primarily an import market with a few exportable surpluses. Ten years ago the EC was broadly self-sufficient in a wide range of farm goods, in spite of the accession of the UK with its historical markets for imports of food. Now the EC is one of the largest exporters of the products that it used to import – cereals, beef, sugar and dairy products. In 1986, exports of agricultural products from the EC actually surpassed those from the USA (see Figure 9.1), though the EC is also a larger importer than the USA of agricultural commodities. This emergence of the EC as a major exporter has meant that the economic pressures on the EC to reform are similar to those faced by the USA.

There are, however, some major differences. Chief among these is the man–land ratio in agriculture – the average size of farm. In the USA, the average size of farm is 438 acres (177 hectares); in the EC it is only 42 acres (17 hectares). The different farm size structure has implications for policy. There is in the USA a tendency for the largest farms to be in areas with poorer land, whereas in the EC the smallest farms often seem to be in areas with the poorest soil. The result is that the distribution of income may be much more skewed in EC agriculture, if larger farm size does not compensate for lower soil quality. This means that one could expect policy to play a much greater role in Europe to ensure an equitable income distribution. Reform efforts in the EC are significantly hampered by this aspect of policy: liberal solutions to the market imbalance problems are often seen to have inequitable distributional impacts.

Budget pressures clearly have dominated the political debate over agricultural policy reform in both the US and the EC in recent years. What seems true in both cases is that budget issues come to the fore when a sudden increase appears in budget cost. This pattern is illustrated by looking at the annual change in budget expenditures in both the USA and the EC, and is done in Figure 9.2. Reform in the USA was stimulated by the cost increases of the 1976–8 period, but derailed by the budget cost reductions at the end of that decade. Interest in reform similarly peaked in 1982–3 but lost steam when budget costs dipped in 1984, largely as a result of the 1983 drought. Reform became an issue again in 1985–6, but is again being influenced by a drought-induced fall in support costs. In the EC, the pressure on the policy appears more continuous, as a result of more steady budget growth. But the periods in which the budget has fallen, in 1974 and 1981 (and again in 1988), have corresponded to times of relaxation of the efforts of policy-makers to reform the CAP. Higher world prices at those times also contributed to the impression that policy reform was less urgent or even that it was unnecessary.

The basic similarities in the situation facing US and EC agriculture have led to serious conflicts regarding export subsidies and export credits in the markets for such products as wheat, dairy products, beef and sugar. The use

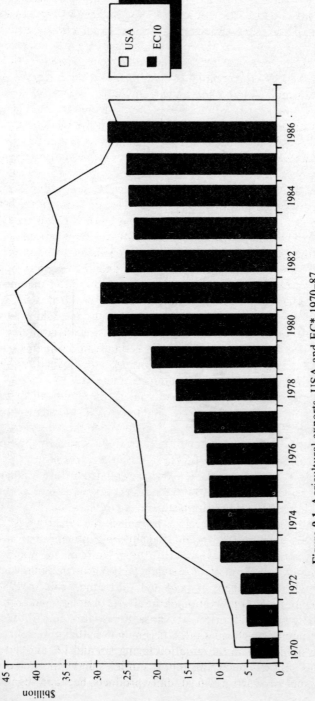

Figure 9.1 Agricultural exports, USA and EC* 1970–87.
Source: Newman *et al.* (1987) *EC exports exclude intra-EC trade.

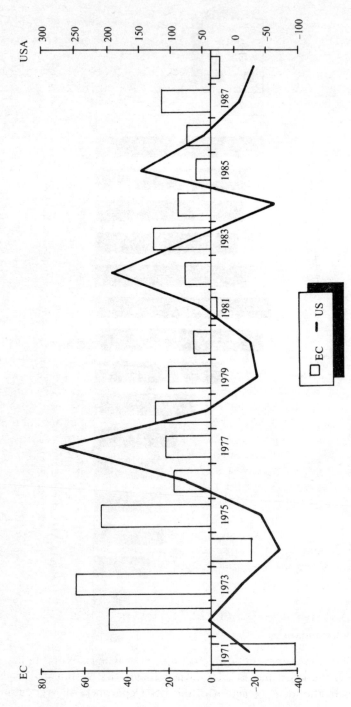

Figure 9.2 Annual change in programme costs, USA and EC (percentage change from previous year).
Source: Figures 2.1 and 5.8

of aggressive export subsidies (including liberal export credits) to expand markets and dispose of surpluses has been a major distinguishing feature of agricultural trade. In no other major economic sector is so much production put into world markets at less than domestic production cost. Moreover, the situation seems to have deteriorated in recent years. If one country engages in such practices, other exporters have to follow the lead or lose markets. The risk of allowing these practices to continue unabated is that they sour trade relations in other fields. In addition, the uncertainty generated in agricultural markets by subsidies gives confused signals to other producers, including those in developing countries attempting to put their own agricultural sectors on a sound footing. The USA and the EC share a common interest in the avoidance of costly subsidy wars. The problem is that neither can afford to give up its policies unilaterally.

The more traditional trade problem of access to import markets raises particular difficulties at a time of high domestic unemployment and relatively low farm incomes. The products involved include cereals, oilseeds, dairy products, meats, sugar, fruit and vegetables. Protectionism is now significantly greater in agricultural than in manufactured trade, though the degree of protection afforded to developed country agriculture tends to rise and fall with world market prices. The reduction in trade barriers in manufacturing has left agriculture out on a limb.

Specific US–EC issues of market access have undergone some modification as trade flows themselves have changed. In 1980 the EC was a major importer of corn and other coarse grains for animal feed. Increased production and a switch in feed ingredients away from cereals have changed that picture. With the emergence of the EC as a major cereal exporter, access to European grain markets has become less of an issue. But the non-grain feeds, imported in part to replace high-cost grains in Europe, have also provided an adequate replacement in the diplomatic diet. The EC would like to control such access, presently guaranteed under the GATT, to ease the burden of cereal surpluses. Similarly, the EC has often sought to support the market for domestic butter and olive oil by taxing substitute vegetable oils. The USA naturally resists this as an affront to the massive soybean trade with Europe. The EC suggestion to allow for the 'rebalancing' of agricultural support in the Uruguay Round negotiations is the latest manifestation of this long-running dispute.

9.3 SIMILARITIES AND DIFFERENCES IN THE POLICY PROCESS
9.3.1 Policy formulation

There are both similarities and differences in the way agricultural policy is formulated in the USA and EC. US farm bills are first formulated in the Executive with the locus of action in the US Department of Agriculture

(USDA) and the office of the Secretary of Agriculture. The EC policy process is comparable to the extent that CAP proposals are formulated in the European Commission, the executive agency of the European Community, with the locus of action in DG-VI and the office of the Agriculture Commissioner. The Secretary of Agriculture and the Agriculture Commissioner have the ability to control the formulation of agricultural legislation in their offices, though they depend heavily on the bureaucracy.

The USDA bureaucracy and DG-VI appear similar in that they are large multi-faceted bureaucracies with significant management responsibilities. Both have close links to the farm lobby and a strong organizational interest in maintaining the status quo for commodity price support policies. The USDA bureaucracy was not a force for reform in either the 1981 or 1985 farm bills. Top officials in DG-VI only played a critical role in the development of milk quotas because the situation was desperate and required decisive action. Both bureaucracies appear to place the maintenance of high and stable farm incomes high in their scheme of values. Both seem most concerned about technical questions and implementability.

The incentives for the US Secretary of Agriculture and EC Agriculture Commissioner diverge more considerably. Both are political appointees, but their accountability is different. The Secretary is appointed by the President and has a responsibility to carry out administration priorities. Significantly different policies could be pursued by Secretaries in subsequent administrations. The EC Agriculture Commissioner, selected by the President of the Commission from the nationally appointed Commissioners, is accountable to the entire Commission. The Agriculture Commissioner tends to act on the basis of what the full Commission, through a mutual accommodation process, considers the Community interest. His positions thus are unlikely to have ideological purity or to change a great deal from one Commission to the next. Both the EC Agriculture Commissioner and the US Secretary of Agriculture are constrained by the need to have their proposals approved, respectively, by the Council of Agriculture Ministers and the US Congress.

The US Secretary of Agriculture and the EC Agricultural Commissioner generally took positions during the 1980s favourable to greater market orientation for commodity policies, largely because the political environment has demanded reductions in surpluses and expenditures. Not surprisingly, the US Secretary took clearer and stronger pro-reform positions, strongly reinforced by the Reagan administration commitment to deregulation and reduced government spending. Both Secretary and Commissioner faced substantial opposition in the legislative process and the final legislation substantially compromised their proposals. Paradoxically, the Commissioner appears to have had more success in influencing the final policy outcome, particularly in the stabilizers debate.

US farm bills have long been comprehensive packages delicately balanced to ensure political acceptability. The EC milk quota and stabilizer packages show similar qualities. US and EC policy-makers have some similar and some different concerns. Both have to balance farm income considerations with concern about budget cost. US policy-makers must in addition balance the benefits between commodity interest groups, while EC policy-makers have to balance the benefits provided to member states. The need to develop complex legislation in a tight time-frame creates a need to streamline the policy process. This need was evident in the formulation of the 1985 US farm bill in Assistant Secretary Lesher's office and the development of the EC stabilizers proposal by the *ad hoc* 'inner circle' of the Commission.

A major difference exists between EC and US agricultural policy formulation processes in the initiation of legislation. The EC Council of Ministers can only work on the basis of Commission proposals. The Council cannot formally propose legislation, though in practice the President of the Council often puts together a compromise package which the Commission accepts as an amendment. By contrast, the US Congress and its Agriculture Committees can amend or reject administration proposals and substitute new ones in their place. Indeed, the 1981 and 1985 farm bills were largely fashioned in the House and Senate Agricultural Committees and sub-committees. Congressional policy formulation adds an element of incoherence to US policy-making for which there is no exact EC equivalent. It allows legislators to consider different options simultaneously, as with supply controls, decoupling and adjustment of the deficiency payments system during the 1985 Food Security Act debate. However, consideration of multiple options tends to overwhelm the system, running the risk that no option will receive very careful consideration. Also, a proposal formulated in Congress tends to reflect compromise between various farm interests; it may appear internally inconsistent; and may not relate easily to any recognized conception of national interest, or to the problem at hand. To a certain extent the EC Council of Ministers also fomulates policy in that it suggests ideas which the Commission comes under heavy pressure to accept. However, the Commission still maintains control over the proposals before the Council considers and hence protects the coherence of EC policy positions.

9.3.2 The legislative response

Legislative approval of agricultural policy proposals takes place in the EC Council of Ministers and the US Congress. The most striking similarity between the two legislative processes is their compartmentalization. Proposed legislation in different subject areas is considered by different Councils of Ministers in the EC and between different committes and sub-committees in the US Congress. This functional division encourages parochialism. It is very difficult for the individuals participating in the process to look at the proposed legislation in its totality. The US policy process has further compartmentalization in that the Senate and House Agricultural Committees must pass on the same legislation. Compartmentalization raises the bargaining costs of reaching a final agreement, thus contributing to policy inertia. It also results in the legislative process consuming an inordinate amount of time.

Another factor contributing to decision delay is the requirement for consensus. The past practice of unanimity in the EC Council of Ministers required almost total consensus on the critical issues, although the use of majority voting has increased since 1987. The US Congressional agriculture Committee process also requires a high level of consensus, even though legislation can be approved by simple majority vote. The overall voting power of farm legislators is so small on the floor of both chambers, that the Agriculture Committees cannot hope to prevail if their membership is deeply divided.

The legislative process favours agricultural interests in both the US and EC. In the EC, the primary decision-making body is the Council of Agriculture Ministers, which has agriculture as its constituency. In the US Congress, the key decisions are made in the Agriculture Committees, whose members disproportionately represent agricultural districts. Non-agricultural interests have difficulty gaining attention until legislative action has proceeded to the full Congress or to the European Council, by which stage the policy is pretty well shaped. Differences appear in the agricultural interests which are favoured. The US process inherently favours commodity groups, representing the principal products produced in individual Congressional districts. It also favours agri-business. The US system allows these interests to contribute heavily through Political Action Committees (PACs) to congressional campaigns. National farm organizations dominate in the Council of Ministers because of their close linkages to agriculture ministers and ministries. In some ways national farm organizations can accommodate agricultural reform more easily than commodity groups in that they can balance gain in some areas with losses in others. Some US commodity groups will inevitably lose without any compensating gain, thus tending to increase their opposition to change.

Strong pressures exist in both US and EC legislative processes to increase agricultural programme costs. Consensus-building requires payoffs for the various actors. When the costs of given policies are uncertain, as with commodity price support programmes, legislative actors have every incentive to assume the lowest cost parameters, thus providing the largest pie for distribution. Both US and EC processes suffer from the lack of an effective central legislative co-ordination mechanism, thus making it difficult to balance agriculture with other priorities. One factor does operate in the USA to ensure budgetary discipline for which there is not an equivalent in the EC – the threat of a presidential veto. This threat played a significant role in forcing House and Senate to cut back their authorized expenditures in both the 1981 and 1985 farm bills.

The role of legislative broker is extremely important in both the USA and EC in working out final deals which satisfy the various bargaining actors and work at the same time to solve the problem at hand. This role is played by the Agricultural Committee chairmen and Congressional floor leadership in the USA and the President of the Council in the EC. The leadership role these actors play creates incentives to develop effective solutions. Senator Robert Dole and Republican Congressman Tom Foley were instrumental in forging the legislative consensus for both 1981 and 1985 US farm bills. M. Rocard shaped the final consensus in the Council of Agriculture Ministers for milk quotas, while Ignaz Kiechle did the same thing for stabilizers.

9.4 POLICY INERTIA AND INCREMENTALISM

In Chapter 1 we posed some hypotheses about the process of agricultural reform. These suggested that domestic policy would be slow to adjust to the changing nature of the domestic and international market. We have seen the continuation of high price supports in both the USA and EC, putting considerable strain on the policy instruments. Our evidence has shown the difficulties in making farm policy responsive to budget pressures. To blame this inertia on the power of farm lobbies does not seem particularly helpful. Indeed it borders on the tautological: farm lobbies must be 'strong' because of the slow response of the policy to changed circumstances. The discussion of institutional objectives and incentives provides other possibilities. The major farm policies survive because of the particular sets of institutions involved in the setting of the policy and the structure of the decision framework in which they operate, as well as the pressures from interest groups.

In the EC, the persistence of outdated policy instruments, such as the use of intervention buying under conditions of chronic surplus, seems largely a function of the glacial pace of decision-making within the Community. The structure of Regulations can only be changed by broad consensus (until recently, virtual unanimity) in the Council of Ministers. Together with the tortuous process of moving a proposal from technical analysis to political reality, this has largely stifled creative policy-making. Though farm groups act as an important input into the various national positions, they cannot be held responsible for the paralysis in the CAP's development. In a rapidly changing domestic and international environment, the need to respond with policy modifications is apparent. Analysis of the institutional incentives against change in policy instruments may suggest better strategies to achieve future reform.

The high level of prices which have been supported under the current agricultural policies in both the EC and the USA does, however, owe more to pressures by groups which would be disadvantaged by price cuts. In Europe, the elaborate system of 'green' exchange rates, and the border taxes and subsidies which go along with this system, point to the sensitivity of national price levels. The annual price decisions supply the focus for pressure from farm groups. So long as this process continues, the institutions will have to face such pressure. Suggestions to make price decisions 'automatic', based on prices in competitor countries or on EC market balance, or to fix prices ahead for several years, are natural responses to the situation. The Commission clearly has an incentive to downplay the importance of the annual price negotiations, though it has traditionally used the occasion to gain Council approval of policy changes.

Though the explanation of policy paralysis and high prices in the EC is illuminated by looking at the incentives of the participating institutions, the situation could have only survived because of the budgetary procedures. In particular, the lack of any link between price decisions and financial consequences has set the CAP apart from most public policies and has created incentives for irresponsibility in the Council. National interests are paramount in setting price levels. Agricultural ministers not held accountable for the budgetary consequences of their actions have little reason to slow down the gravy-train of CAP spending. The 'reforms' of February 1988 begin to address this issue. It remains to be seen whether such action significantly alters the set of incentives which currently determine the performance of the CAP.

The organizational process and government politics paradigms provide important insights into why agricultural policy reform has proven so difficult in both the USA and EC. Past policies tend to persist until consensus is reached about how to change them. The complex political and bureaucratic processes of pluralistic democratic societies make such consensus extremely difficult to achieve. Agricultural policy is now so complicated that it must be compartmentalized and formulated in isolation from other policies. This almost guarantees that the actors with the greatest knowledge of agricultural issues play a central role. But, those actors with the greatest expertise are likely to have a strong commitment to the current policy. Even to the extent that outsiders can become involved, they are likely to be overwhelmed in a bargaining process which puts a premium on expertise. Relating agricultural policy to other priorities is expensive and bureaucratically difficult. It can only occur at the highest policy levels, where decision-makers, who suffer from a lack of expertise and have many other things to think about, are severely constrained by the information and options filtered from below.

One factor stands out above all others in the previous chapters' discussions about agricultural reform in the EC and USA – the enormous inertia of the policy process. The basic commodity price support policies are deeply ingrained and have proved remarkably unresponsive to the huge food surpluses and escalating budget costs they have created. The organizational process paradigm provides important insights into why this is the case. Most important, there is no unitary actor to make decisions. Instead, responsibility is essentially divided between the Commission and Council of Ministers in the EC and between the Executive and Congress in the USA, with power in each organization further divided among component groups.

We have seen how parochial interests influence the behaviour of the various organizational actors in the reform debate. Resolving the conflicts between organizations and individuals involves a complicated time-consuming bargaining process. The many steps are difficult to complete even when the differences do not seem very great. The various organizations have a collective interest in conserving time and effort, and hence look for ways to simplify decisions. This means that they tend to satisfice (choose the first acceptable option) and act only when they must, and then only to the extent necessary to 'cope' with the crisis. To the extent that change is necessary, a strong tendency exists to adapt familiar ideas (standard operating procedures), easier to deal with than new ideas which have more uncertain consequences and are likely to prove more difficult to implement. Examples of such familiar ideas are EC guarantee thresholds and US set-asides.

The respective structures of EC and US policy-making processes create strong biases against policy reform. The most serious problem is that the agricultural policy-making and budget processes tend to operate independently, with a consequent difficulty in bringing budgetary interests to bear. In the EC, the Budget Council can only provide the most general constraints on the Agriculture Council. The Congressional Budget Committees have a comparable lack of influence over the Agriculture Committees. The problem is greatly aggravated in that commodity programmes create entitlements whose costs evade easy prediction and give rise to interest groups dedicated to their defence.

The government politics paradigm further explains the agricultural policy inertia. Division of power implies bargaining between individuals, each of whom pursues his or her own interests. We have seen that both US farm bill debates and EC reform package debates involve a long sequence of bargaining situations, each of which takes time to complete. Each participant has an incentive to try to 'win' the bargaining game. In the absence of overwhelming power, this implies persuading adversaries and building winning coalitions, which, in turn, places a premium on acceptability. Acceptability is most easily achieved by options which do not vary much from existing policy, reflecting previous consensus among the actors. Radically different ideas cannot usually be operationalized into policy without heavy bargaining costs. No actor wants to incur such costs unless other acceptable options do not exist and unless it is clear that the new idea will work to solve the current problem. Unfortunately, new ideas do not generally have completely predictable consequences. Finally, since bargaining implies compromise, new ideas are likely to become highly attenuated before translation into policy.

Some individual characteristics of the EC and US bargaining processes make change particularly difficult. The EC is impeded by having legislative authority divided between sectoral Councils of Ministers, in the past operating to a large extent under the constraints of unanimity.[1] US flexibility suffers because consensus must be achieved between two chambers of Congress, each of which can write its own farm bill, and between Congress and the Executive branch, which can have another completely different farm bill. Inertia is reinforced in both the EC and USA by the fact that key policy actors have a vested interest in the status quo – the Agricultural Committees and sub-committees in the US Congress and the Council of Agriculture Ministers.

The public choice paradigm also helps explain EC and US resistance to agricultural reform. This paradigm predicts that individuals will maximize values and interests which are important to them. Individuals are likely to commit resources to influence the policy process in direct proportion to the degree to which their interests are at stake. Price support policies in both the EC and USA create large rents and financial interests for farmers, which they have a strong interest in mobilizing to protect. They have much less impact on individual consumers and taxpayers, who thus have little incentive to mobilize to counter the farm lobby. Policy-makers, particularly elected ones, have little incentive to reform agricultural policy if they feel that the unfavourable reaction from farmers will more than counter-balance favourable reactions from other sectors in society.

The problems which policy-makers have in maximizing values contribute to inertia. The individuals playing critical roles in EC and US agricultural policy-making have significant administrative responsibilities, which limit the time they can spend on analysis. They also usually have a number of different values to consider simultaneously, which means that more attention must be given to balancing values than to maximizing them. EC and US policy-makers must balance programme cost with farm income, political feasibility and implementability. Sudden changes in policy, though they might be indicated by surpluses and high budgetary costs, create problems for farm income and political feasibility. There is a natural tendency to move incrementally to keep the task of balancing values manageable.

Policy-makers seldom have an interest in increasing market orientation, the most often stated goal of agricultural reform. Market orientation implies deregulation and greater reliance on market mechanisms. While there are usually gains in economic efficiencies, these gains may not easily translate into short-term political benefits. On the other hand, short-term political costs are almost invariably created. Deregulation threatens the bureaucracy, whose mission in life is to administer the regulated policy. It also abolishes rents, guaranteeing opposition from those who lose their special benefits. The net gains from increased efficiency through deregulation tend to be widely distributed through society, with no individual gaining enough to justify political action. Losers will tend to have more incentives for political action than winners. (Bauer *et al.*, 1963, p. 397).

The political incentives against deregulation are not completely symmetrical in the USA and EC because the perceived consequences are different. The general consensus seems to be that the USA would gain from international deregulation through increased agricultural exports because of a comparative advantage in agriculture, while the EC would lose trade share because of a comparative disadvantage. Thus US officials take a more favourable view towards agricultural reform than EC officials do. Some EC member states, particularly France, could see their agricultural exports increase with deregulation, but others, notably West Germany, fear that their agricultural industry would be adversely affected. The prospect of change in the distribution of agricultural benefits among EC member states does little to increase the incentive for EC officials to promote increased resource efficiency.

Policy complexity itself promotes policy inertia and incrementalism. Over the years, both the CAP and US agricultural policy have become increasingly complicated, largely as a result of the political compromise necessary to achieve policy approval. There are now so many details that no one can hope to understand them all. Yet it is often not possible to isolate some aspects of agricultural policy for change, because the different aspects are highly interconnected. When agricultural reform is considered, the consequences of the proposed changes for the full range of existent agricultural policies must be considered. Even if the consequences of proposed actions can be calculated, a possibility still exists that a delicate balance between different interests will be upset. Thus, complexity increases uncertainty which, in turn, increases the tendency to 'muddle along', creating even greater complexity, which will be even more difficult to alter in the future.

Policy complexity has other consequences adverse to reform. First, a complex policy requires a large bureaucracy to administer it, but large bureaucracies inherently protect the status quo. Second, complexity raises the ante for influencing the policy process. Only the farm lobby has enough at stake to justify the commitment of resources to mastering the policy detail requisite for meaningful participation in the policy process. Agricultural policy cannot respond steadily to mild discontent. Rather, discontent is ignored until it builds to such a high level that the response is fitful.

Much of the preceding analysis in this chapter does not apply exclusively to agriculture, but generally to domestic policy in pluralistic democratic nations. One factor seems unique to agriculture – the strong homogeneity and group identity of farmers. Farmers in both the EC and USA have tended to work together to protect group interests in a way that must be the envy of groups benefiting from other policies. This may be because farmers think of themselves as distinctive in society, sharing a way of life experienced by no other group. The nature of farm group influence does, however, seem somewhat different on the two sides of the Atlantic. In the USA the farm vote is not very important, but the campaign contributions which farm groups give are significant. In Europe campaign contributions are less important, but farmers have significant voting strength, and often control critical swing votes in a number of countries, particularly West Germany.

Another factor unique to agriculture hinders commodity policy reform in both the EC and USA – the enormous public sympathy for the plight of farmers, which operates on both sides of the Atlantic. The public tends to think that farmers have a very difficult life and are under-rewarded for the important task of food production which they perform. Some of this probably reflects the stage which the industrialized nations have reached in the transformation of farming. Most people in the USA and Europe are only two or three generations removed from the land. They are still close enough to remember the hardships of farming in the past. They are thus willing to treat agriculture differently from other productive sectors and continue to support benefits for farmers. The public sympathy for farming aids the political strength of the farm lobby and makes it very difficult to mobilize a public constituency for reform.

The different emphases of US and EC policy have some implications for the volatility of public-opinion influence. EC policies, guaranteeing a certain level of commodity prices, minimize the possibility of a sudden farm income crisis such as occurred in the USA in 1985. It was this income crisis which generated a groundswell of US public support that frustrated a strong reform impulse. EC mechanisms also assure stable consumer prices, which militate strongly against consumer rebellion. No such mechanisms exist in the USA, but the tendency of the current crisis of overproduction to lower consumer prices has the same effect.

A number of other factors operating in either the USA or EC impede agricultural reform capacity. In the USA, one such factor is the Congressional coalition between legislators who support commodity programmes in return for rural support for food stamps. Another is the increased fragmentation of Congressional authority. In the EC, the threat of a policy veto in the Council of Ministers clearly impedes reform of the CAP.

9.5 THE IMPACT OF CRISIS ON POLICY REFORM

We have seen that, in spite of all the obstacles, the agricultural policy processes can respond to crisis and produce a measure of reform. The USA froze crop bases and yields for deficiency payments programmes in the 1985 farm bill and created a conservation reserve designed to remove 40 million acres from production. The EC imposed milk quotas in 1984 and stabilizers in 1988. All of these reforms came during a budget crisis when policy-makers were concerned about rapidly increasing expenditures. We have seen that a budget crisis provides a strong impetus for agricultural reform. There are a number of reasons why this is the case.

Perhaps most important, a budget crisis creates a zero-sum bargaining game, which in turn changes the power and incentives of the various actors. We have seen evidence in both the EC and US agricultural reform debates of a number of zero-sum game symptoms. These have generally been more obvious in the EC, which cannot legally run a budget deficit. First, the farm lobby appears increasingly divided as different farm interests compete for scarce funds, resulting in a loss of influence. This factor was observable in the EC milk quotas debate, but much more obvious in the consideration of stabilizers. It was somewhat apparent during the US Congressional discussions of the 1981 farm bill, but muted in the 1985 Food Security Act debate, when public outcry at the plight of farmers created a national consensus that farm spending should be increased. The split in the US farm lobby seems to be increasing again today in the USA, largely because of the budgetary bite of the deficit reduction programme (the Gramm–Rudman–Hollings Act).

Second, a zero-sum game creates competition between farm and non-farm programmes for scarce funds. This provides the impetus for budget actors to participate more in the making of agricultural policy in order to control spending and distribute resources equitably. The Office of Management and Budget played a significant role in both the 1981 and 1985 US farm bill debates. The evidence from the milk quota and stabilizers debates shows the EC Budget Commissioner as an increasingly important actor in CAP formulation. It may not be entirely coincidental that the last two EC Agriculture Commissioners, Frans Andriessen and Ray MacSharry, have been former national finance ministers. Competition for scarce resources also tends to shift the locus of decision-making higher in the political process to officials who can adjudicate between competing claims for funds, thus broadening the interests which agricultural policy must take into account. In the USA, the White House and Congressional leadership showed a strong predisposition to involvement in agricultural policy-making in the 1980s. In the EC, with agricultural issues increasingly shuttled to the European Council, the role of heads of government is greatly enhanced. At the level of the Commission, it is interesting to note that the

President of the Commission, another former finance minister, was heavily involved in the stabilizers debate. The locus of decision-making in the Commission was an *ad hoc* 'inner circle' consisting of the President, the Budget Commissioner and the Agriculture Commissioner.

Budgetary crises, by threatening the survival of an organization, tend to shift the incentives for policy-makers' behaviour toward promoting the interests of the threatened group. The EC milk quotas and stabilizers debates have shown CAP decision-makers willing to sacrifice narrow agricultural interests to the long-term survival of the CAP. The differences between the various sections of DG-VI, and between DG-VI and the Agriculture Commissioner and his Cabinet, seem also to have been subordinated to the need to cut CAP costs. In the past, there appears to have been little inclination to sacrifice agricultural policy for the greater benefit of the EC; indeed, the success of the CAP, the most integrated EC policy, was often equated with the success of the EC. The stabilizers debate provides evidence that this view may be changing. People were willing to sacrifice elements of the CAP to reach an agreement which would allow the movement towards a single European market to proceed smoothly. The greatest problems in terms of subordinating narrow interests have come at the level of the Council of Agriculture Ministers. The Council concedes a willingness to sacrifice national interests to the survival of the CAP, but individual agriculture ministers have retarded the reform process by trying to minimize their own country's sacrifices while maximizing those of others.

The shift in interest priorities has been much less visible in the USA than in the EC – probably because the sense of crisis has appeared less severe. The Reagan administration made a significant effort to subordinate agricultural programmes to budgetary discipline, but the general inconsistency in administration budgetary priorities between defence and domestic programmes worked to undercut the President in USDA and Congress. Escalating farm expenditures in the 1980s would probably have put narrow farm interests on the defensive in the 1985 farm bill debate, had it not been for the farm debt crisis.

Finally, a budget crisis creates political incentives to pay more attention to efficiency. When funds are limited, the case for efficient use of resources is intrinsically strengthened. For agriculture, pressures are created to reduce commodity price supports closer to market clearing levels, to eliminate wasteful storage costs and export subsidies. There seems little doubt that efficiency increased in importance during the 1980s as a generally accepted value for the CAP, because of the widespread perception that the spending escalation could not go on. Those who advocated criteria other than efficiency were clearly on the defensive in both the milk quotas and stabilizers debates. There is a limit, though, to the efficiency impetus created by a budget crisis. As soon as enough resources have been saved to deal with the crisis, pressure is removed to take any further action. That, too, was evidenced in the EC milk quotas and stabilizers debates.

In the USA agricultural production efficiency has a stronger policy goal than in Europe. This tendency was reinforced in the 1970s, during the period of rapid growth of agricultural exports. Congress felt that the price support levels set in the 1981 farm bill would not hinder efficient production. However, the subsequent collapse of the export boom and world prices, along with the failure to give the Executive leeway to adjust price supports, contributed very significantly to the loss of production efficiency. The agricultural policy cost escalation between 1981 and 1985 generated pressures to recover efficiency by lowering both loan rates and target prices. However, the farm debt crisis undercut the target price portion of this effort.

The reform momentum set in motion by a budget crisis does not remain for long when the crisis recedes. It takes a continuing impetus for change to overcome the status quo tendencies inherent in both EC and USA agricultural policy processes. This seems evidenced in 1989 when the reform process slowed considerably as spending pressures declined. The movement towards policy reform in the EC in the period after February 1988 has been driven more by the need to make agricultural markets more compatible with the removal of internal trade barriers than to save budget cost. This motive has led to changes in both the beef and sheepmeat regimes in 1989.

9.6 THE IMPACT OF INTERNATIONAL PRESSURES ON REFORM

Both US and EC case studies have shown that international political pressures do not play a major role in domestic agricultural policy reform. There are a number of reasons why this is the case. Perhaps most important, foreign nations do not have any way of participating directly in the domestic bargaining process. Hence, they are severely disadvantaged in attempting to influence outcomes. Second, little incentive exists for domestic policy-makers to heed foreign advice. Their positions generally depend on domestic constituencies and foreign nations cannot directly help or hurt them in pursuing their individual and organizational objectives. Interestingly, in this regard, the agricultural trade and domestic agricultural policy bureaucracies are separated. The people responsible for trade negotiations are not the individuals who play key roles in domestic agricultural policy, with the exception of the US Secretary of Agriculture and the EC Agriculture Commissioner.[2] Third, the domestic bargaining process is already so complex and balance so difficult to achieve, that none of the participants has any incentive to complicate the decision-making process still further by introducing foreign concerns.

As the EC stabilizers debate shows, foreign pressures can provide an impetus to action when the general threat of a deterioration in relations appears. They may also deter certain actions, such as the US ability to prevent the EC from imposing meaningful restrictions on soybean and corn gluten feed imports. However, foreign pressures cannot dictate exactly what the USA or EC will do. In general, they have an effect on the domestic policy bargaining process to the extent that they create economic shocks, or influence economic trends and the political environment. Increased EC export subsidies from 1980 to 1985 (along with the strengthening of the dollar), contributed to the decline of US cereal export markets, and thus helped to galvanize the Congressional effort to lower loan rates and increase export subsidies in the 1985 Food Security Act. These export subsidies helped to increase the cost pressures on the CAP (along with the concurrent weakening of the dollar) and, hence, helped catalyse the stabilizers debate.

This suggests that there can indeed be a strong link between EC and US farm policy reform even if each is apparently unresponsive to foreign pressures. This indirect link can be illustrated with a stylized example. Imagine a situation in which the probability of EC reform was judged at 40 per cent and that of US reform placed at 60 per cent. If the two reform processes were independent, then the joint probabilities of the four possible reform–non-reform combinations would be as shown in Figure 9.3(a). There would be a 36 per cent chance of US reform combined with EC non-reform, a 16 per cent chance of EC reform combined with no US reform, and a 24 per cent chance of each of the other two outcomes. However, it seems implausible that there is no association between the reform prospects in the USA and the EC. It seems more reasonable to assume, within the same overall probabilities of reform, that the outcomes are not independent. Figure 9.3(b) shows the situation if reform in the USA decreases the likelihood of EC reform – by raising world prices and reducing the pressure on the CAP. On the assumption that lack of reform in the USA increases the chance of EC reform – for instance by increasing the budget cost of the CAP – the probabilities of the off-diagonal outcomes increase. In this illustration, the likelihood of the US reforming and 'saving' the CAP from the need to reform increases from 36 to 50 per cent. Figure 9.3(c) shows the opposite tendency, towards increased probabilities of matching reforms (or non-reforms). This could be the case if reform were to be co-ordinated in the GATT Round. In this case, the probability of both the EC and the USA undertaking reforms is assumed to increase to 35 per cent. This implies lower probabilities for the off-diagonal elements and presumably less potential for continued trade conflict.

These conditional probabilities encapsulate a complex of underlying political and economic realities. The question whether EC reform helps or hinders US reform, and vice versa, raises issues to do with domestic politics, commodity market conditions, and the nature of the trading system. A review of these linkages is necessary before attempting an answer to the

EUROPEAN COMMUNITY	UNITED STATES: Reform	UNITED STATES: No reform
Reform	24	16
No reform	36	24

(a) Independent probabilities of reform

EUROPEAN COMMUNITY	UNITED STATES: Reform	UNITED STATES: No reform
Reform	10	30
No reform	50	10

(b) Negative association between reform probabilities

EUROPEAN COMMUNITY	UNITED STATES: Reform	UNITED STATES: No reform
Reform	35	5
No reform	25	35

(c) Positive association between reform probabilities

Figure 9.3 Illustrative probabilities of reform in the USA and EC

question. We shall look first at the role that international developments play in policy-making; then at the particular commodity market linkages which bear the brunt of the conflicts between the EC and the USA; and finally at the extent to which common concern over the fortune of the trading system can lead to agreements which will determine the agricultural reform agenda.

9.7 INTERNATIONAL DEVELOPMENTS AND NATIONAL POLICY

The issue of the role of international developments in domestic policy decisions can be split into two parts, representing a passive and an active linkage between trade and domestic policy. The passive linkage is the influence that external conditions have on policy attitudes, objectives, instruments and costs. The active linkage is the extent to which domestic policy is itself formed with the international situation in mind – to influence international developments, to stimulate trade in particular ways, or to promote change in the policies of other countries. If the passive linkage is dominant, one might expect the 'off-diagonal probabilities' discussed above to be enhanced. Reform in one country takes the heat off another. If the active linkage is at all strong, the 'diagonal' outcomes, of corresponding actions in each country, become more plausible. Domestic reforms are a part of the strategy for trade reform and are offered up on the bargaining table to gain similar concessions from others.

In the case of the EC, the argument for a passive link between international conditions and domestic policy change appears strong. As discussed in Chapter 2, CAP reform was swept off course (or rendered less urgent) in 1975 and 1981, in both cases by a significant rise in world prices. World prices are the major determinant of the variation in export subsidy costs. An upward movement of such costs is the usual signal for policy change: a fall in outlays for export subsidies generally takes the pressure off the policy for that commodity. A case in point is the rise in dairy product prices on world markets in the early 1980s. Following an agreement with New Zealand to hold back exports in 1981 (using the framework of the International Dairy Agreement, which came out of the Tokyo Round) the world market price of butter and skimmed milk powder rose significantly. Over $1 billion was cut from the cost of the milk programme as the export subsidy bill dropped by 37 per cent between 1980 and 1981. The CAP was 'saved' from financial disaster. Unfortunately, the salvation was only temporary. Underlying imbalances between supply and demand had not changed, and the dairy policy was in trouble again within two years.

Rising world prices not only reduce the budget pressure for policy change in the EC but also seem to relax the vigilance of the Commission in its quest for a restrictive price policy. It is clearly more difficult to argue for domestic price restraint when world prices are rising. Again, the experience of the 1973–5 and 1980–1 periods, when world prices for several commodities rose sharply, indicates the impact of these events on domestic price levels. The public perception of possible shortages, encouraged by the rhetoric of interest groups, was translated into higher prices even though in most cases the level of protection was still significant and the surpluses still existed. Inflationary pressures linked by the oil-price increases in those two periods also acted to weaken the resolve of those aiming to keep down prices.

In the politics of farm price-setting, what goes up takes time to come down. The periods of high world prices and relaxed domestic price restraints have been followed by a wider gap between world and domestic prices. World prices fell back rapidly in 1976 and 1982, although in the latter case the strength of the dollar masked the full impact on the EC until 1985.

Domestic prices cannot fall fast in nominal terms – though they do occasionally decline. In periods of inflation there is some scope for reducing domestic incentives. When inflation is low and world prices are falling, levels of protection can rise rapidly. This appears particularly true in the EC since 1984. Exacerbated by the 1982 decision to tie the ECU used for agricultural prices to the Deutschmark (by giving it a premium over the monetary ECU equal to the degree of appreciation of the Deutschmark), the EC's policy of a price freeze has corresponded to a steady increase in the level of protection.

The USA also reacts to the state of the world market in setting domestic policy. In the USA, the impact is felt directly in farm income as well as indirectly on budget cost. With the additional policy instrument of set-asides and other forms of acreage control, the policy reaction is more complex. The high price period in the mid-1970s gave the Nixon administration the flexibility to remove acreage controls and to deregulate the sugar market. With prices above the support levels, new forces came into play. Exports of some products were restricted to keep down domestic prices, causing serious damage to the USA's image as a reliable supplier in times of shortage. When, by 1977, prices had returned to a more normal level, US policy resumed its role in supporting markets. Acreage controls were reintroduced and price supports raised. However, the export boom lasted through 1981, implying relatively low support costs and levels of protection.

World market developments in the 1980s, coupled with the behaviour of the US dollar, hit US farm policy even more dramatically. The 1981 farm bill, as discussed in Chapter 7, was largely premised on high levels of exports at high prices. The next few years saw a precipitous drop in US export volumes, followed by weak prices in the major grain and oilseed markets. The high target prices built into the 1981 farm bill paralleled the generous price increases effected by the EC in the same period. In both cases, the taxpayer cost rose to fill the gap between expectations and reality. After a drop in 1984, reflecting the 1983 drought in the Midwest, budget costs rose to nearly $26 billion by 1986 – from a mere $4 billion in 1981. EC spending rose from $13 billion to $22 billion over the same period.

By the time of the 1985 farm bill, the realities of lower export volumes and prices had made themselves felt. The USA was losing market share in a weak market. In spite of outspending the EC on farm support, the value of agricultural exports actually dropped below that of the Community in 1986. The main reason for the change in market shares was undoubtedly the strength of the dollar, which rose by over 40 per cent relative to the major EC currencies in the period 1983–5 before falling back to its earlier levels (see Figure 9.4).

Policy linkages through world price movements are a fact of life: other linkages come through more conscious acts of policy. The EC and the USA

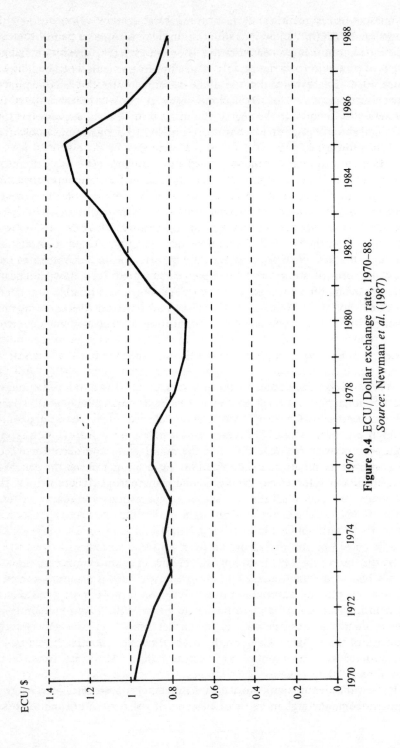

Figure 9.4 ECU/Dollar exchange rate, 1970–88.
Source: Newman *et al.* (1987)

have attempted to influence each other's domestic policy by actions as well as words. They also attempt to influence third countries as a part of foreign policy. This use of agricultural policy as an instrument to achieve change abroad can range from the gentle application of pressure to the blatant manipulation of markets. Perhaps because of a more flexible farm policy and a less disparate set of political interests, the USA has been tempted to use agricultural trade and policy as an instrument more often than has the EC. The 1980 embargo on grain sales to the Soviet Union is an example of a swift decision by the USA; the EC at that time showed how difficult it was to obtain any firm policy response from the member states.

The more relevant example of the use of farm policy to influence the decisions of others, in the present context, is the use of the Export Enhancement Programme (EEP) in recent years by the USA. The ability to offer export credits and guarantees has long been a part of US trade policy, but direct export subsidies had generally not been used since the early 1970s. The EEP was a deliberate attempt to put pressure on the EC, through the increased competition in markets in which the Community had gained (or regained) a foothold.

The analysis of EC and US agricultural policy in earlier chapters suggests reasons why passive links may more easily influence policy-making than active ones. We have noted the considerable inertia in both US and EC policy processes. Once a policy consensus has been achieved it tends to persist until the necessity for change is forced upon the policy actors. Passive forces in the form of economic trends and economic shocks can affect the interests of outside groups and policy actors sufficiently to shake the policy consensus if they are strong enough. We have seen that passive forces become particularly persuasive when they contribute to a budget crisis, as evidenced, in the case of the EC, by the milk quotas debate in 1983–4 and stabilizers debate in 1987–8, and, in the case of the USA, by the 1985 farm bill. Passive forces can create a policy environment where there is no alternative to policy change.

The domestic agricultural policy process appears less attuned to active links. It is difficult for compartmentalized, inward-looking actors to consider directly the international situation as they bargain together to formulate policy. Bureaucratic processes are intrinsically reactive. They cannot look ahead very well or plan strategies to pursue common interests with other countries. Threats and promises from outside actors usually have little impact because they usually cannot be brought to bear on policy-makers' domestic constituencies. For instance, the USA can do little directly to influence the EC Council of Agriculture Ministers, whose constituencies are national farm groups relatively impervious to US pressures. Active pressures in policy areas outside agriculture have little influence on agricultural policy-makers, because of the considerable difficulty non-agricultural policy-makers have in influencing the agricultural policy process. Direct outside pressures can only influence the domestic bargaining process when they affect the economic situation to which policy-makers react. However, this kind of pressure requires a considerable sacrifice from the country creating it, which may prove too costly to justify the effort or may not be politically acceptable.

9.8 FEASIBLE TYPES OF AGRICULTURAL REFORM

Experience of US and EC agricultural policy reform confirms the casual expectation that proposals imposing direct price cuts face the most severe opposition from the farm lobby. As indicated above, price cuts challenge the very legitimacy of farm organizations. The EC settled on milk quotas largely because milk price cuts were unacceptable to farmers and their representatives. The farm lobby also went out of its way to prevent direct price cuts in the stabilizers debate. The West Germans pushed set-asides and the French pushed co-responsibility levies in a partially successful effort to limit price cuts. US politicians opposed to rising agricultural expenditures were unable to prevent price increases in the 1981 farm bill. With expenditures much higher at the time of the 1985 Food Security Act, they had to settle for a conservation reserve, a slight nominal decline in target prices during the last three years of a five-year bill, and a freezing of programme bases and yields.

Neither the USA nor EC has made much progress in shifting farm subsidies to direct income support. This is not surprising given that a shift to direct income supports smacks of welfare and raises the question whether the general welfare programme standard for giving benefits on the basis of need should be applied to farm programmes. Moreover, it makes visible the full costs of agricultural support by shifting costs from consumers to taxpayers through the budget. There is no reason to think that farmers would not accept direct income payments if no other support were available, but this is not the situation that they presently face.

Though the influence of the farm lobby is probably declining in both the USA and EC, it is still strong enough that reform measures must prove at least minimally acceptable to farmers in order to succeed. Quotas meet this test because they protect existing farm incomes. Set-asides and paid conservation reserves are also acceptable because of their income-preserving character. If voluntary, they are even more acceptable because the farmer is provided with options. Decoupling measures such as the Boschwitz–Boren proposal (see Chapter 7) which would pay farmers a flat rate per acre of land and allow them to grow what they want for sale on an open market have an intrinsic appeal, both because they protect farm income and because they give farmers greater autonomy in their planting decisions. Measures taken in the name of conservation cannot easily be opposed by the farm lobby: such measures have an unusually strong public-support base which may even transcend the support for farming. The unexpectedly strong showing of the 'green' parties in the European elections in June 1989 has heightened the importance of environmental issues in the agricultural policy agenda. The popular notion in the EC of 'extensification' – promoting farming that does not use large quantities of agricultural chemicals, nor require intensive livestock rearing – also poses a challenge for agricultural interests. They may find such developments preferable to lower prices and higher output intensity. Other reform measures, as happened with the freezing of bases and yields in the USA, may slip through without the opposition of farmers, either because the consequences are unclear or because the farm lobby is so busy dealing with more visible issues, such as price cuts, that it cannot mount a campaign in opposition.

9.9 LESSONS FOR POLICY-MAKERS

This study of US and EC agricultural policy-making suggests a number of factors that individuals involved with policy reform might consider. One such factor is the question of timing. It is often the case that the bargaining costs of achieving change are so great that reform proposals do not succeed unless the economic forces, political developments and political environment indicate the necessity for change, which happens only when a spending crisis appears. An intensive political effort to make significant changes to policy instruments in the absence of an environment demanding reform produces only frustration and squandering of political capital. To be sure, modifications in existing policy instruments can occur in the absence of a spending crisis, particularly where they do not attract the attention of the farm lobby. Change is also possible where it has ambiguous consequences, such as the freezing of bases and yields in the 1985 US farm bill. But without a crisis it appears that comprehensive change is impossible. On the other hand, it seems wise for reform advocates to develop and publicize their arguments well in advance of a crisis, so that key officials in the public and private sector can become familiar with them. When the crisis actually occurs, decision-makers will not have time to develop and explore new ideas, but will look for a familiar option which will allow them to 'cope' with the situation.

A second factor which those involved in reform might consider is the intrinsic tendency toward mutual accommodation (partisan mutual adjustment) apparent in both US and EC agricultural policy processes. Well-integrated comprehensive proposals are almost inevitably watered down through compromise in the political process, creating a certain amount of policy incoherence. A proposal based on simple ideological principle may provide a strong initial bargaining position. However, sticking to principle to overcome the 'messiness' of compromise seems doomed to failure in pluralistic political processes, where benefits must be provided to a majority coalition. This may in part explain the difficulties faced by the Reagan administration proposal for trade liberalization in the Uruguay Round.

Third, when attempting to promote a reform proposal, one should be mindful of the still strong power of the farm lobby in both the USA and EC. Farm organizations will continue to have more incentive than any other groups to influence agricultural policy legislation, both because their members will probably have to absorb the majority of the adjustment costs of agricultural policy reform and because the legitimacy of these organizations is linked inextricably to agricultural policy. The farm lobby may no longer have the power to block change. However, it still retains the power to influence the type of change which will occur. The advocates of reform proposals should attempt to gain support from at least some important elements of the farm community and acquiescence from much of the rest of that community if they hope to succeed.

Fourth, reform advocates should be mindful of the strong base of public support farmers have in both the USA and EC. A very strong possibility always exists that the farm lobby will be able to mobilize the public to prevent change unless the public can be convinced that the proposed measures will not hurt farming and farmers. Stating the reality more positively, the proponents of reform should seek to demonstrate to the public that their proposals will be good for farming, particularly for the farmer who is not rich, who employs good land management and soil conservation techniques and who minimizes the uses of chemicals and pesticides in producing healthy food. Public support for agricultural reform can never be taken for granted. In particular, consumer groups almost never have a strong enough incentive or base of support to exercise influence on the agricultural policy process.

Fifth, it would seem helpful to limit international agreement to the necessary general commitment to take action by individual nations. To seek international agreement dictating to individual nations exactly what they should do would seem to ignore the realities of domestic politics and process. Measures dictated from the outside almost inevitably unite domestic forces against change, which portends badly in a world without strong international authority. If, on the other hand, governments, such as those of the USA and EC, are left to determine for themselves the actual measures they will take to fulfil their international commitments, the outlook for progress in reform is much better. Domestic leeway maximizes the probability of measures which can generate the support of a winning coalition of politicians and administrators.

NOTES

1. This was never true for the Budget Council in establishing the annual budget where 'qualified majority' always applied.
2. The EC Agriculture Commissioner is not responsible for trade negotiations. Some previous Agriculture Commissioners showed little interest in trade matters. That was not the case for Andriessen, who has now moved into the Trade post. Perhaps there will now be greater integration between trade and agricultural policy.

BIBLIOGRAPHY

Allen, Kristen (1988). 'Reflections from the Past, Challenges for the Future: An Examination of U.S. Agricultural Policy Goals', National Center for Food and Agricultural Policy and National Planning Association, Washington, DC, November.

Allison, Graham T. (1971). *Essence of Decision: Explaining the Cuban Missile Crisis,* Boston: Little, Brown and Company.

Australian Bureau of Agricultural and Resource Economics (1988). *Early Action on Agricultural Trade Reform,* Discussion Paper 88-3, Canberra, ABARE.

Avery, Graham (1984). 'Europe's Agricultural Policy: Progress and Reform', *International Affairs,* vol. 60, no. 4, Autumn, pp. 643-56.

Avery, Graham (1985). 'Guarantee Thresholds and the Common Agricultural Policy', *Journal of Agricultural Economics,* vol. XXXVI, Sept 1985, pp.355-65.

Avery, Graham (1987a). 'Agricultural Policy: European Options and American Comparisons', *European Affairs,* no. 1, Spring, pp. 62-73.

Avery, Graham (1987b). 'Farm Policy: Chances for Reform', *The World Today,* vol. 43, nos 8-9, pp. 160-5.

Averyt, William F. (1977). *Agropolitics in the European Community: Interest Groups and the Common Agricultural Policy,* New York: Praeger.

Barton, Weldon V. (1976). 'Coalition Building in the United States House of Representatives: Agricultural Legislation in 1973' in James E. Anderson, ed., *Cases in Public Policy-making,* New York: Praeger.

Bauer, Raymond A., Ithiel de Sola Poole and Lewis Anthony Dexter (1963). *American Business and Public Policy,* New York: Atherton.

Bonnen, James T. (1987). 'Institutions, Instruments and Driving Forces Behind U.S. National Agricultural Policies', paper prepared for the binational symposium on US-Canadian Agricultural Trade Challenges sponsored by the National Center for Food and Agricultural Policy, Resources for the Future, Washington, DC, and the C.D. Howe Institute of Canada, Wayzeta, MN, 22-24 July.

Braybrooke, David and Charles E. Lindblom (1963). *A Strategy of Decision,* Glencoe Ill: The Free Press.

Browne, William P. (1988a). 'The Fragmented and Meandering Politics of Agriculture' in M. Ann Tutwiler, ed., *U.S. Agriculture in a Global Setting; An Agenda for the Future,* National Center for Food and Agricultural Policy, Annual Policy Review 1987-88, Washington, DC: Resources for the Future.

Browne, William P. (1988b). *Private Interests, Public Policy, and American Agriculture,* Lawrence: University Press of Kansas.

Browne, William P. and James T. Bonnen (1987). 'The Political Economy of United States Agriculture', unpublished paper, December.

Brownstein, Ronald (1984). 'In Era of Deficits, Farm Price Supports Seem Likely Targets for Cuts, *National Journal,* 11 February, pp. 270-3.

Buchanan, J.M., R.D. Tollison, and G. Tullock (1981). *Toward a Theory of a Rent-seeking Society,* College Station: Texas A and M University Press.

Campbell, John (1986). 'The Food Security Act of 1985: Implications for the Grains

Sector', unpublished thesis, Department of Agricultural Economics, University of Sydney, December.

Cheeseright, Paul (1985). 'Lobbying the E.C.: A Diffuse Process', *Europe*, November/December, pp. 18–19.

Clymer, Adam (1986). 'Poll Finds Most Americans Cling to Ideals of Farm Life', *New York Times*, 25 February, p. A22.

Cochrane, Willard W. (1965). *The City Man's Guide to the Farm Problem*, Minneapolis: University of Minnesota Press.

Cochrane, Willard W. (1986). 'A New Sheet of Music: How Kennedy's Farm Advisor Has Changed His Tune About Commodity Policy and Why', *Choices*, 1st Quarter.

Cochrane, Willard W. and Mary E. Ryan (1976). *American Farm Policy, 1948–1973*, Minneapolis: University of Minnesota Press.

Commission of the European Communities (1968). 'Memorandum on the Reform of Agriculture in the European Economic Community', COM (68) 1000, Part A, Brussels.

Commission of the European Communities (1973). 'Improvement of the Common Agricultural Policy', COM (73) 1850, Brussels.

Commission of the European Communities (1975). 'Stocktaking of the Common Agricultural Policy', COM (75) 100, Brussels.

Commission of the European Communities (1978). 'Future Development of the Common Agricultural Policy', COM (78) 700, Brussels.

Commission of the European Communities (1980). 'Reflections on the Common Agricultural Policy', COM (80) 800, Brussels.

Commission of the European Communities (1981a). 'Commission Report on the Mandate', COM (81), Brussels, 24 June.

Commission of the European Communities (1981b). 'Guidelines for European Agriculture', COM (81) 608, Brussels.

Commission of the European Communities (1983). 'Common Agricultural Policy – Proposals of the Commission', COM (83) 500, Brussels.

Commission of the European Communities (1984). 'Agriculture in the United States and in the European Community: A Comparison', *Green Europe*, 4/84.

Commission of the European Communities (1985a). 'Perspectives for the Common Agricultural Policy', COM (85) 333, Brussels.

Commission of the European Communities (1985b). 'A Future for Community Agriculture', COM (85) 750, Brussels, December.

Commission of the European Communities (1986). 'The Agreement on Agriculture of 16 December 1986'.

Commission of the European Communities (1987a). 'Making a Success of the Single European Act. A New Frontier for Europe', COM (87) 100 final, Brussels, 15 February.

Commission of the European Communities (1987b). 'Report by the Commission to the Council and Parliament on the Financing of the Community Budget', COM (87) 101 final, Brussels, 28 February.

Commission of the European Communities (1987c). 'Review of Action Taken to Control the Agricultural Markets and Outlook for the Common Agricultural Policy', COM (87) 410 final, Brussels, 3 August.

Commission of the European Communities (1988a). *The Agricultural Situation in the Community*, EC Publications Office, Luxembourg.

Commission of the European Communities (1988b). *Disharmonies in EC and US Agricultural Policy Measures*, Luxembourg.

Commission of the European Communities (1988c). *Europeans and Their*

Agriculture, Directorate-General Information, Communication, Culture, Brussels, Spring.

Cox, Graham, Philip Lowe and Michael Winter (1986). 'From State Direction to Self Regulation: The Historical Development of Corporatism in British Agriculture', *Policy and Politics* vol. 14, no. 4 pp. 475-6

Cox, Graham, Philip Lowe and Michael Winter (1987). 'Farmers and the State: A Crisis for Corporatism', *Political Quarterly*, vol. 58, pp. 73-81.

Cyert, R. and J. March (1963). *A Behavioral Theory of the Firm*, Englewood Cliffs, NJ: Prentice Hall.

Daft, Lynn M. (1986). 'The 1985 Farm Bill', *Choices*, 1st Quarter.

Destler, I. M. (1980). *Making Foreign Economic Policy,* Washington, DC: Brookings Institution.

Destler, I. M. (1986). *American Trade Politics: System Under Stress*, Washington DC: Institute for International Economics and the Twentieth Century Fund.

Downs, Anthony (1957). *An Economic Theory of Democracy*, New York: Harper and Row.

Downs, Anthony (1967). *Inside Bureaucracy*, Boston: Little, Brown.

European Community (1987). 'Single European Act', *Official Journal of the European Communities*, vol. 30, L169, 29 June.

European Institute of the Public Administration (1986). 'Alternative Support Measures for Agriculture,' Report of the Round Table, Maastricht, 12-14 November.

Fearne, Andrew (1988). 'The Annual Price Review: A Framework for Decisionmaking', University of Newcastle upon Tyne Discussion Paper, February.

Fennell, Rosemary (1979). *The Common Agricultural Policy of the European Community*, Oxford: BSP Professional Books.

Franklin, Michael (1988). *Rich Man's Farming: The Crisis in Agriculture*, London and New York: Royal Institute of International Affairs.

George, Alexander (1980). *Presidential Decisionmaking in Foreign Policy: The Effective Use of Information and Advice*, Boulder, CO: Westview Press, Ch. 2.

Guither, Harold D. (1980). *The Food Lobbyists: Behind the Scenes of Food and Agri-Politics*, Lexington, MA: Heath.

Guither, Harold D. (1986). 'Tough Choices: Writing the Food Security Act of 1985', American Enterprise Institute Occasional Paper, December.

Hagedorn, Konrad (1983). 'Reflections on the Methodology of Agricultural Policy Research', *European Review of Agricultural Economics*, vol. 10 pp. 303-23.

Hagedorn, Konrad (1985). 'CAP Reform and Agricultural Economics: A Dialogue of the Deaf?' in Jacques Pelkmans, ed., *Can the CAP be Reformed?*, Masstricht: European Institute of Public Administration, 1985.

Hagstrom, Jerry, (1984). 'Candidates Woo Farmers as Agricultural PACs Step up Their Contributions', *National Journal*, 3 March, pp. 420-4.

Hallberg, Milton C. (1988). *The US Agricultural and Food Systems: A Postwar Historical Perspective*, Northeast Regional Center for Rural Development, Pennsylvania State University, University Park, Pennsylvania, October.

Harris, Simon, Alan Swinbank and Guy Wilkinson (1983). *The Food and Farm Policies of the European Community*, Chichester and New York: John Wiley and Sons.

Harvey, David R. (1982). 'National Interests and the CAP', *Food Policy*, August.

Harvey, David R. (1985). 'Costs, Benefits and the Future of the Common Agricultural Policy', *Journal of Common Market Studies*, vol. XXIV, no. 1, September, pp. 3-20.

Harvey, David R. (n.d.) 'Public Choice and Non-market Decisionmaking', unpublished manuscript.

Hathaway, Dale E. (1986). 'Trade Negotiations: They Won't Solve Agriculture's Problems', *Choices*, 4th Quarter.

Hathaway, Dale E. (1987). *Agriculture and the GATT: Rewriting the Rules*, Washington, DC: Institute for International Economics.

Hermann, A. H. (1988). 'Eurotwists to Make Britain Toe the Line', *Financial Times*, 3 March.

Hill, Brian E. (1984). *The Common Agricultural Policy: Past, Present and Future*, London and New York: Methuen.

Hirschman, A. O. (1975). *Exit Voice and Loyalty, Responses to Declines in Firms, Organizations and States*, Cambridge, MA and London: Harvard University Press.

Ikerd, John E. (1987). 'Running out of Room to Swerve between Domestic and Export Policies', *Choices*, 2nd Quarter.

International Policy Council on Agriculture and Trade (1988). 'The Mid-Term Review and the GATT Negotiations on Agriculture', October.

Jarchow, Gerd (n.d.). 'Developments in the Common Agricultural Policy', unpublished paper.

Jervis, Robert (1976). *Perception and Misperception in International Politics*, Princeton, NJ: Princeton University Press.

Josling, Tim and Wayne Moyer (1989). 'The Common Agricultural Policy of the European Community: A Public Choice Interpretation' in Roland Vaubel and Thomas D. Willet, eds, *The Political Economic of International Organization: A Public Choice Approach*, Boulder, CO: Westview Press.

Koester, Ulrich and Stefan Tangermann (1986). 'Agricultural Protectionism in the European Community', Paper presented at a workshop on Agricultural Policies and Trade, East-West Center, Honolulu, Hawaii, 17–20 February.

Lindblom, Charles E. (1959). 'The Science of Muddling Through', *Public Administration Review*, vol. 19, Spring.

Lindblom, Charles E. (1965). *The Intelligence of Democracy*, New York: The Free Press.

Mahler, Vincent H. (1986). 'A Comparison of Agricultural Policies in the European Community and the United States: The Case of Sugar Policy', paper prepared for delivery at the annual meeting of the American Political Science Association, Washington, DC.

Mangold, D. (1987). 'Aspects of Agricultural Policy in the European Community 1986/87', *Review of Marketing and Agricultural Economics*, vol. 55, no. 2, August, pp. 117–39.

March, James (1965). *Handbook of Organizations*, Chicago: Rand, McNally.

March, James and Herbert Simon (1958). *Organizations*, New York: Wiley.

Martin, Marshall, A. *et al.* (1986). 'Most Farmers Got What They Wanted', *Choices*, 3rd Quarter.

Mayhew, David R. (1974). *Congress: The Electoral Connection*, New Haven, CT and London: Yale University Press.

Miner, William M. and Dale E. Hathaway (eds) (1988). *World Agricultural Trade: Building a Consensus*, Institute for Research on Public Policy/Institute for International Economics, Ottawa and Washington, DC.

National Center for Food and Agricultural Policy (1988a). 'Issues and Options for U.S. Agricultural Policy', Briefing Book, July.

National Center for Food and Agricultural Policy (1988b). 'Agriculture in the Uruguay Round of the GATT', Briefing Book, August.

National Center for Food and Agricultural Policy and Center for Agricultural and Rural Development (1988). 'De-coupling Farm Programs', briefing book issued in conjunction with Washington Briefings held on 28 April, Iowa State University.

Neustadt, Richard (1980). *Presidential Power*, New York: John Wiley and Sons.

Neville-Rolfe, Edmund (1984) *The Politics of Agriculture in the European Community*, London: Policy Studies Institute.

Newman, Mark, Tom Fulton, and Lewrene Glaser (1987). *A Comparison of Agriculture in the United States and the European Community*, USDA/ERS Foreign Agricultural Economic Report no. 233, Washington, DC, October.

OECD (1987). *National Policies and International Trade*, Paris: OECD.

OECD (1988). *Agricultural Policies, Markets and Trade: Monitoring and Outlook, 1988*, Paris: OECD.

Olson, Mancur (1965). *The Logic of Collective Action: Public Goods and The Theory of Groups*, Cambridge, MA: Harvard University Press.

Paarlberg, Robert L. (1988). *Fixing Farm Trade: Policy Options for the United States*, Cambridge, MA: Ballinger/Council on Foreign Relations.

Parikh, K. S., G. Fischer, K. Frohberg and O. Gulbrandsen (1988). *Toward Free Trade in Agriculture*, Laxenburg, Austria: Food and Agriculture Program, International Institute of Applied Systems Analysis.

Penn, J. B. (1977). 'The Federal Policy Process in Developing the Food and Agriculture Act of 1977', in USDA/ERS, *Agricultural-Food Policy Review*, ERS-AFPR-1, Washington, DC, January.

Petit, Michel (1985). *Determinants of Agricultural Policies in the United States and the European Community*, International Food Policy Research Institute, Research Report 51, IFPRI, Washington, D.C.

Petit, Michel, Michele de Benedictis, Denis Britton, Martin de Groot, Wilhelm Henrichsmeyer and Francesco Leshi (1987). *Agricultural Policy Formation in the European Community: The Birth of Milk Quotas and CAP Reform*, Amsterdam: Elsevier.

Quiggin, John (1987). 'Egoistic Rationality and Public Choice: A Critical Review of Theory and Practice', *Economic Review*, March vol. 63, no. 180, pp. 10–21.

Rauch, Jonathan (1985a). 'Writing a Blank Check', *National Journal*, 23 March, pp. 625–31.

Rauch, Jonathan (1985b). 'A Rock and a Hard Place', *National Journal*, 7 September, pp. 1981–85.

Rauch, Jonathan (1985c). 'Farmers' Discord over Government Role Produces a Farm Bill that Pleases Few', *National Journal*, November 9, pp. 2535–9.

Rauch, Jonathan (1986). 'The Great Farm Gamble', *National Journal*, 29 March, pp. 759–2.

Rauch, Jonathan (1989). 'Farm Welfare', *National Journal*, 16 November, p. 2624.

Rausser, Gordon C. (1982). 'Political Economic Markets: PERTs and PESTs in Food and Agriculture', *American Journal of Agricultural Economics*, December, pp. 821–3.

Renshaw, Derwent. (1986). 'The European View: U.S./EC Struggle over Agricultural Markets', *Choices*, 4th Quarter.

Ritson, Christopher (1979). 'An Economic Interpretaion of National Approaches to CAP Prices', paper for the Second Wageningen Seminar on the Role of the Economist in Policy Formation, Wageningen, August.

Robbins, William (1986). 'Surge in Sympathy for Farmer's Found', *New York Times*, 25 February, p. 1.

Roningen, V. O.and P. Dixit (1987). 'Impact of Removal of Support to Agriculture in Developed Countries', paper presented at the International Agricultural Trade Research Consortium Meeting, Airlie House, December.

Rossmiller, George E. and M. Ann Tutwiler (1986). 'Will the New Farm Bill Help US Farmers Compete on World Markets', paper presented at Twin Cities Agricultural Roundtable, Minneapolis, MN, 26 March.

Runge, Carlisle Ford (1988). 'The Assault of Agricultural Protectionism', *Foreign Affairs*, vol. 67, no. 1.

Runge, C. Ford and Daniel W. Halbach (1987). 'Neopopulism and the New Agriculture', *Review of Marketing and Agricultural Economics*, vol. 55, no. 2, August.

Runge, Carlisle Ford and Harald von Witzke (1985). 'Institutional Innovation in the Common Agricultural Policy of the European Community', University of Minnesota Department of Agricultural and Applied Economics, June.

Sanderson, Fred, H. (1983). U.S. Farm Policy in Perspective', *Food Policy*, February.

Sanderson, Fred H., T. K. Warley and Tim Josling (forthcoming). 'The Future of International Agricultural Relations: Issues in the GATT Negotiations', in Fred Sanderson (ed.), *Agricultural Protectionism in the Industrialized World*, Resources for the Future: Washington, DC.

Schelling, Thomas (1960). *The Strategy of Conflict*, Cambridge, MA: Harvard University Press.

Schnittker, John A. (1987). 'Coping with Excess Capacity: Speculations on the Coming Agricultural Policy Envirnmont', *Choices*, 2nd Quarter.

Senior Nello, Susan (1984). 'An Application of Public Choice Theory to the Question of CAP Reform', *Review of European Economics*, vol. 11 pp. 261-83.

Simon, Harold (1957). *Models of Man*, New York:

Stokes, Bruce (1984). 'Falling Exports, Rising Support Payments Throwing Farm Economy out of Sync', *National Journal*, 24 November pp. 2250-4.

Stokes, Bruce (1985a). 'A Divided Farm Lobby', *National Journal*, 23 March, pp. 632-8.

Stokes, Bruce (1985b). 'Pyrrhic Victory', *National Journal*, 7 December.

Stokes, Bruce (1986). 'Powers that Be Carried Farm Bill', *National Journal*, 18 January, pp. 159-60.

Stokes, Bruce (1989). 'Pressures Back Home', *National Journal*, 2 February, 286-91.

Talbot, Ross B. (1983). 'Food in the American Political Economy' in Don F. Hadwiger and Ross B. Talbot, *Food Policy and Farm Programs*, Proceedings of the Academy of Political Science, vol. 34, no. 5, New York.

Tracy, Michael (1987). 'Can the CAP Survive', Paper presented for Second World Basque Congress, Conference on the Basque Primary Sector, Bilbao, 2-6 November.

Tracy, Michael (1989). *Government and Agriculture in Western Europe* 3rd edn, New York and London: Harvester Wheatsheaf.

Tullock, G. (1986). *The Politics of Bureaucracy*, Washington, DC: Public Affairs Press.

Tyers, R. and K. Anderson (1987). 'Liberalizing OECD Agricultural Policies in the Uruguay Round: Effects on Trade and Welfare', Australian National University, Working Paper in Trade and Development 87/10, Canberra.

US Congressional Budget Office (1987). *The Gatt Negotiations and US Trade Policy*, Washington, CBO, July.

US Council of Economic Advisors (1988). *Annual Report to the President*, Washington, DC.

USDA (1987). *Government Intervention in Agriculture: Measurement, Evaluation, and Implications for Trade Negotiations*, Economic Research Service.

USDA (1988a). *Estimates of Producer and Consumer Subsidy Equivalents: Government Intervention in Agriculture, 1982-86*, Economic Research Service Staff Report, April.

USDA (1988b). *Western Europe: Agricultural and Trade Report*, Economic Research Service, Situation and Outlook Series, Washington, DC, June.

Wilson, Graham K. (1977). *Special Interests and Policymaking: Agricultural Policies and Politics in Britain and the United States of America, 1956-70*, London: John Wiley and Sons.

Winters, L. Alan (1987). 'The Political Economy of the Agricultural Policy of Industrial Countries', *European Review of Agricultural Economics*, vol. 14, pp. 290-1.

Witzke, Harald von and C. Ford Runge (1987). 'Institutional Choice in the European Community', paper presented at the Fifth European Congress of Agricultural Economists, Balatonszlepak, Hungary 31 August-4 September.

Zeitz Joachim and Alberto Valdes (1988). *Agriculture in the GATT: An Analysis of Alternative Approaches to Reform*, Research Report no. 70, International Food Policy Research Institute, Washington, DC, November.

INDEX